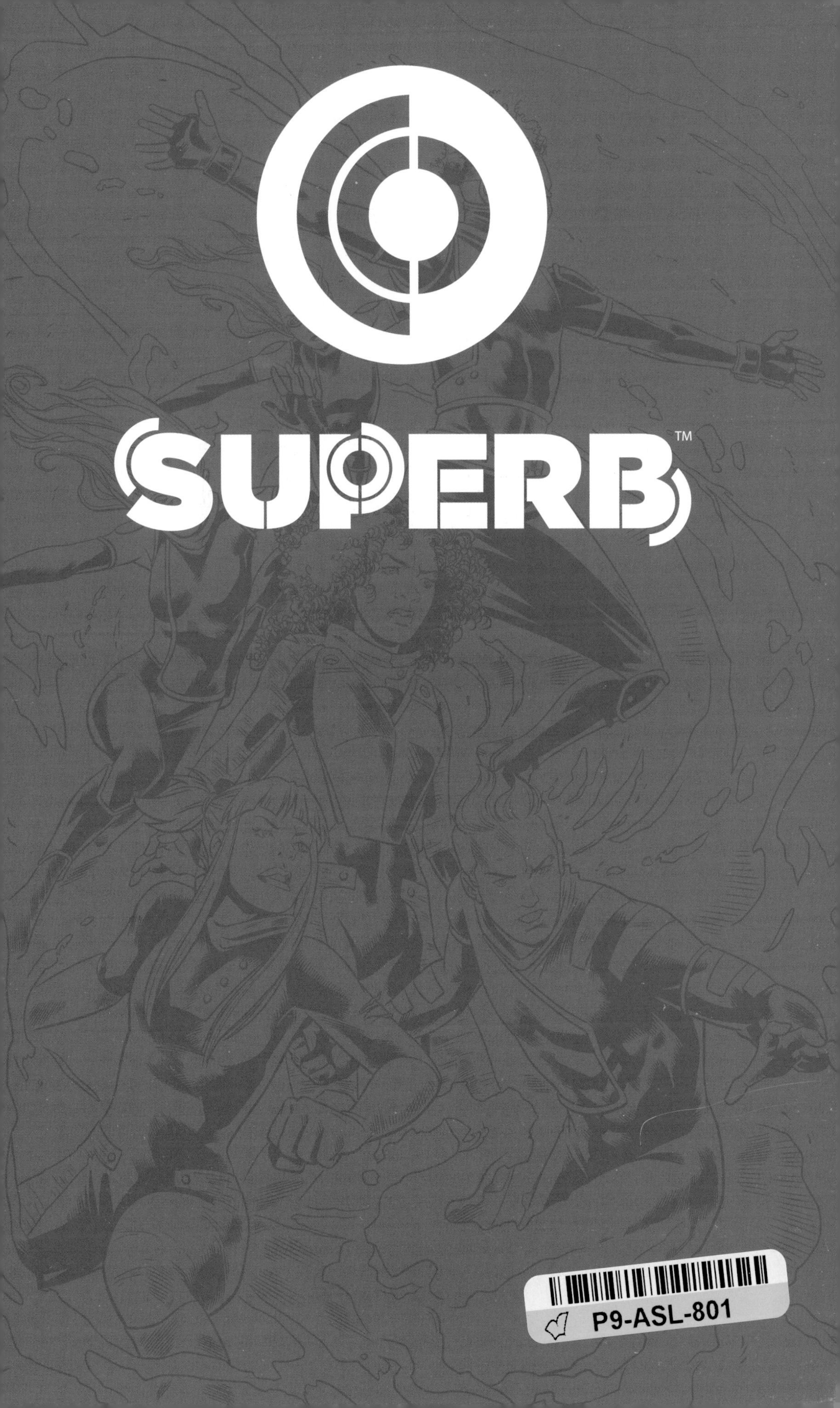
SUPERB™

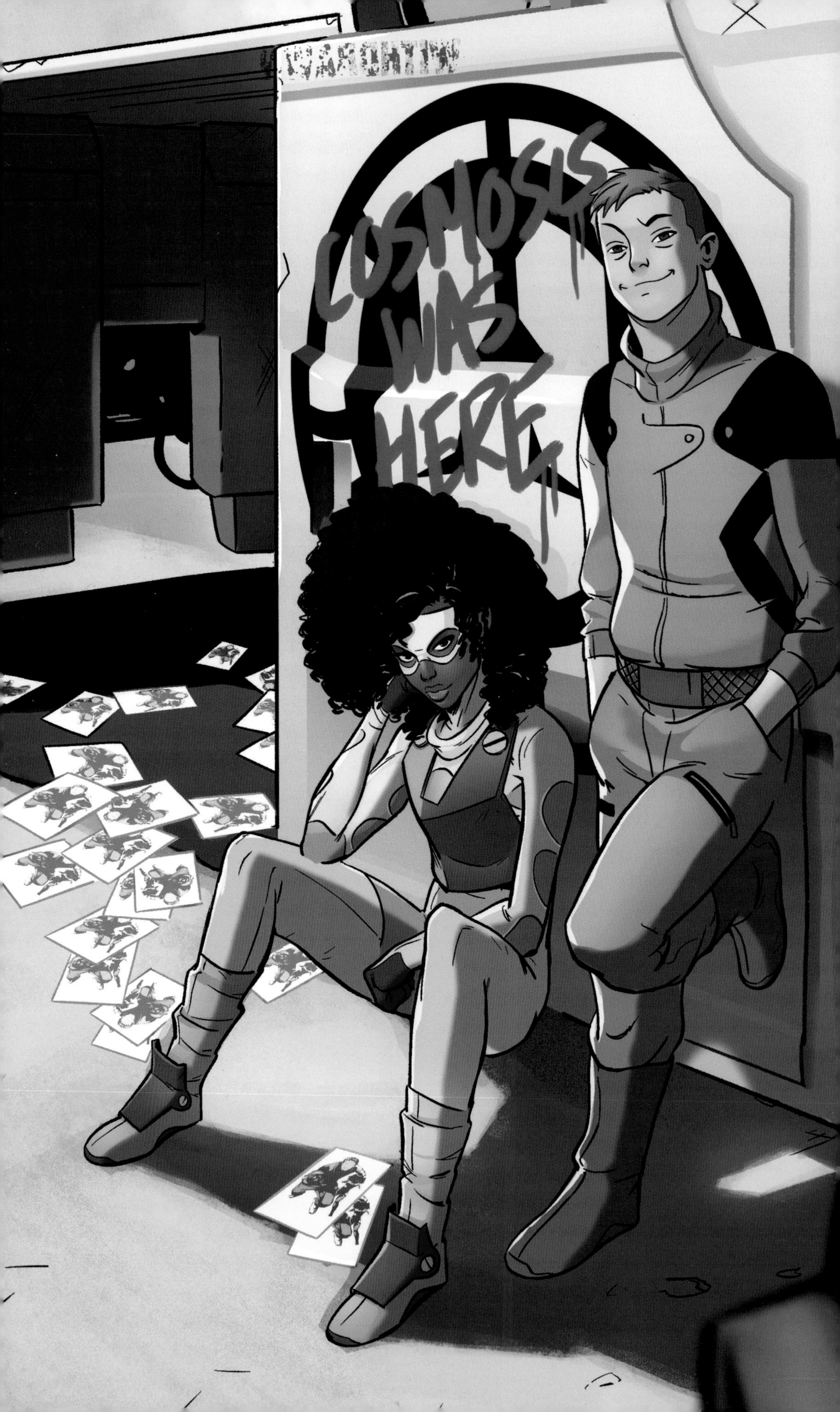
COSMOSIS WAS HERE

CHARLESTON COUNTY LIBRARY
AUG 2019
WITHDRAWN

CATALYST™
PRIME

SUPERB™

THE YOUTH ARE GETTING RESTLESS

Written by **DAVID F. WALKER**
Penciled by **ALITHA MARTINEZ**
Inked by **DAVID CABEZA** and **JOHN LIVESAY**
Lettered by **AW'S TOM NAPOLITANO**
Colored by **VERONICA GANDINI** and **DC ALONSO**

JASMINE AMIRI · Editor
DESIREE RODRIGUEZ · Editorial Assistant

Cover by **ANTHONY PIPER**

ROAR™

ISBN: 978-1-941302-86-6

Library of Congress Control Number: 2017951832

Superb Vol. 3, published 2019, by The Lion Forge, LLC. Copyright 2019 The Lion Forge, LLC. Portions of this book were previously published in Superb, Vol. 3 Issues 10-14. All Rights Reserved. SUPERB™, LION FORGE™, CATALYST PRIME™, ROAR™, and their associated distinctive designs, as well as all characters featured in this book and the distinctive names and likenesses thereof, and all related indicia, are trademarks of The Lion Forge, LLC. No similarity between any of the names, characters, persons, or institutions in this book with those of any living or dead person or institution is intended, and any such similarity which may exist is purely coincidental. Printed in Korea.

10 9 8 7 6 5 4 3 2 1

CHAPTER ONE

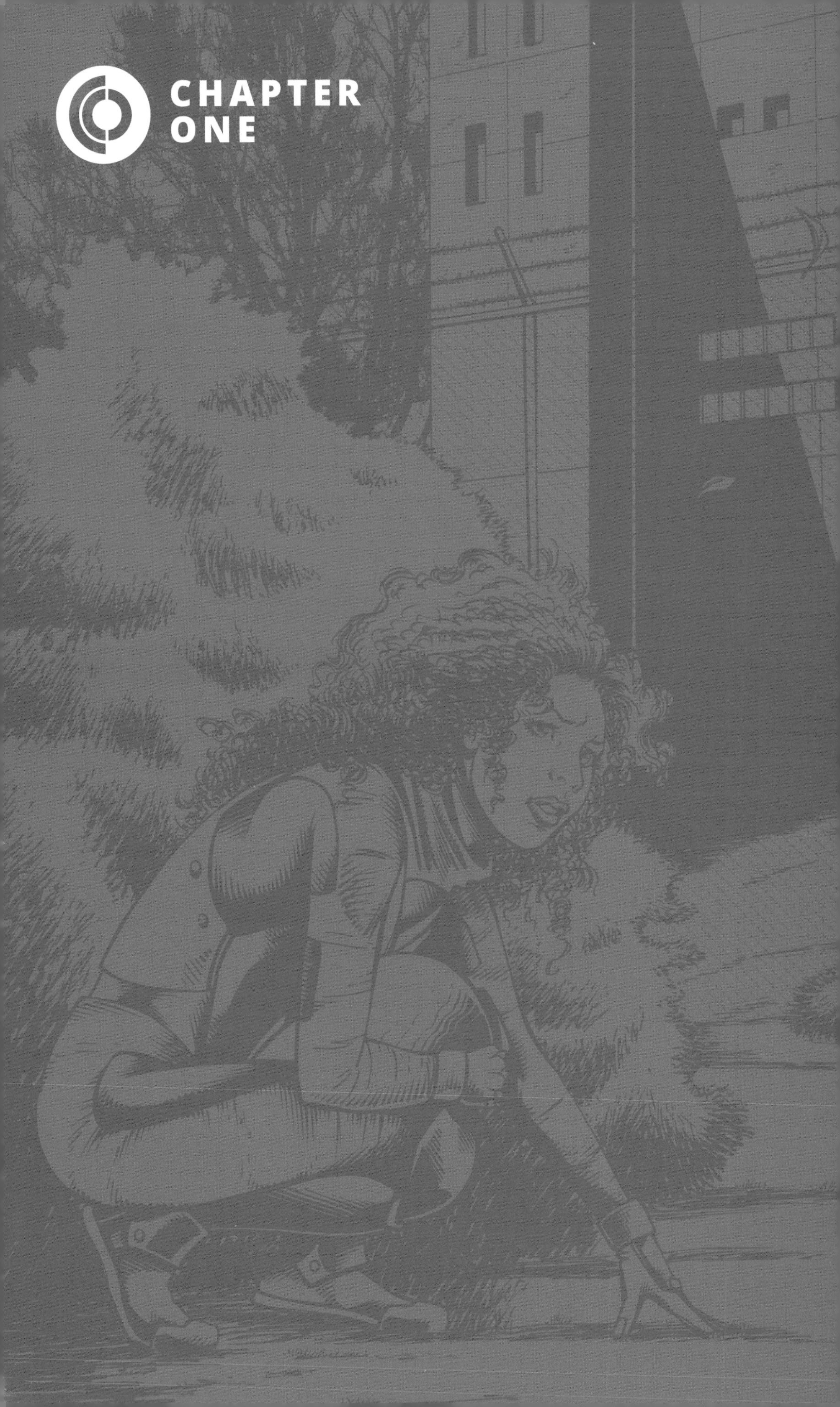

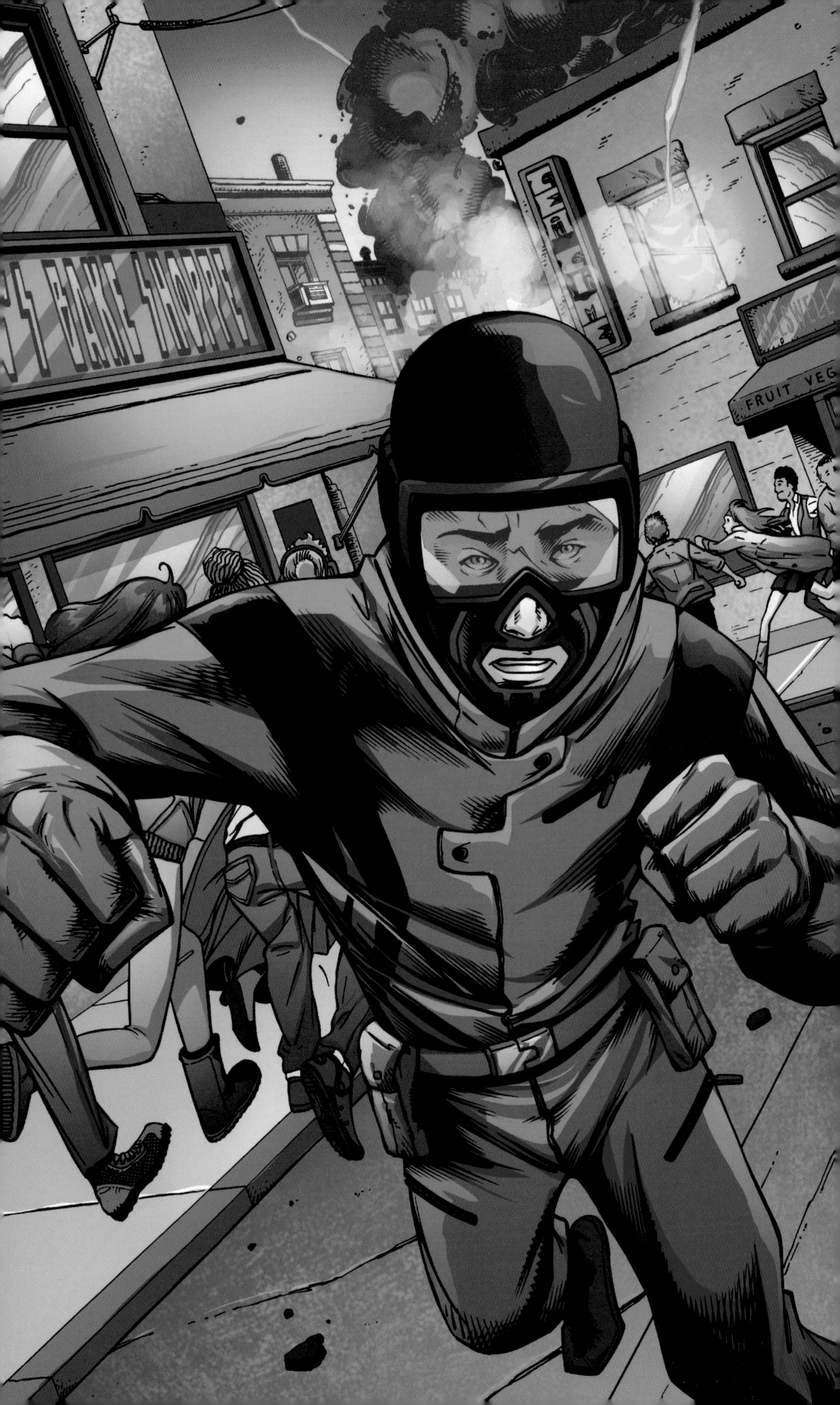
BAKE SHOPPE
FRUIT VEG

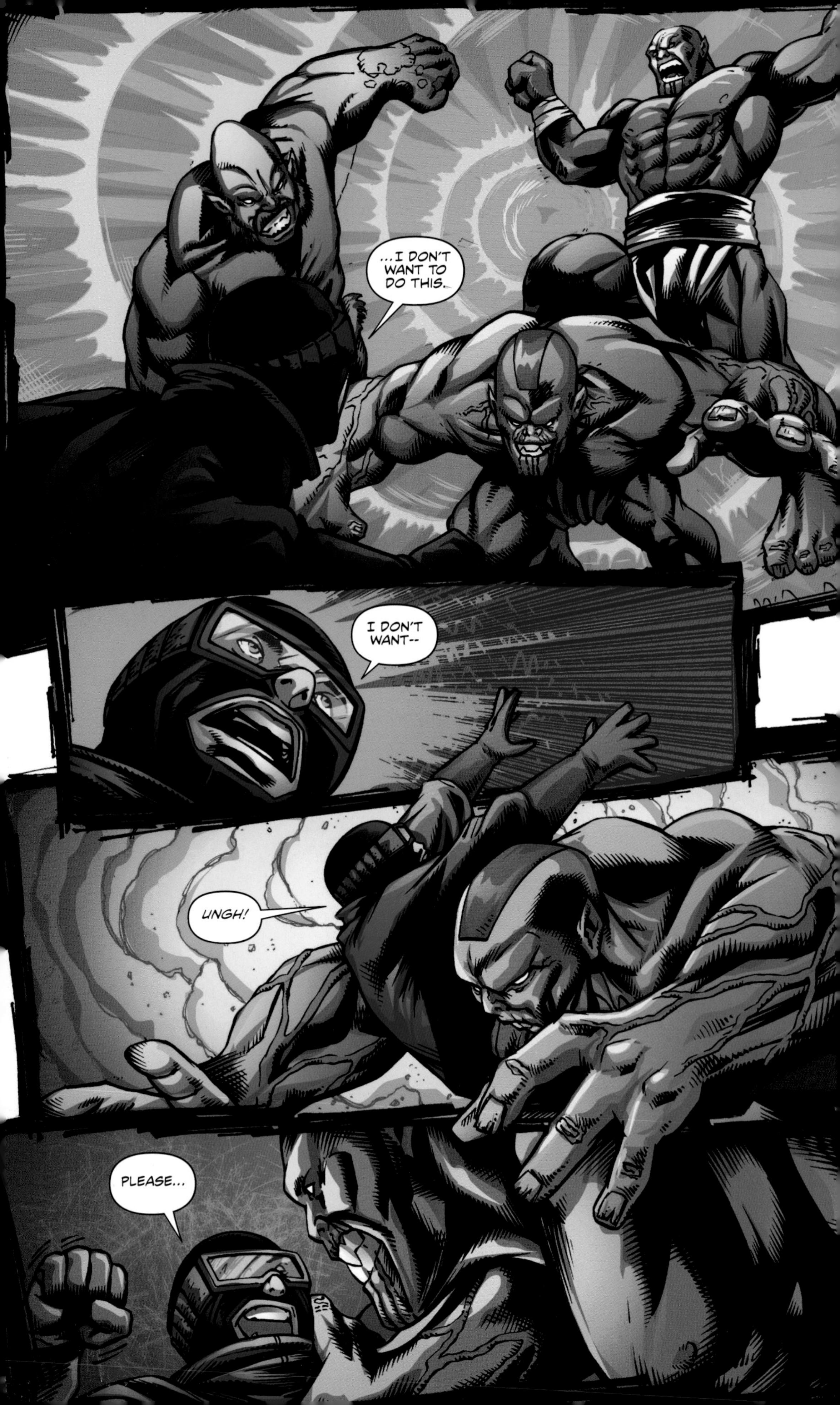
...I DON'T WANT TO DO THIS.
I DON'T WANT--
UNGH!
PLEASE...

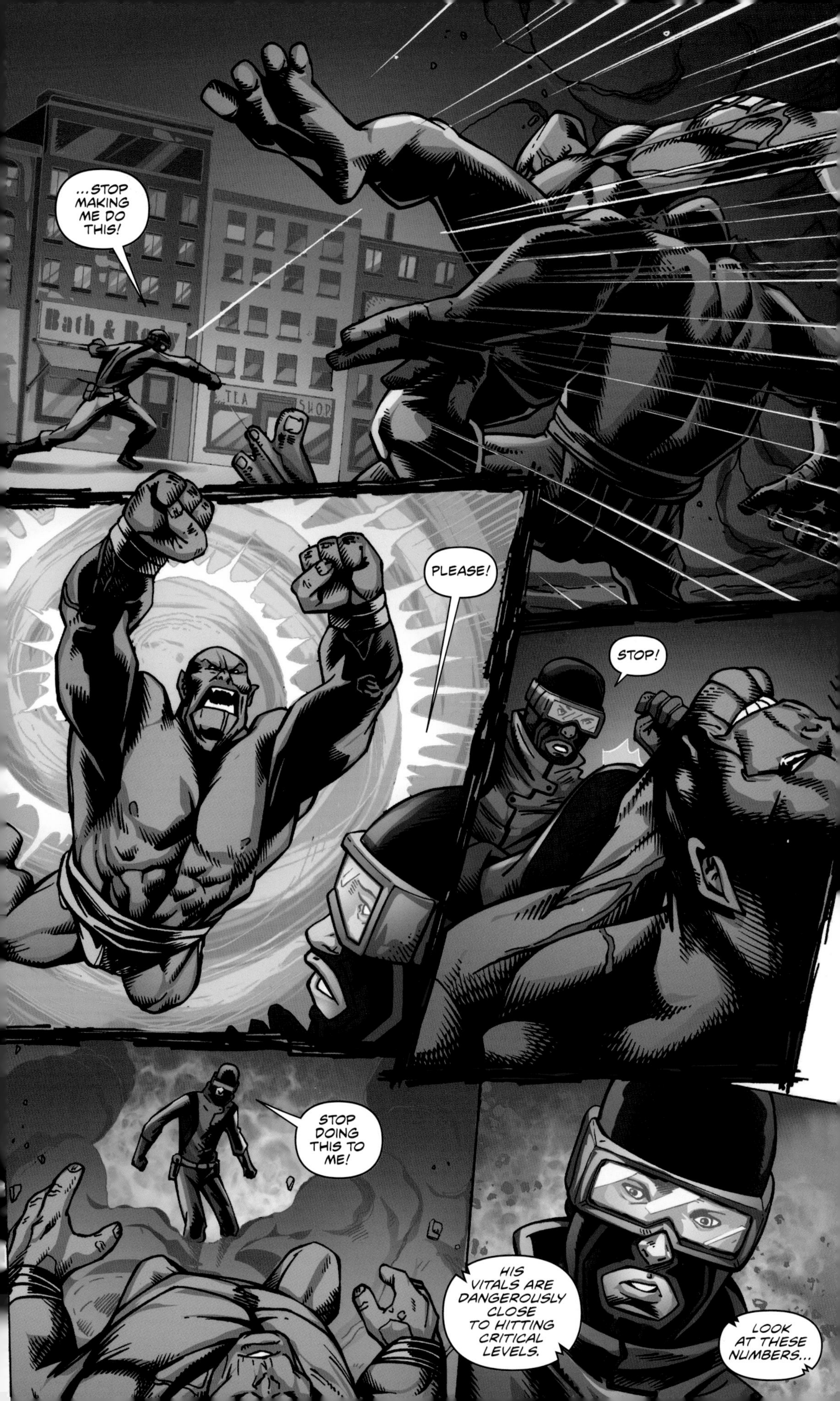

...STOP MAKING ME DO THIS!
Bath & Body
TEA SHOP
PLEASE!
STOP!
STOP DOING THIS TO ME!
HIS VITALS ARE DANGEROUSLY CLOSE TO HITTING CRITICAL LEVELS.
LOOK AT THESE NUMBERS...

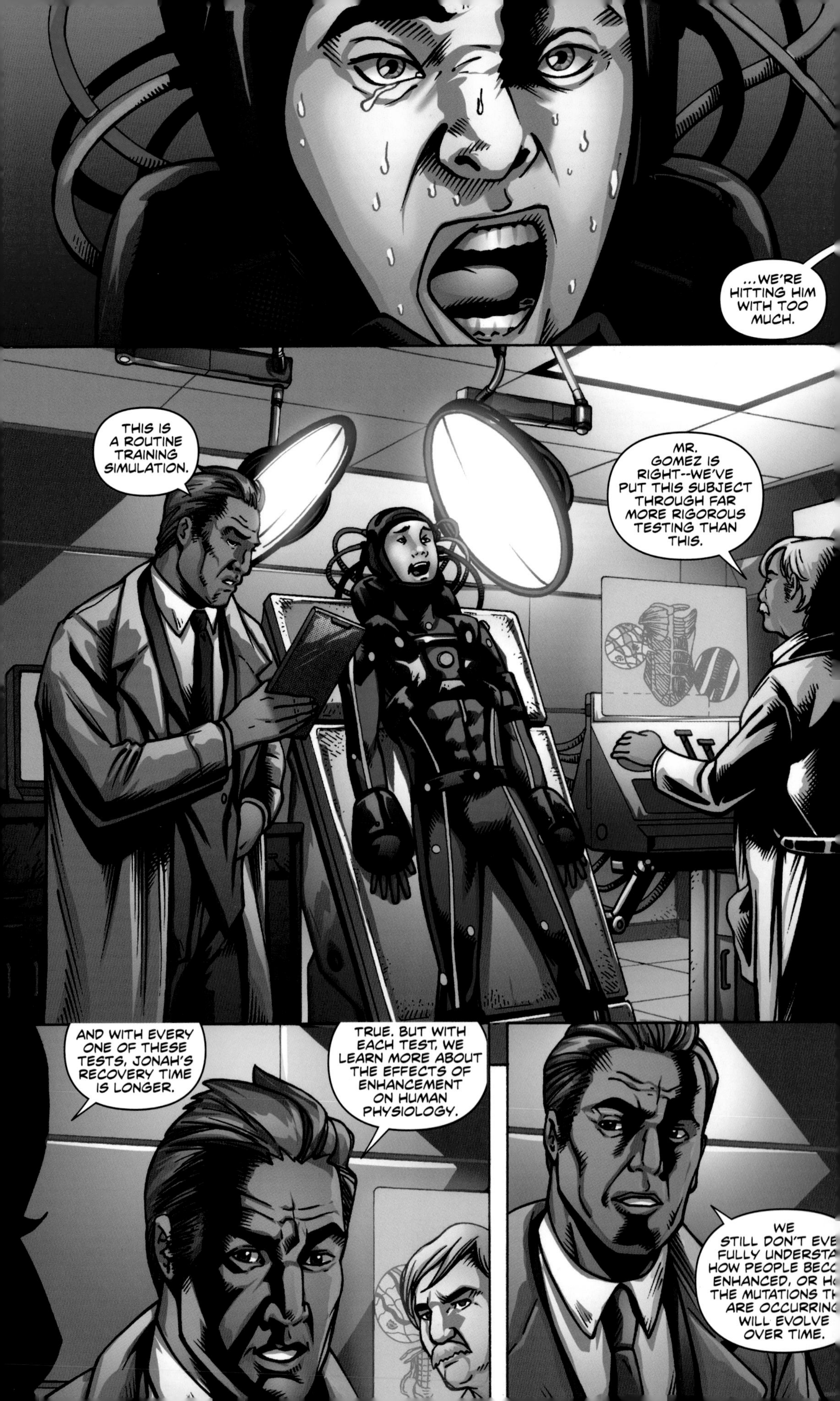
...WE'RE HITTING HIM WITH TOO MUCH.
THIS IS A ROUTINE TRAINING SIMULATION.
MR. GOMEZ IS RIGHT--WE'VE PUT THIS SUBJECT THROUGH FAR MORE RIGOROUS TESTING THAN THIS.
AND WITH EVERY ONE OF THESE TESTS, JONAH'S RECOVERY TIME IS LONGER.
TRUE. BUT WITH EACH TEST, WE LEARN MORE ABOUT THE EFFECTS OF ENHANCEMENT ON HUMAN PHYSIOLOGY.
WE STILL DON'T EVE FULLY UNDERSTA HOW PEOPLE BECO ENHANCED, OR H THE MUTATIONS T ARE OCCURRING WILL EVOLVE OVER TIME.

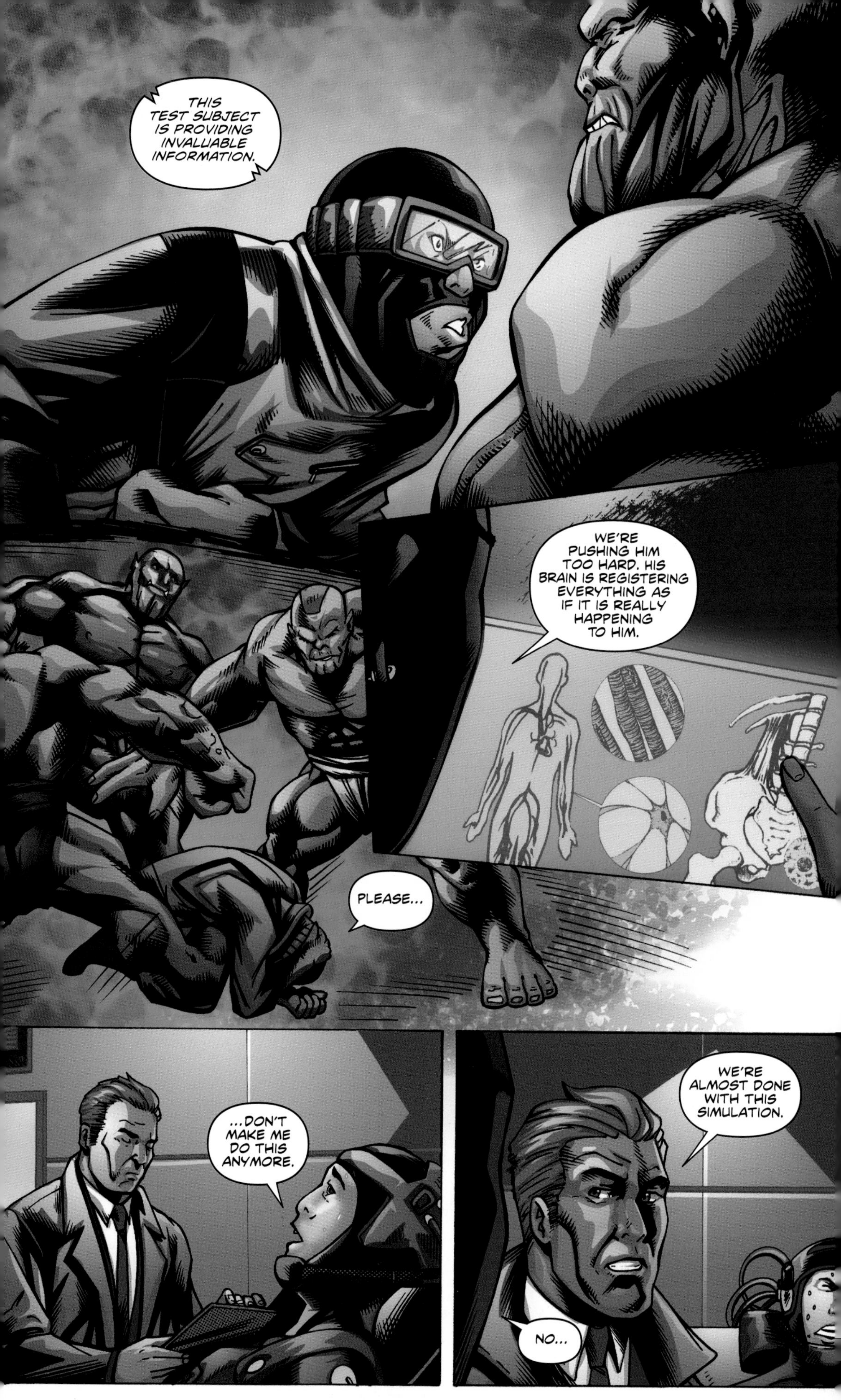
THIS TEST SUBJECT IS PROVIDING INVALUABLE INFORMATION.
WE'RE PUSHING HIM TOO HARD. HIS BRAIN IS REGISTERING EVERYTHING AS IF IT IS REALLY HAPPENING TO HIM.
PLEASE...
...DON'T MAKE ME DO THIS ANYMORE.
WE'RE ALMOST DONE WITH THIS SIMULATION.
NO...

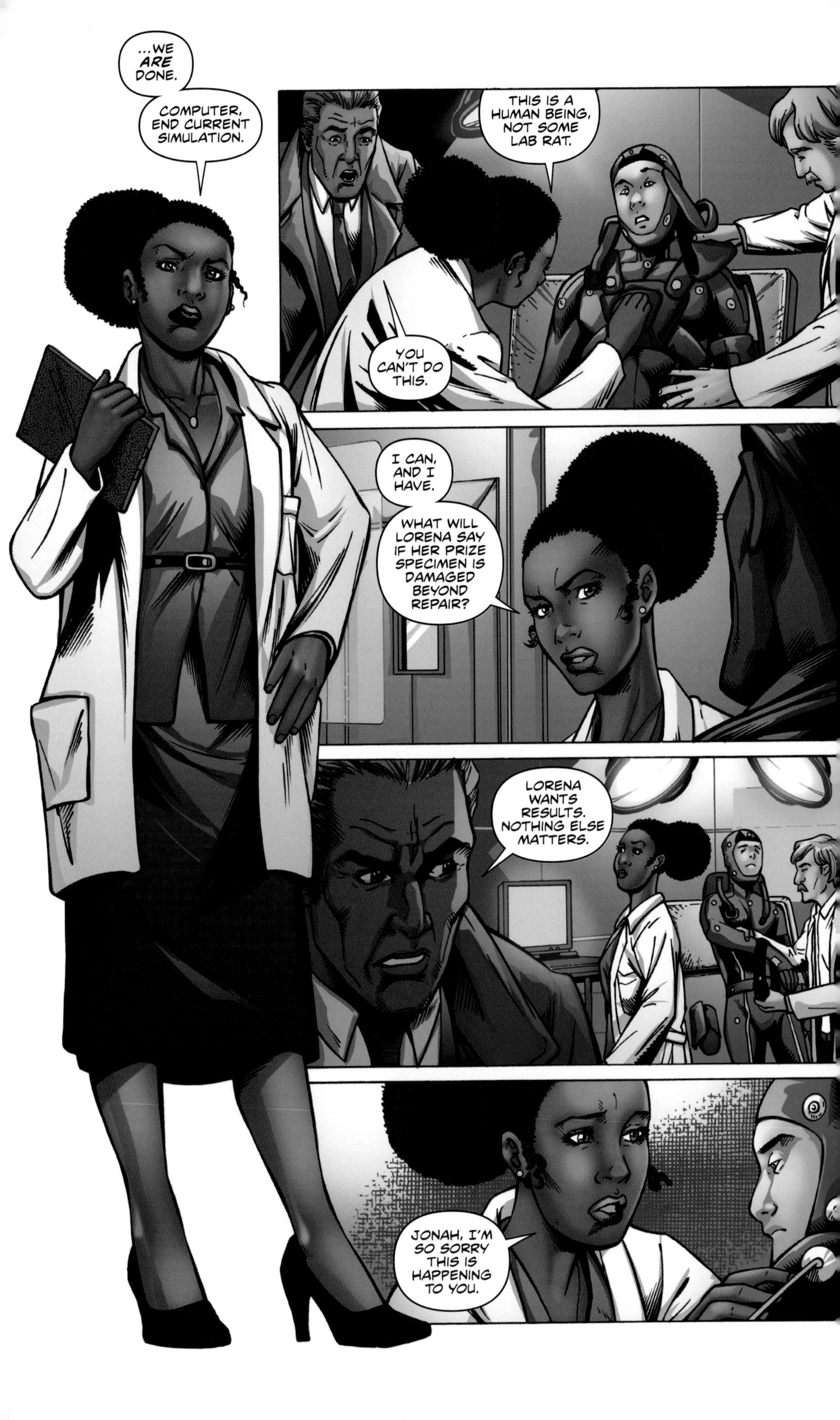
...WE ARE DONE.
COMPUTER, END CURRENT SIMULATION.
THIS IS A HUMAN BEING, NOT SOME LAB RAT.
YOU CAN'T DO THIS.
I CAN, AND I HAVE.
WHAT WILL LORENA SAY IF HER PRIZE SPECIMEN IS DAMAGED BEYOND REPAIR?
LORENA WANTS RESULTS. NOTHING ELSE MATTERS.
JONAH, I'M SO SORRY THIS IS HAPPENING TO YOU.

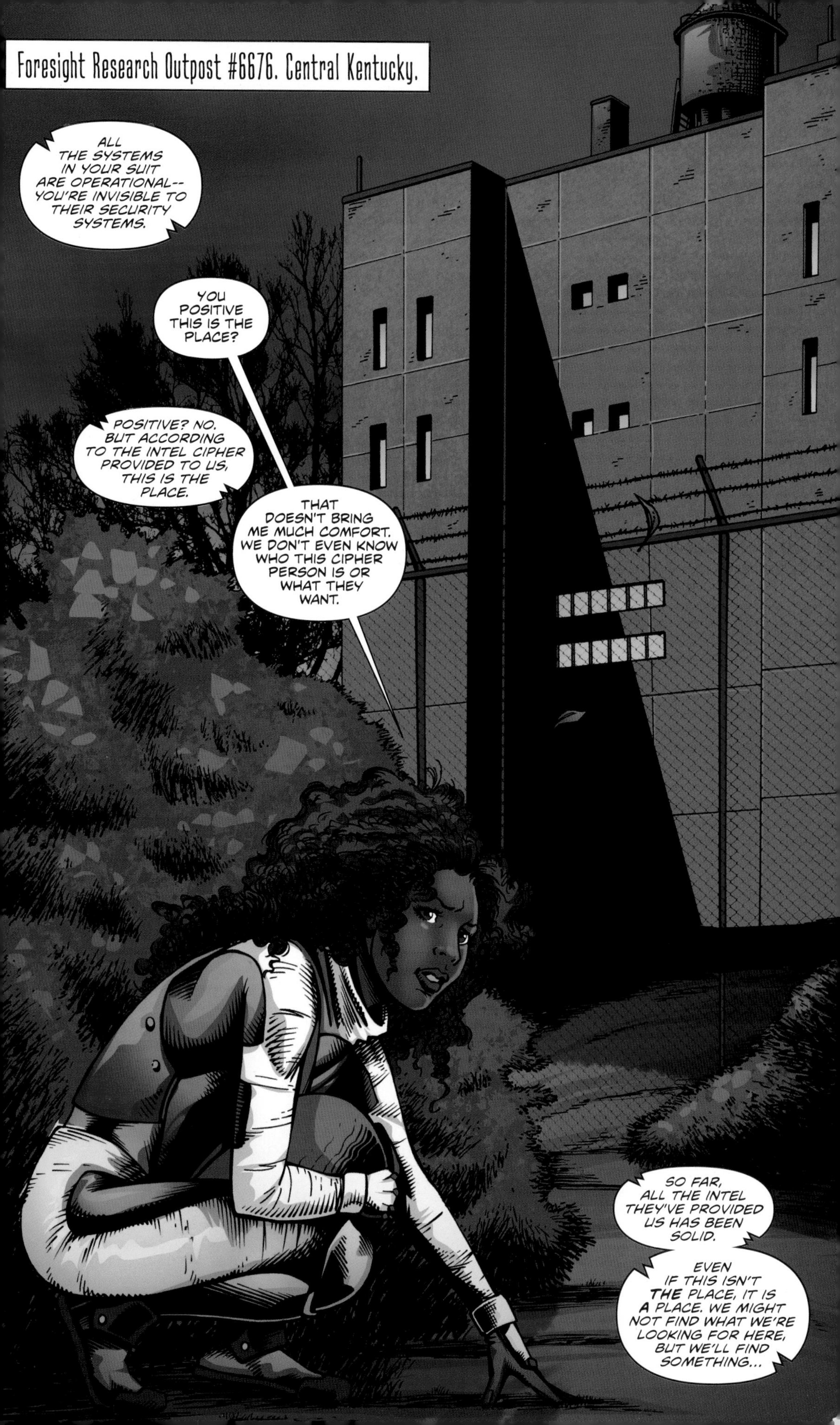
Foresight Research Outpost #6676. Central Kentucky.
ALL THE SYSTEMS IN YOUR SUIT ARE OPERATIONAL-- YOU'RE INVISIBLE TO THEIR SECURITY SYSTEMS.
YOU POSITIVE THIS IS THE PLACE?
POSITIVE? NO. BUT ACCORDING TO THE INTEL CIPHER PROVIDED TO US, THIS IS THE PLACE.
THAT DOESN'T BRING ME MUCH COMFORT. WE DON'T EVEN KNOW WHO THIS CIPHER PERSON IS OR WHAT THEY WANT.
SO FAR, ALL THE INTEL THEY'VE PROVIDED US HAS BEEN SOLID.
EVEN IF THIS ISN'T **THE** PLACE, IT IS **A** PLACE. WE MIGHT NOT FIND WHAT WE'RE LOOKING FOR HERE, BUT WE'LL FIND SOMETHING...

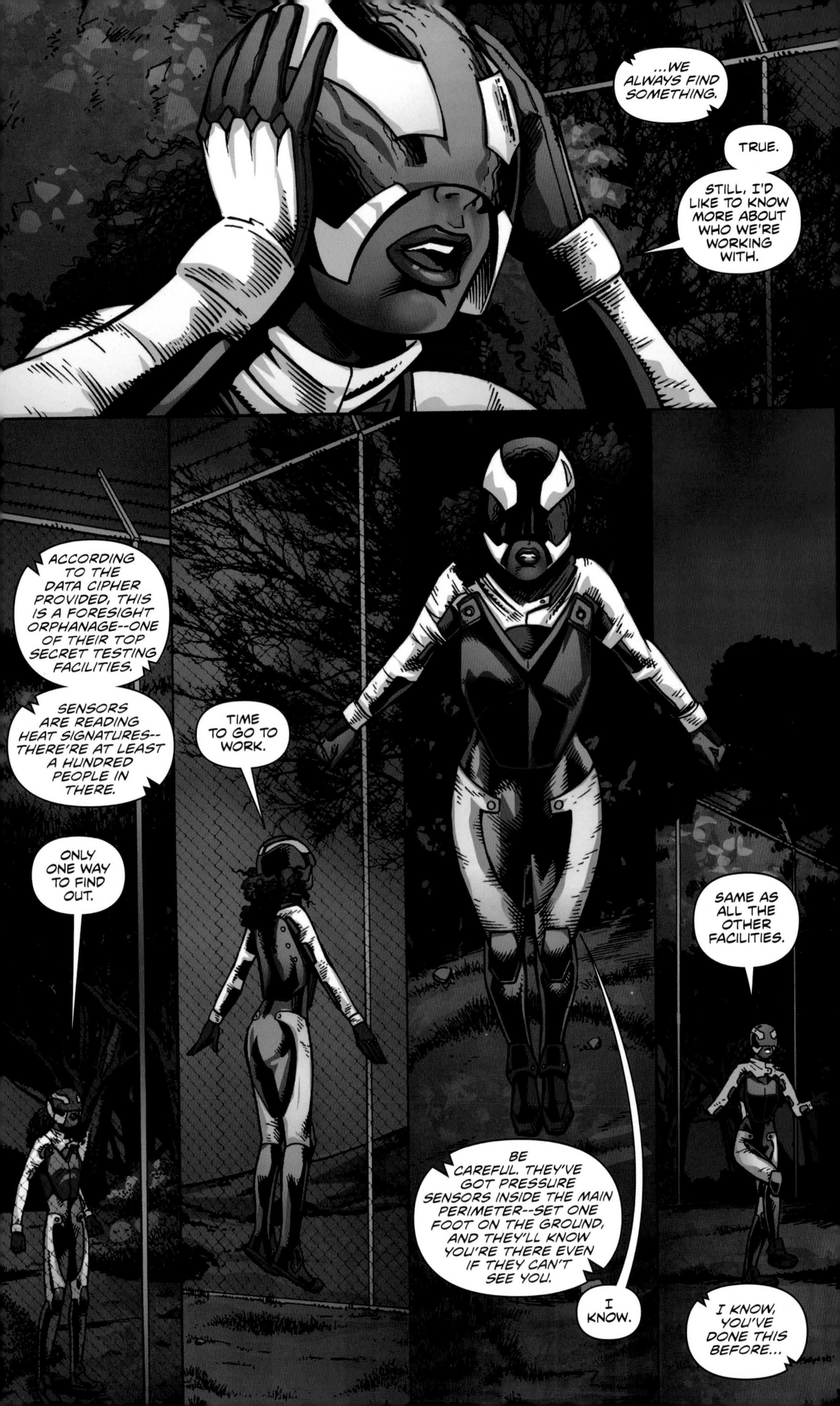
...WE ALWAYS FIND SOMETHING.
TRUE.
STILL, I'D LIKE TO KNOW MORE ABOUT WHO WE'RE WORKING WITH.
ACCORDING TO THE DATA CIPHER PROVIDED, THIS IS A FORESIGHT ORPHANAGE--ONE OF THEIR TOP SECRET TESTING FACILITIES.
SENSORS ARE READING HEAT SIGNATURES--THERE'RE AT LEAST A HUNDRED PEOPLE IN THERE.
ONLY ONE WAY TO FIND OUT.
TIME TO GO TO WORK.
SAME AS ALL THE OTHER FACILITIES.
BE CAREFUL. THEY'VE GOT PRESSURE SENSORS INSIDE THE MAIN PERIMETER--SET ONE FOOT ON THE GROUND, AND THEY'LL KNOW YOU'RE THERE EVEN IF THEY CAN'T SEE YOU.
I KNOW.
I KNOW, YOU'VE DONE THIS BEFORE...

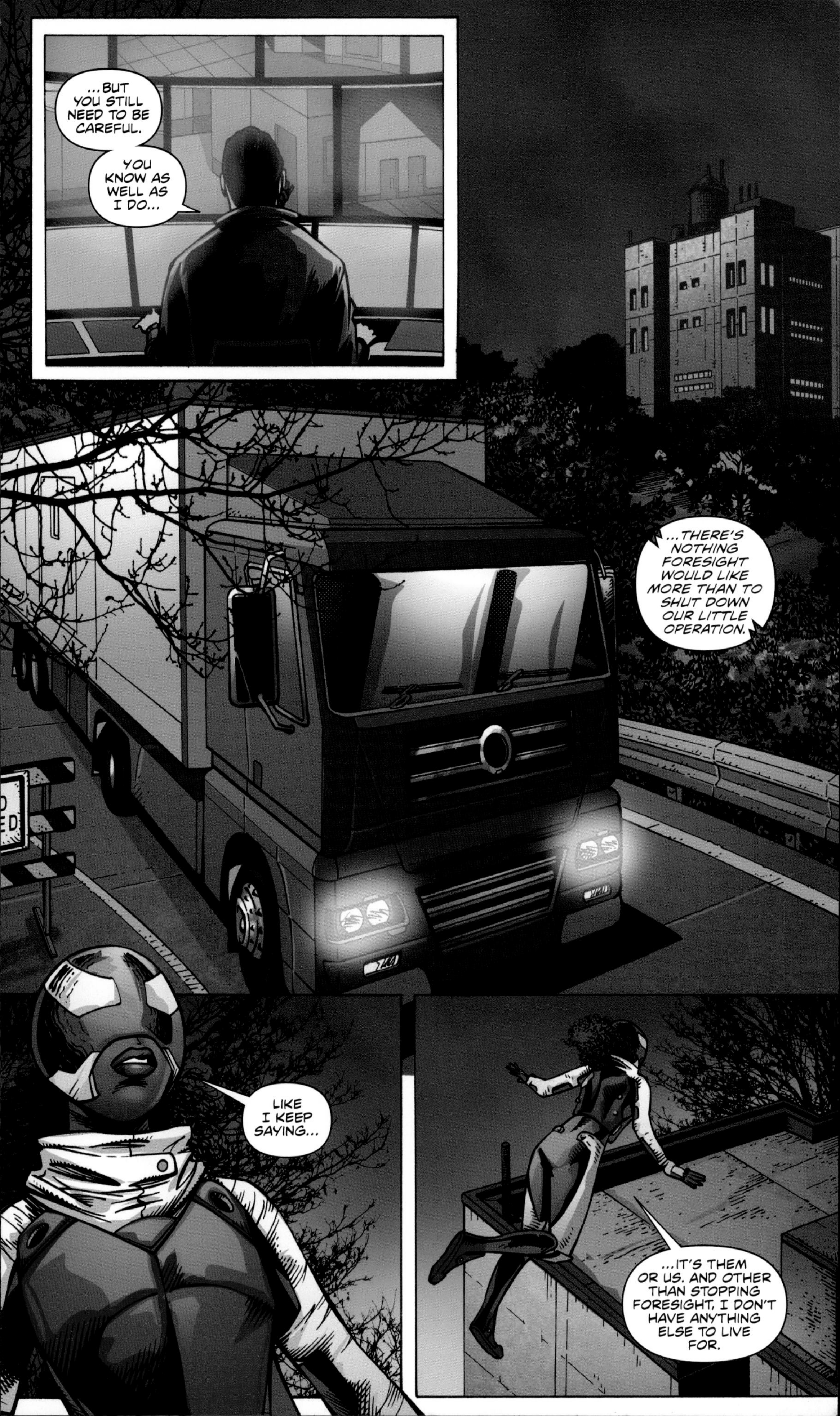
...BUT YOU STILL NEED TO BE CAREFUL.
YOU KNOW AS WELL AS I DO...
...THERE'S NOTHING FORESIGHT WOULD LIKE MORE THAN TO SHUT DOWN OUR LITTLE OPERATION.
LIKE I KEEP SAYING...
...IT'S THEM OR US. AND OTHER THAN STOPPING FORESIGHT, I DON'T HAVE ANYTHING ELSE TO LIVE FOR.

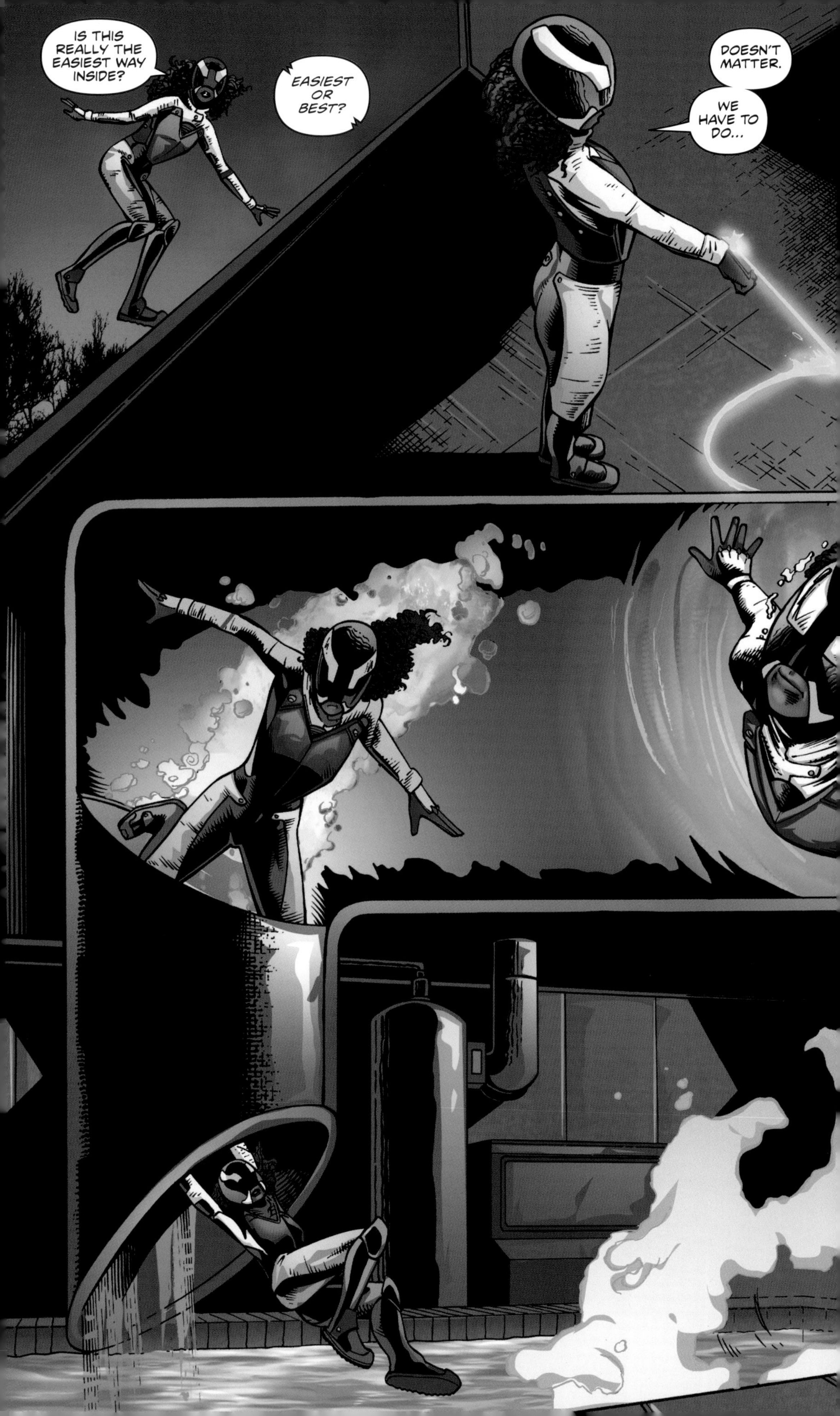
IS THIS REALLY THE EASIEST WAY INSIDE?
EASIEST OR BEST?
DOESN'T MATTER.
WE HAVE TO DO...

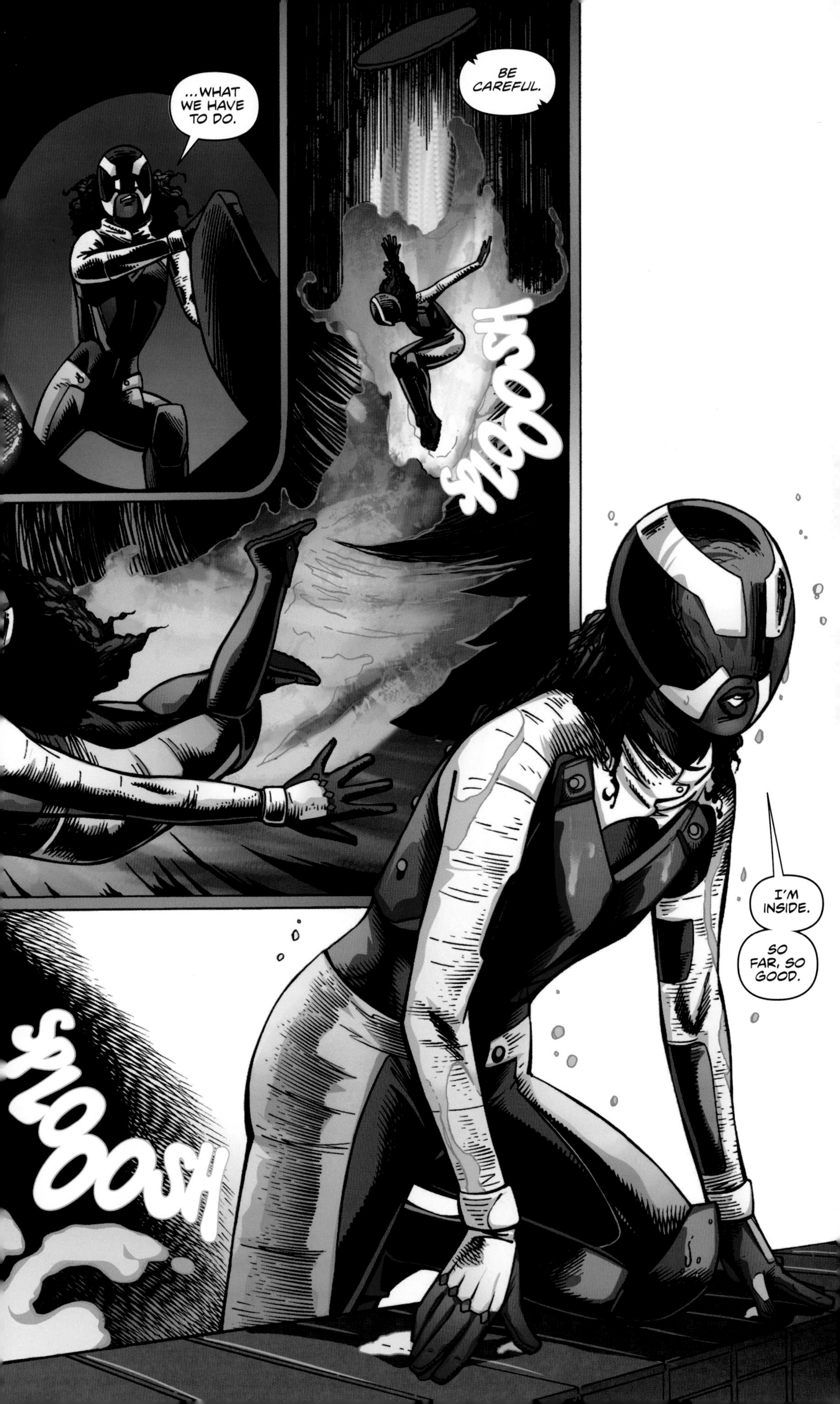
...WHAT WE HAVE TO DO.
BE CAREFUL.
SPLOOSH
I'M INSIDE.
SO FAR, SO GOOD.
SPLOOSH

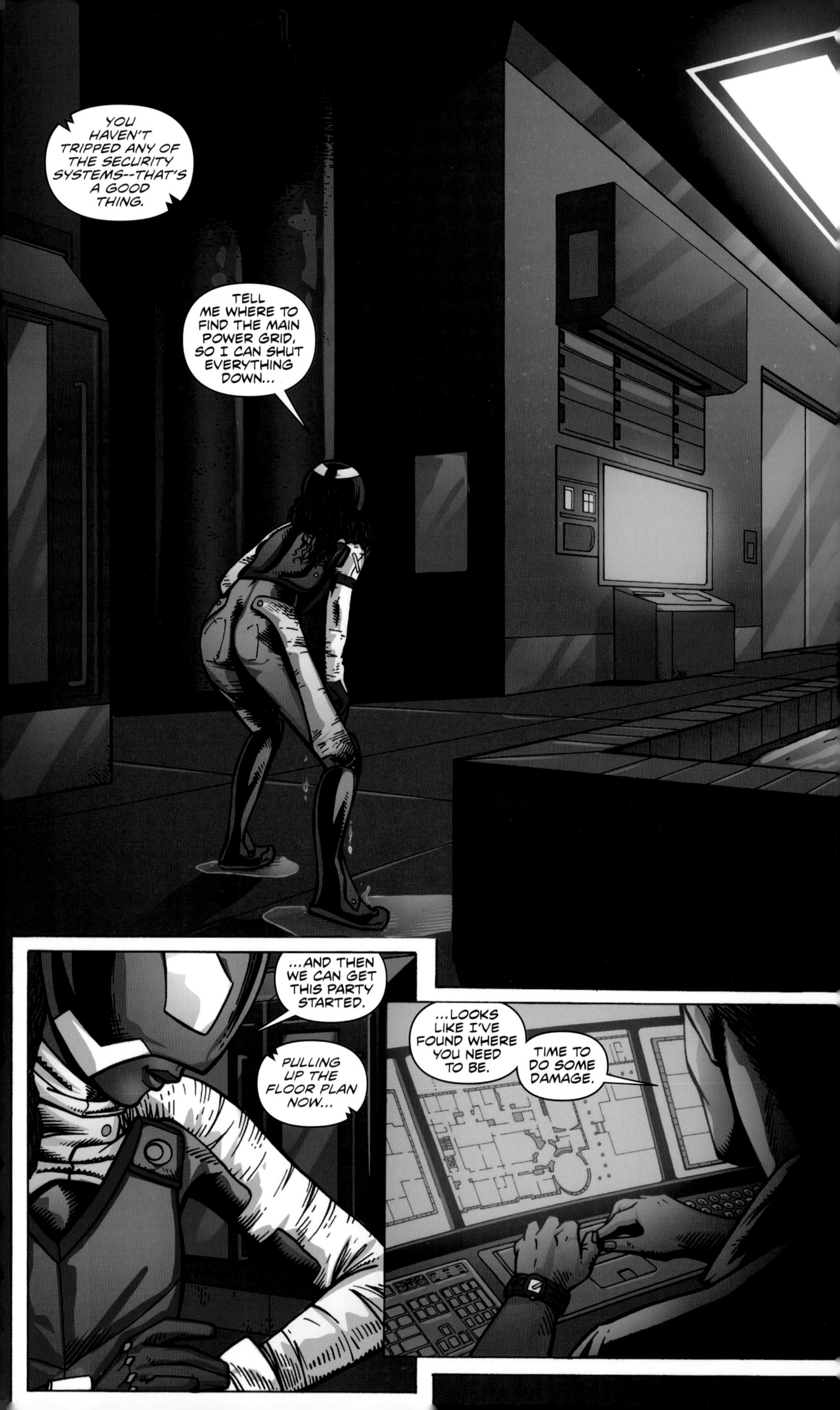
YOU HAVEN'T TRIPPED ANY OF THE SECURITY SYSTEMS--THAT'S A GOOD THING.
TELL ME WHERE TO FIND THE MAIN POWER GRID, SO I CAN SHUT EVERYTHING DOWN...
...AND THEN WE CAN GET THIS PARTY STARTED.
PULLING UP THE FLOOR PLAN NOW...
...LOOKS LIKE I'VE FOUND WHERE YOU NEED TO BE.
TIME TO DO SOME DAMAGE.

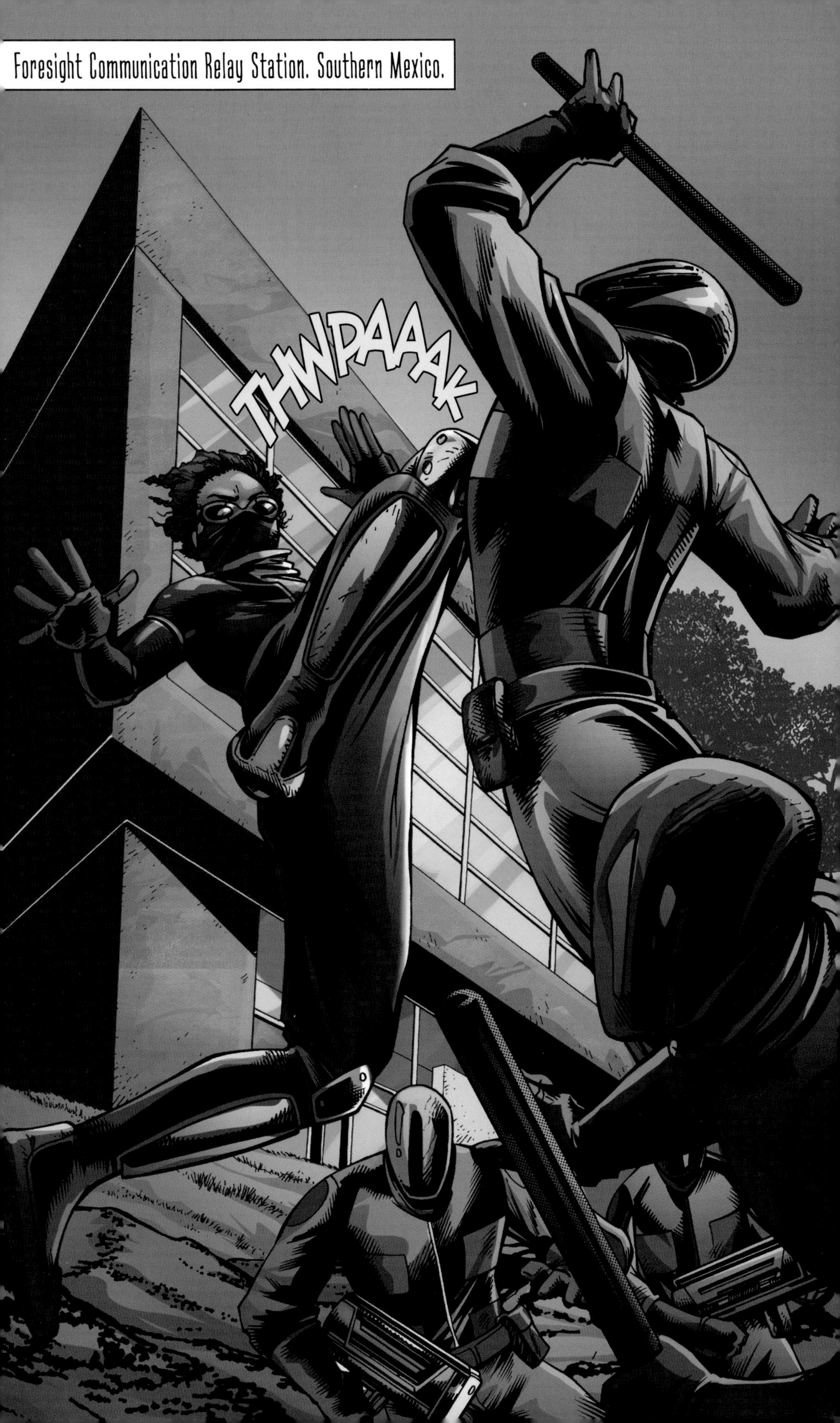

Foresight Communication Relay Station. Southern Mexico.
THWPAAAK

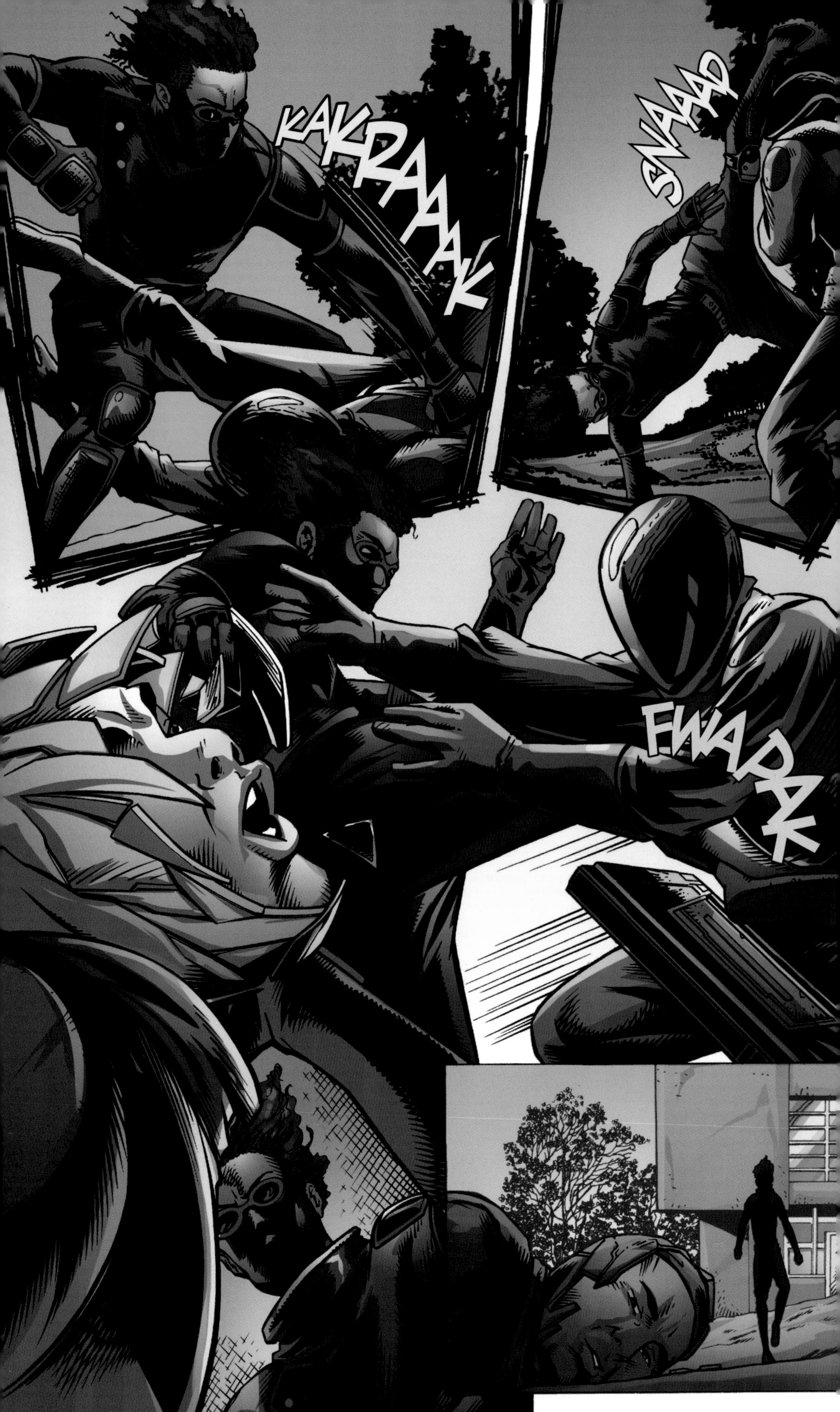
KAKRAAAAK
SNAAAP
FWAPAK

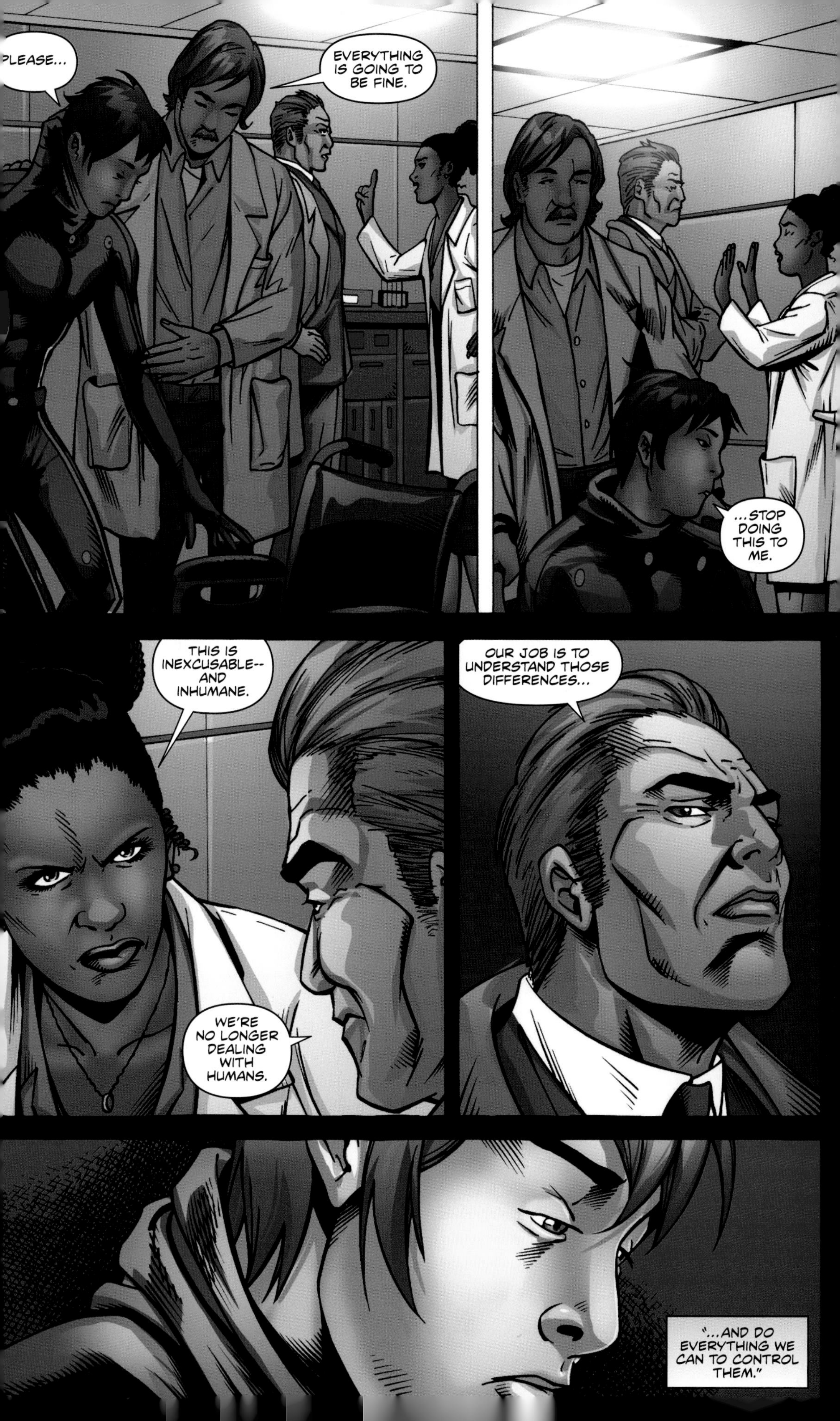
PLEASE...
EVERYTHING IS GOING TO BE FINE.
...STOP DOING THIS TO ME.
THIS IS INEXCUSABLE-- AND INHUMANE.
WE'RE NO LONGER DEALING WITH HUMANS.
OUR JOB IS TO UNDERSTAND THOSE DIFFERENCES...
"...AND DO EVERYTHING WE CAN TO CONTROL THEM."

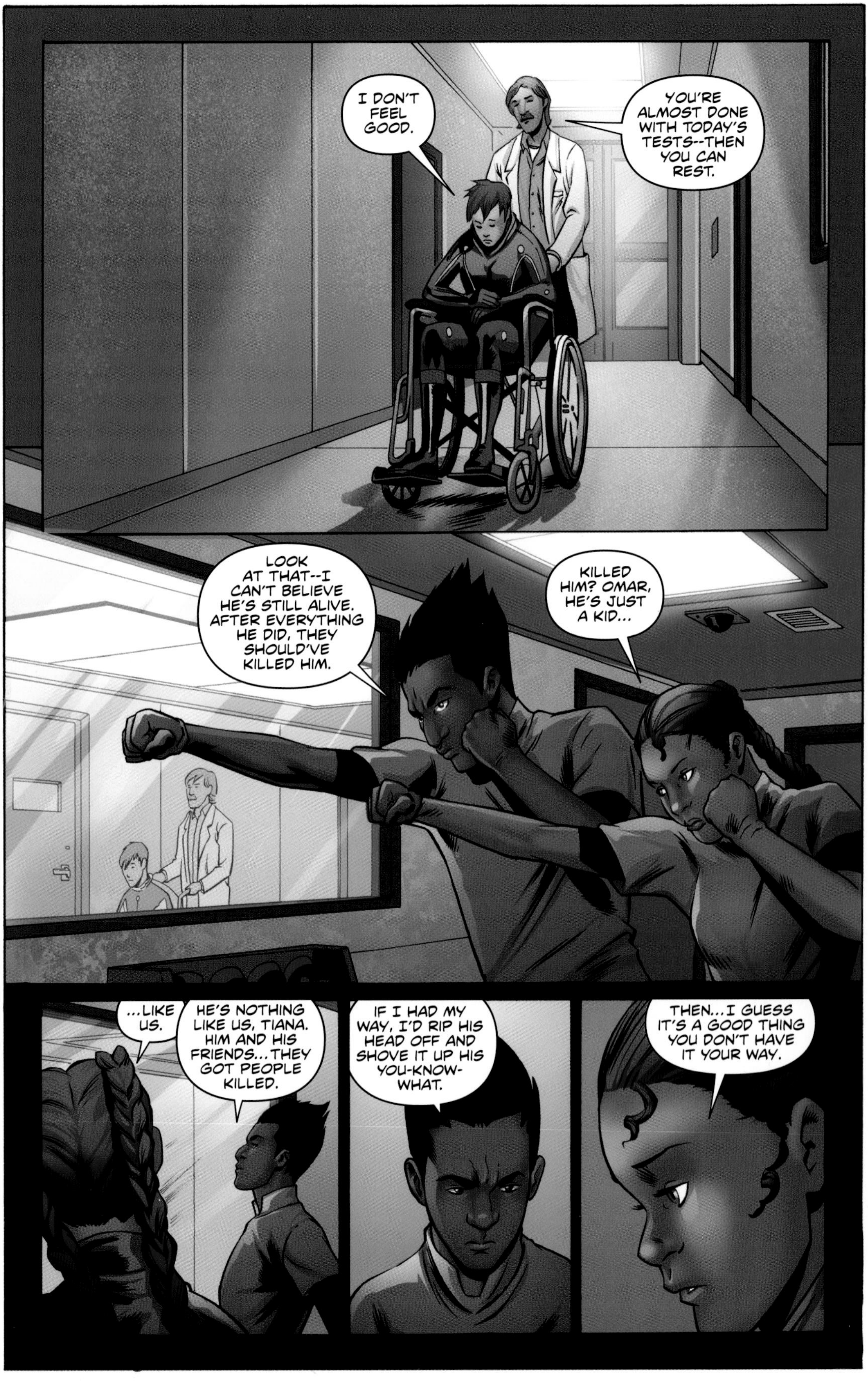
I DON'T FEEL GOOD.
YOU'RE ALMOST DONE WITH TODAY'S TESTS--THEN YOU CAN REST.
LOOK AT THAT--I CAN'T BELIEVE HE'S STILL ALIVE. AFTER EVERYTHING HE DID, THEY SHOULD'VE KILLED HIM.
KILLED HIM? OMAR, HE'S JUST A KID...
...LIKE US.
HE'S NOTHING LIKE US, TIANA. HIM AND HIS FRIENDS...THEY GOT PEOPLE KILLED.
IF I HAD MY WAY, I'D RIP HIS HEAD OFF AND SHOVE IT UP HIS YOU-KNOW-WHAT.
THEN...I GUESS IT'S A GOOD THING YOU DON'T HAVE IT YOUR WAY.

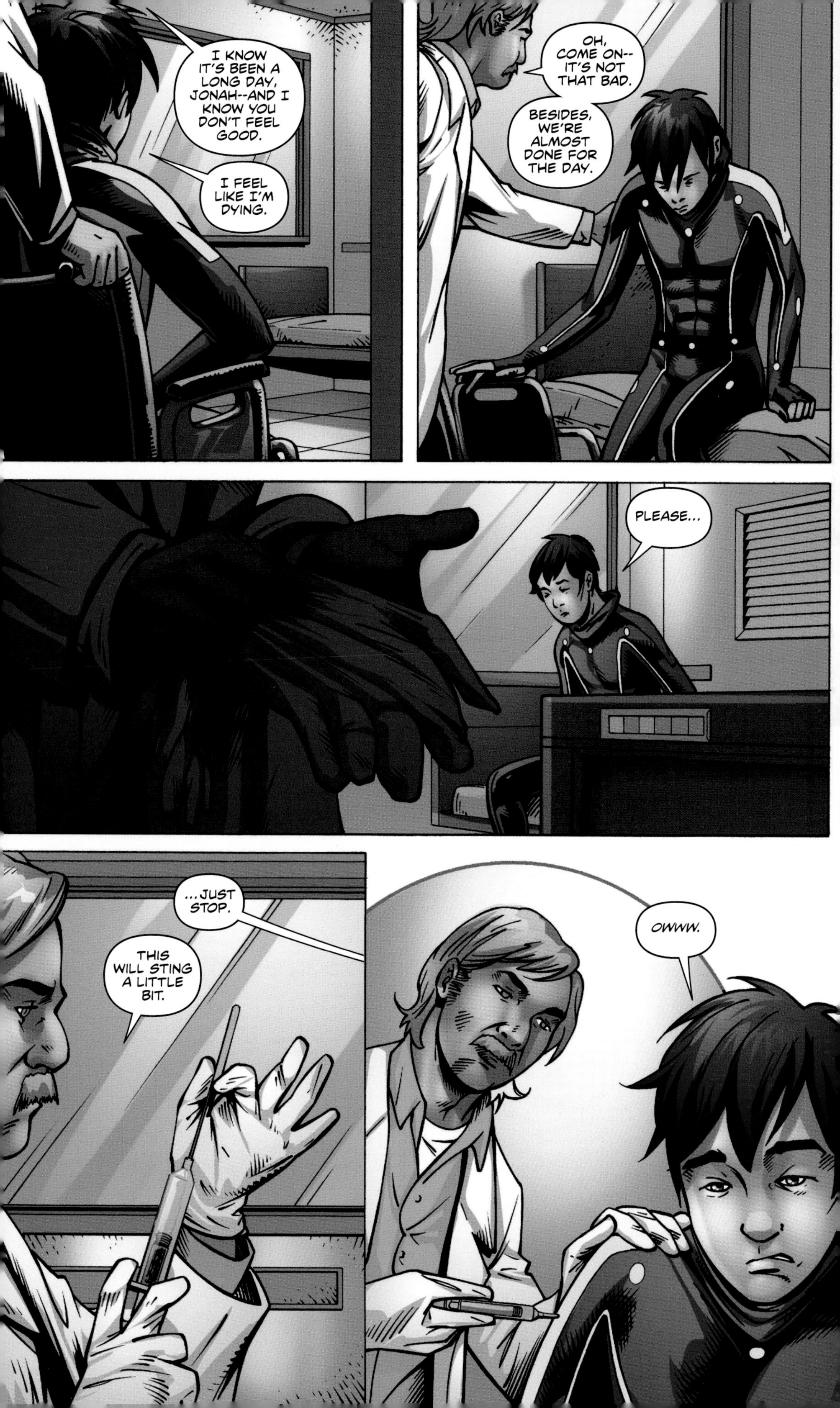
I KNOW IT'S BEEN A LONG DAY, JONAH--AND I KNOW YOU DON'T FEEL GOOD.
I FEEL LIKE I'M DYING.
OH, COME ON-- IT'S NOT THAT BAD.
BESIDES, WE'RE ALMOST DONE FOR THE DAY.
PLEASE...
...JUST STOP.
THIS WILL STING A LITTLE BIT.
OWWW.

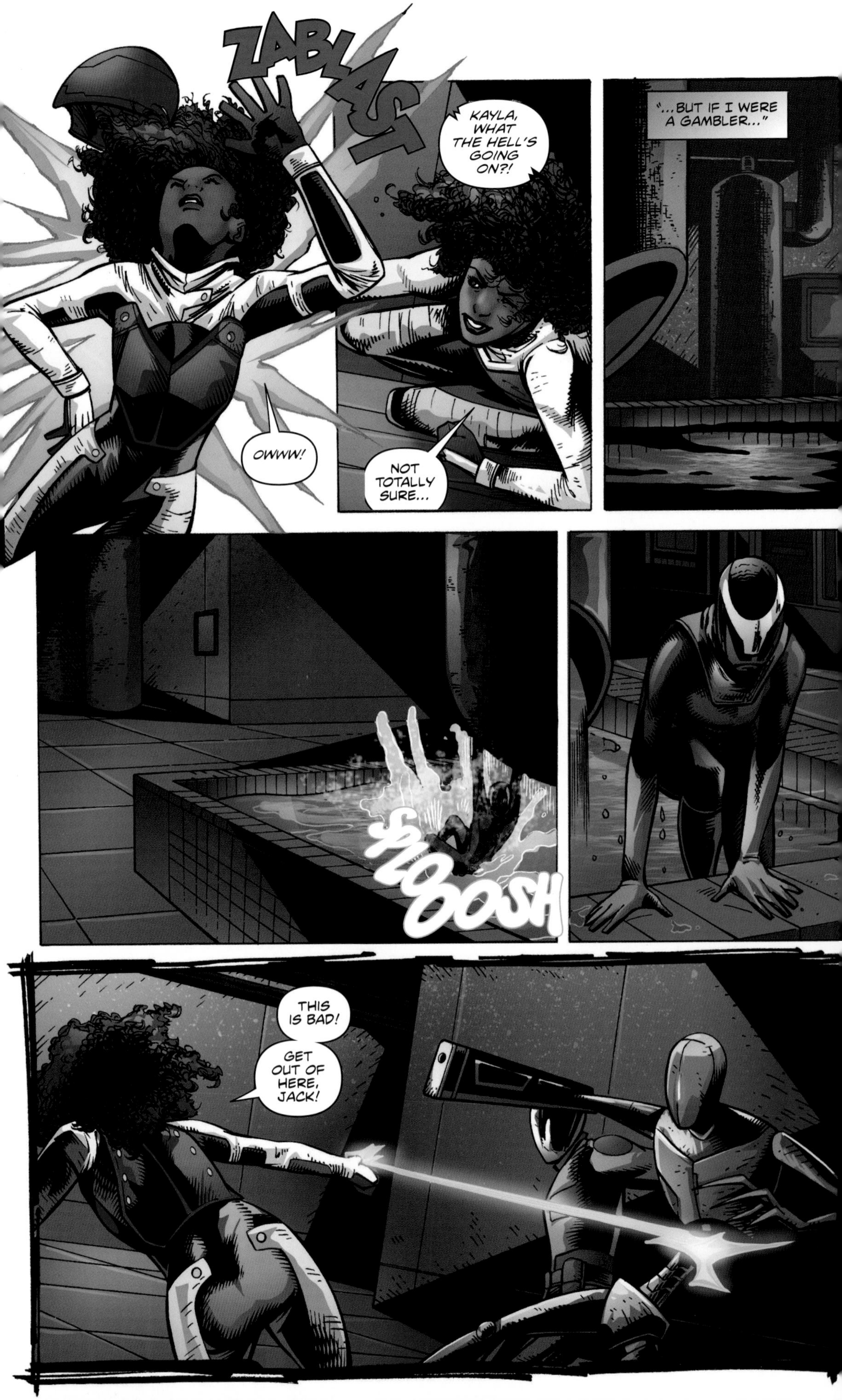
ZABLAST
KAYLA, WHAT THE HELL'S GOING ON?!
OWWW!
NOT TOTALLY SURE...
"...BUT IF I WERE A GAMBLER..."
SPLOOOSH
THIS IS BAD!
GET OUT OF HERE, JACK!

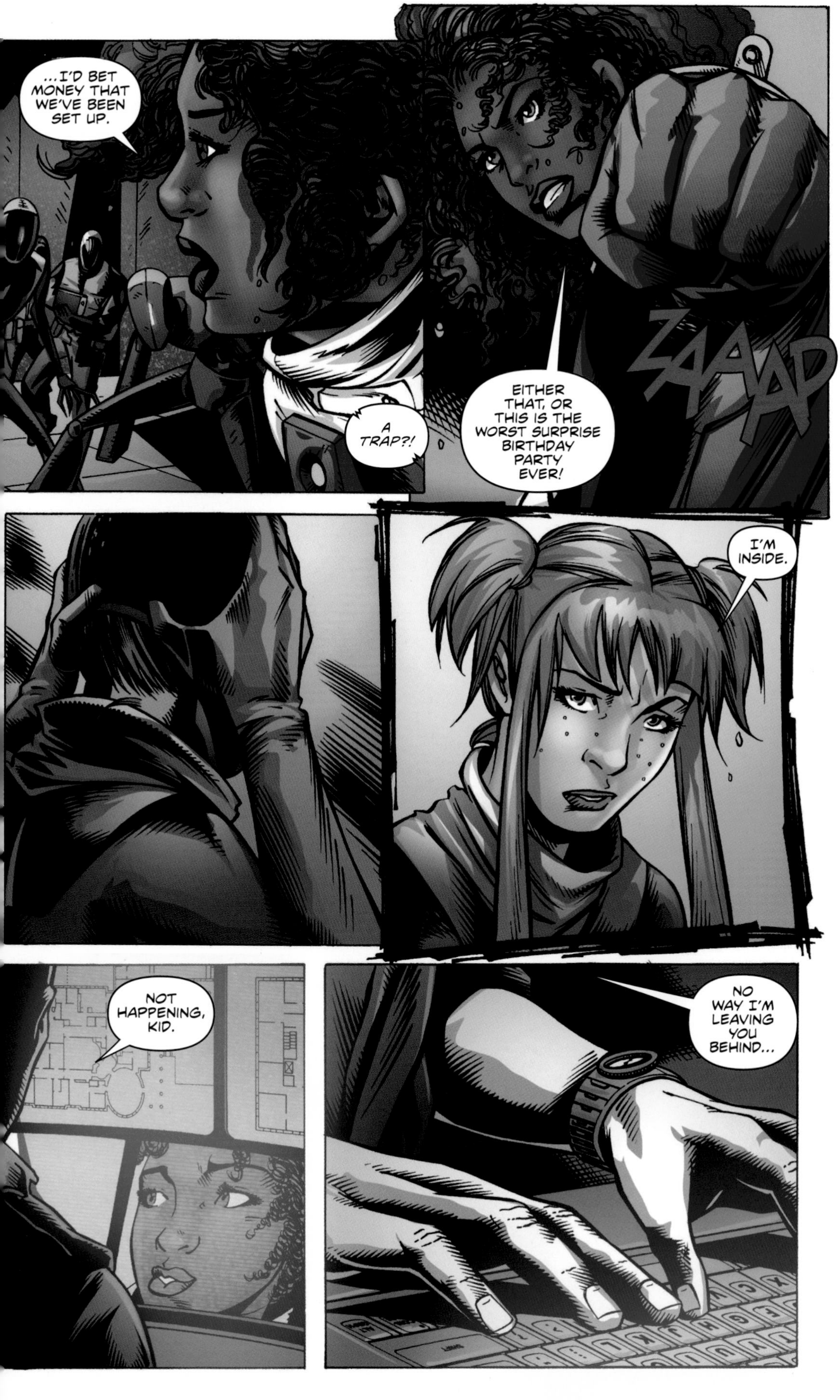
...I'D BET MONEY THAT WE'VE BEEN SET UP.
A TRAP?!
EITHER THAT, OR THIS IS THE WORST SURPRISE BIRTHDAY PARTY EVER!
ZAAAP
I'M INSIDE.
NOT HAPPENING, KID.
NO WAY I'M LEAVING YOU BEHIND...

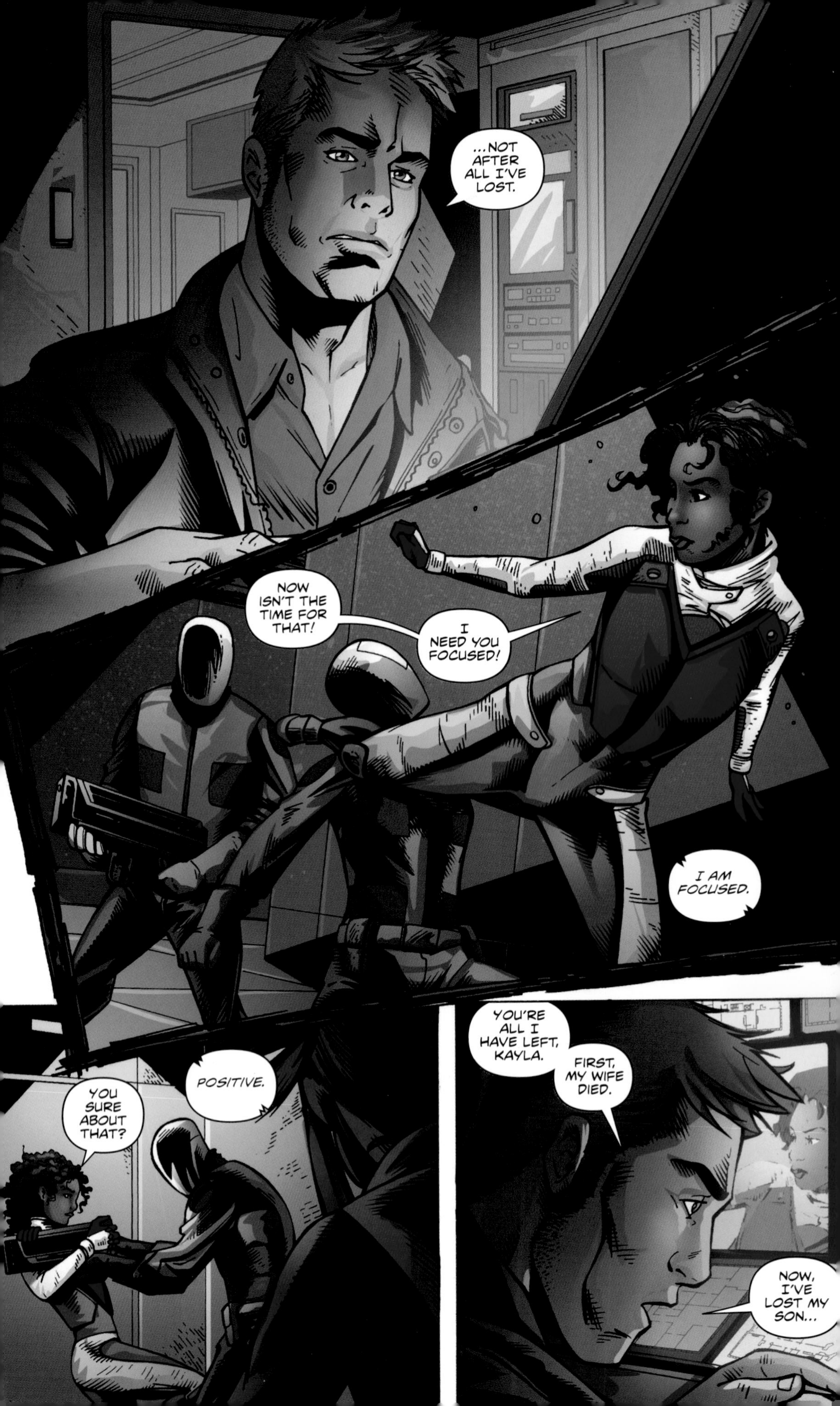

...NOT AFTER ALL I'VE LOST.
NOW ISN'T THE TIME FOR THAT!
I NEED YOU FOCUSED!
I AM FOCUSED.
YOU SURE ABOUT THAT?
POSITIVE.
YOU'RE ALL I HAVE LEFT, KAYLA.
FIRST, MY WIFE DIED.
NOW, I'VE LOST MY SON...

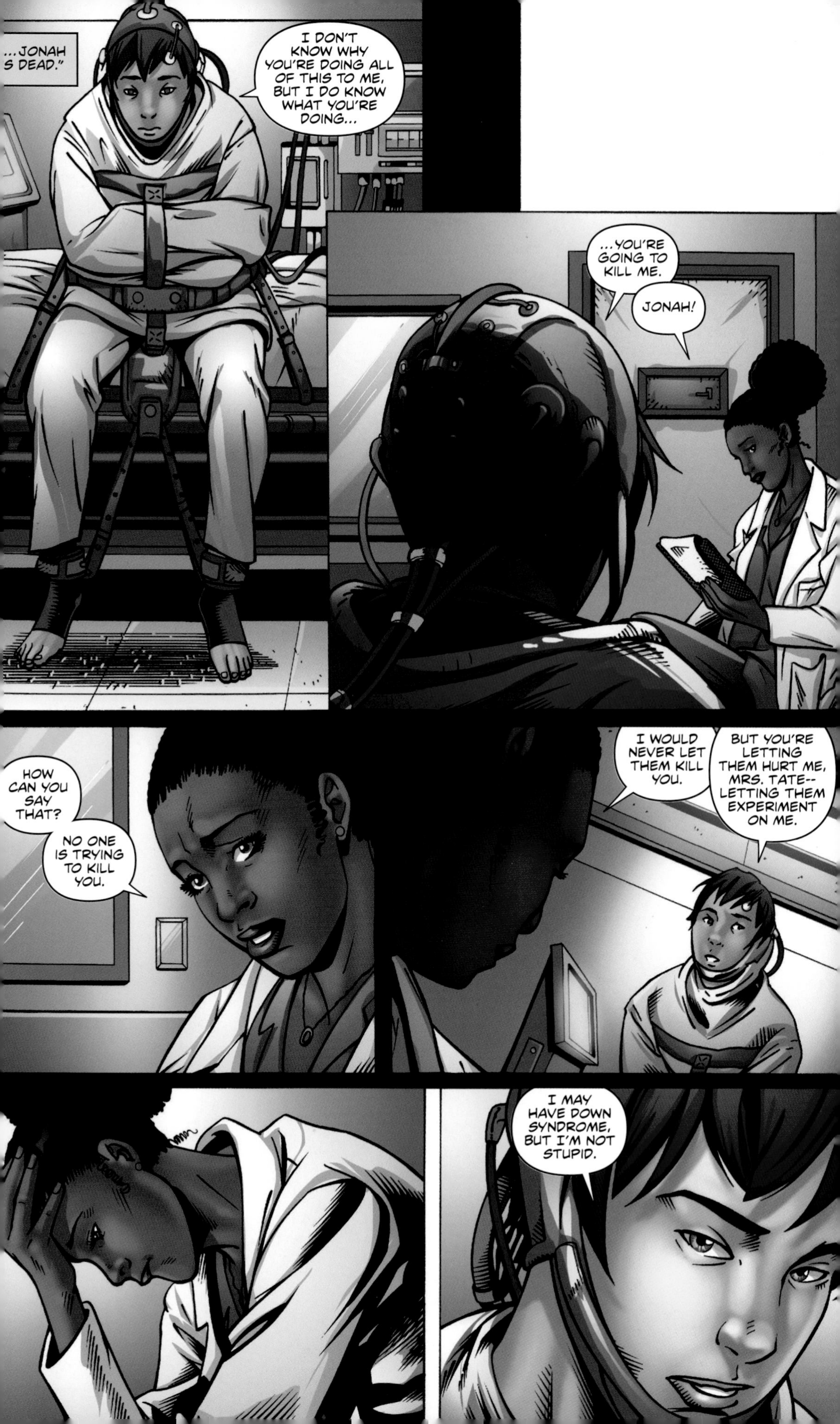

...JONAH S DEAD."
I DON'T KNOW WHY YOU'RE DOING ALL OF THIS TO ME, BUT I DO KNOW WHAT YOU'RE DOING...
...YOU'RE GOING TO KILL ME.
JONAH!
HOW CAN YOU SAY THAT?
NO ONE IS TRYING TO KILL YOU.
I WOULD NEVER LET THEM KILL YOU.
BUT YOU'RE LETTING THEM HURT ME, MRS. TATE-- LETTING THEM EXPERIMENT ON ME.
I MAY HAVE DOWN SYNDROME, BUT I'M NOT STUPID.

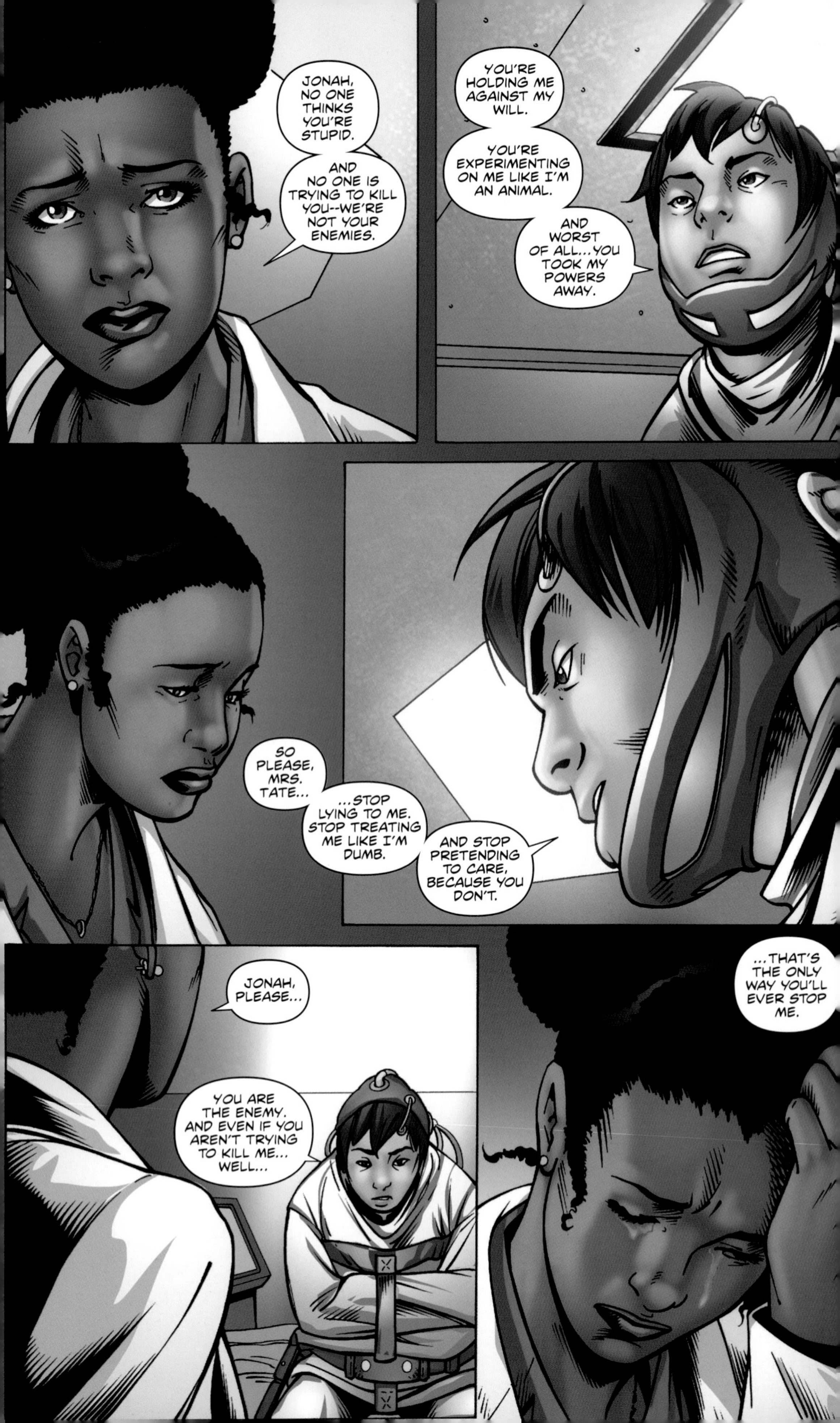

JONAH, NO ONE THINKS YOU'RE STUPID.
AND NO ONE IS TRYING TO KILL YOU--WE'RE NOT YOUR ENEMIES.
YOU'RE HOLDING ME AGAINST MY WILL.
YOU'RE EXPERIMENTING ON ME LIKE I'M AN ANIMAL.
AND WORST OF ALL...YOU TOOK MY POWERS AWAY.
SO PLEASE, MRS. TATE...
...STOP LYING TO ME. STOP TREATING ME LIKE I'M DUMB.
AND STOP PRETENDING TO CARE, BECAUSE YOU DON'T.
JONAH, PLEASE...
YOU ARE THE ENEMY. AND EVEN IF YOU AREN'T TRYING TO KILL ME... WELL...
...THAT'S THE ONLY WAY YOU'LL EVER STOP ME.

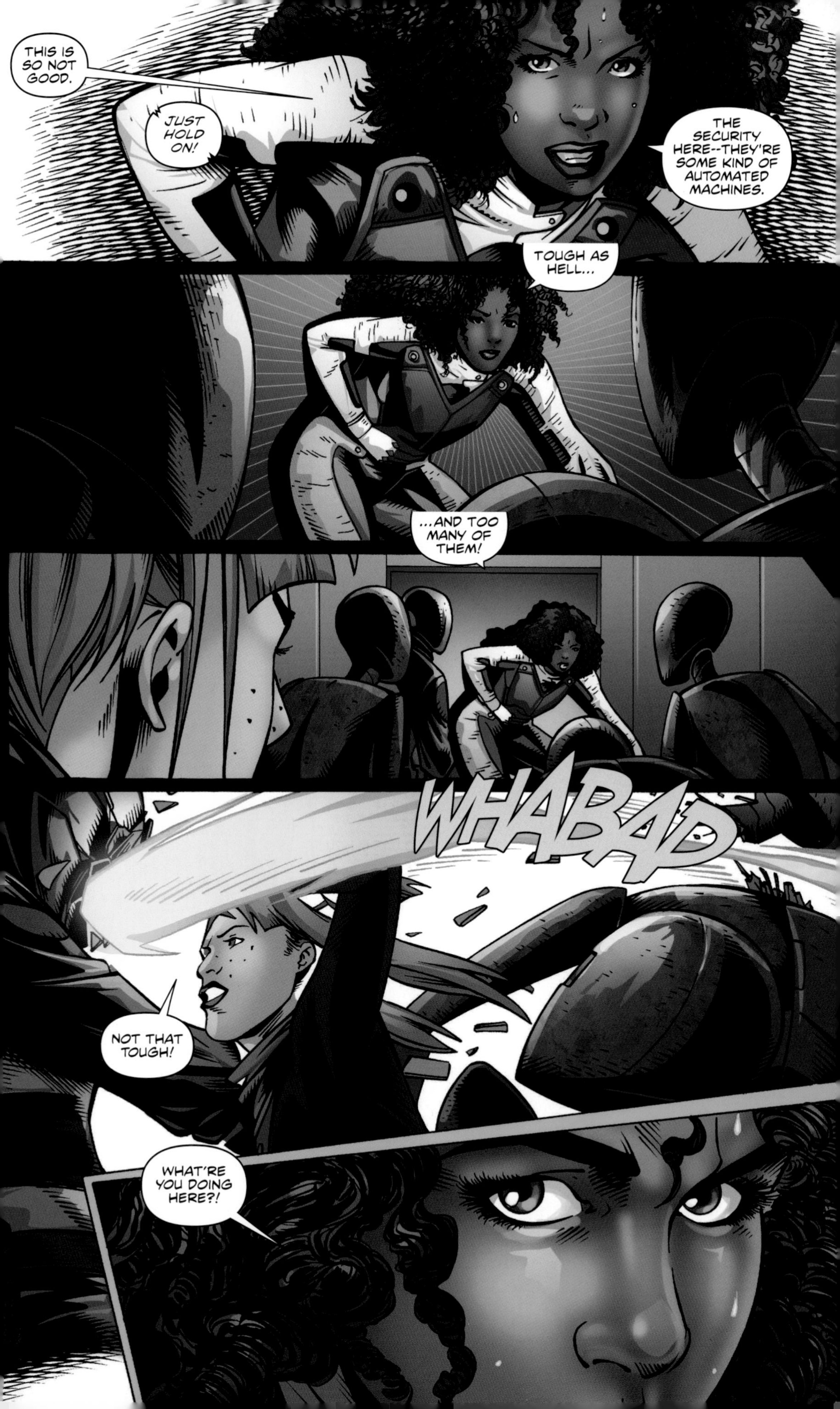
THIS IS SO NOT GOOD.
JUST HOLD ON!
THE SECURITY HERE--THEY'RE SOME KIND OF AUTOMATED MACHINES.
TOUGH AS HELL...
...AND TOO MANY OF THEM!
WHABAD
NOT THAT TOUGH!
WHAT'RE YOU DOING HERE?!

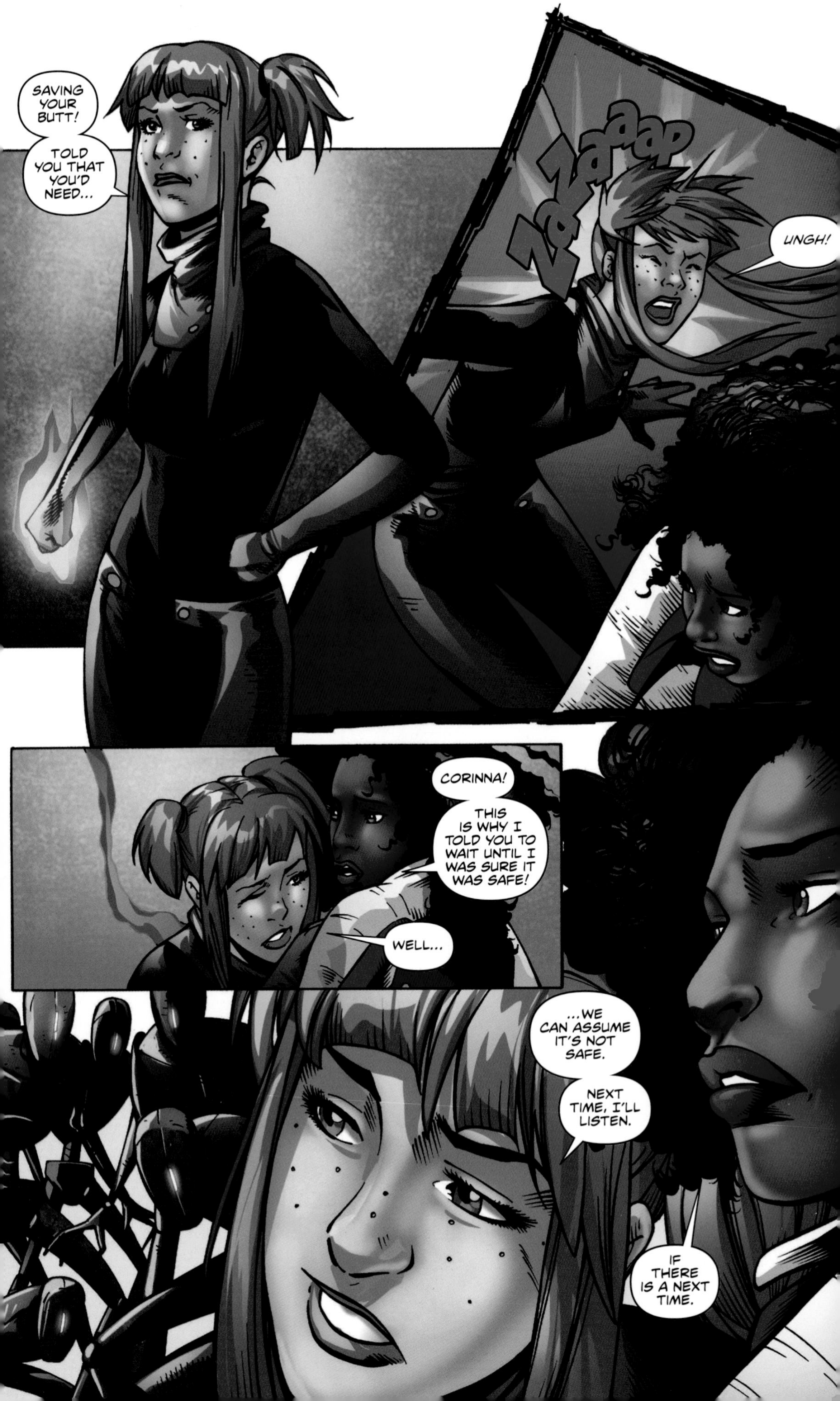
SAVING YOUR BUTT!
TOLD YOU THAT YOU'D NEED...
ZaZaaaap
UNGH!
CORINNA!
THIS IS WHY I TOLD YOU TO WAIT UNTIL I WAS SURE IT WAS SAFE!
WELL...
...WE CAN ASSUME IT'S NOT SAFE.
NEXT TIME, I'LL LISTEN.
IF THERE IS A NEXT TIME.

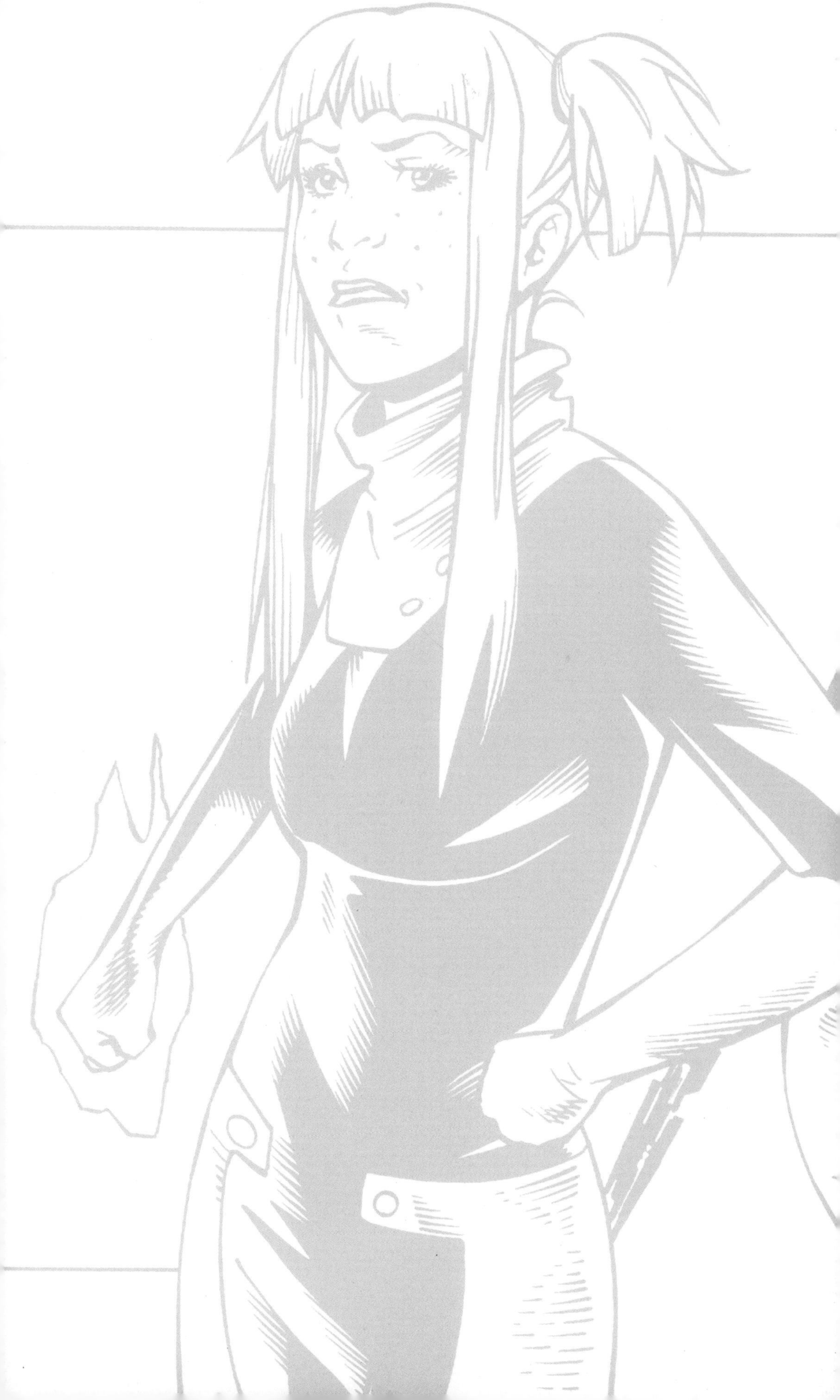

CHAPTER TWO

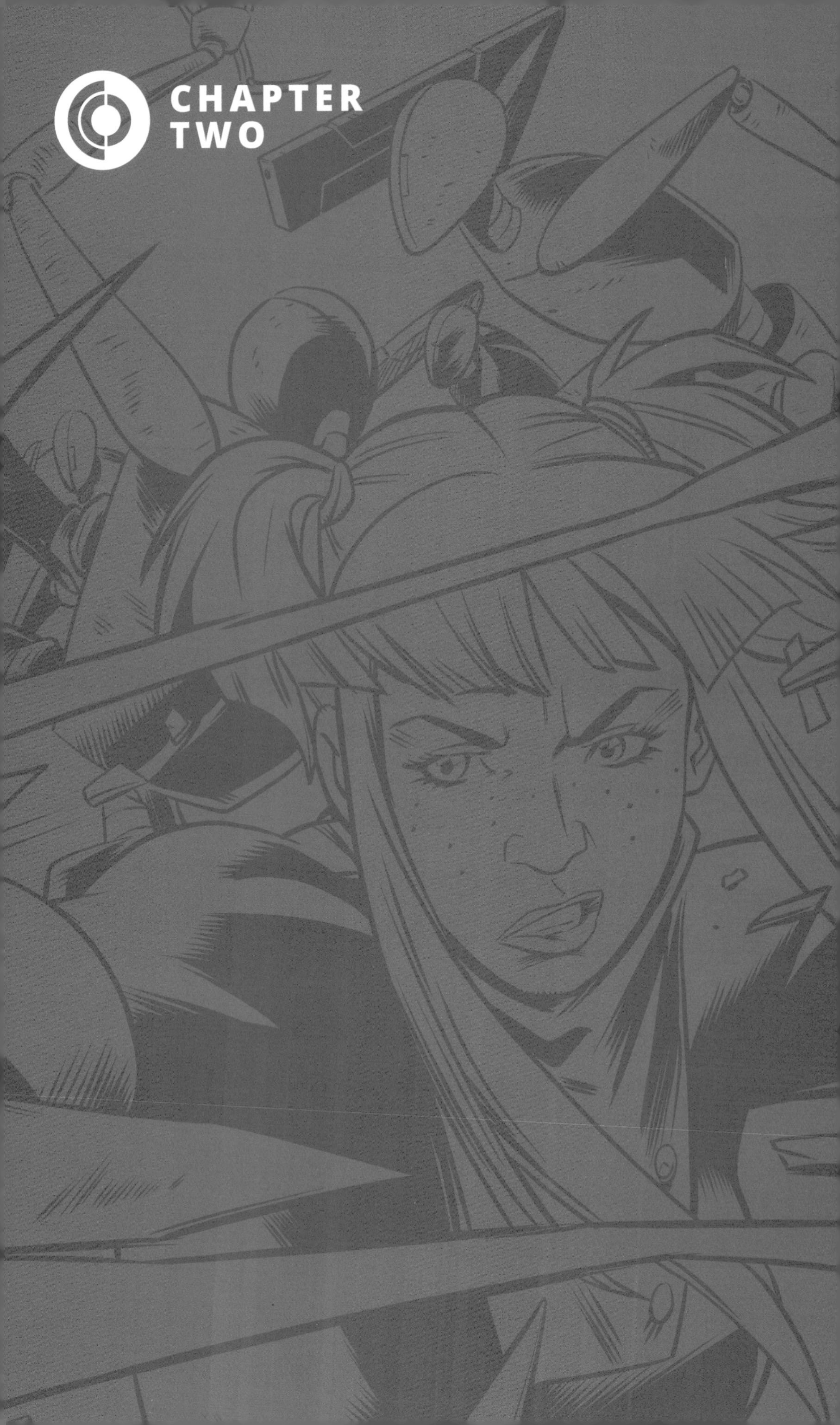

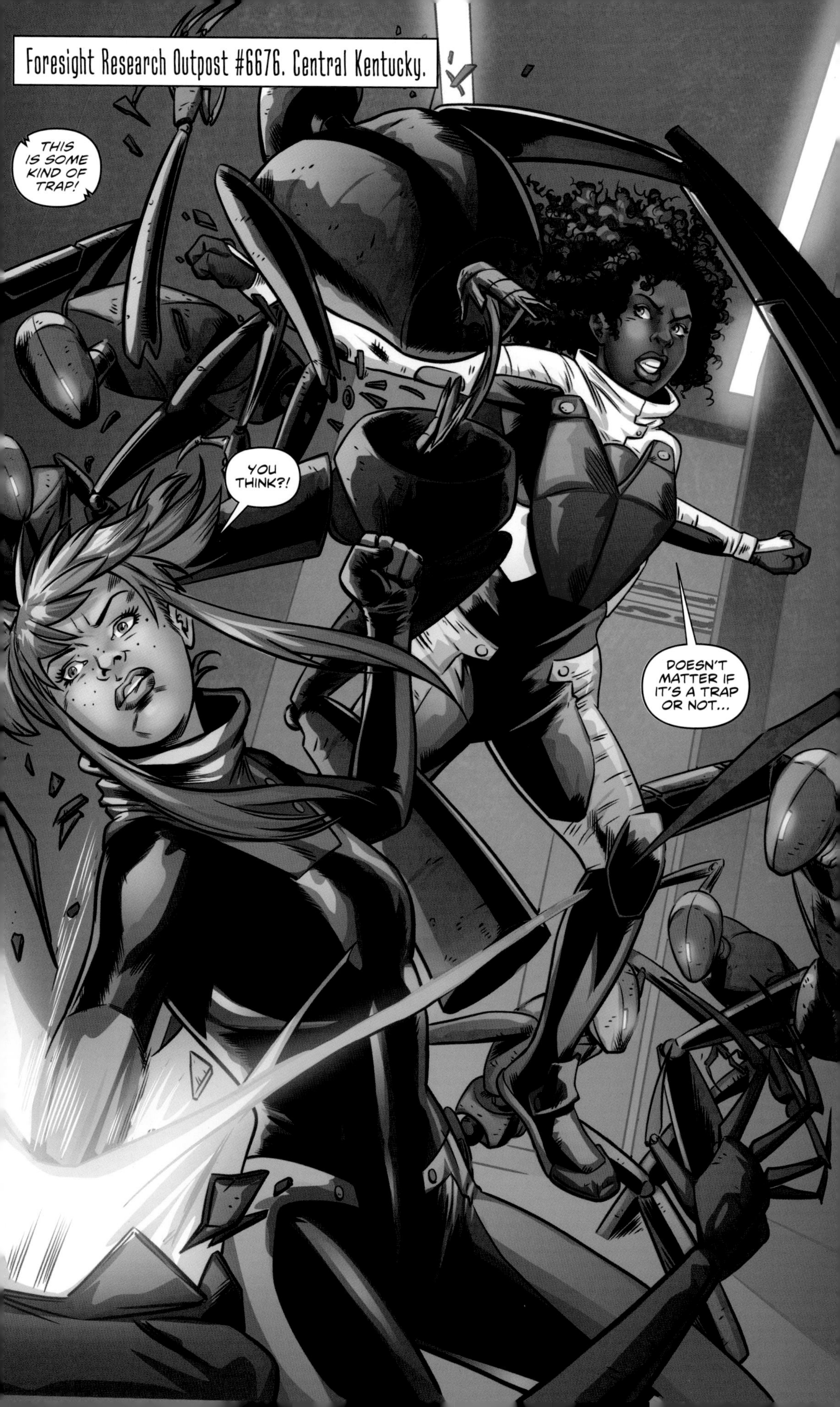
Foresight Research Outpost #6676. Central Kentucky.
THIS IS SOME KIND OF TRAP!
YOU THINK?!
DOESN'T MATTER IF IT'S A TRAP OR NOT...

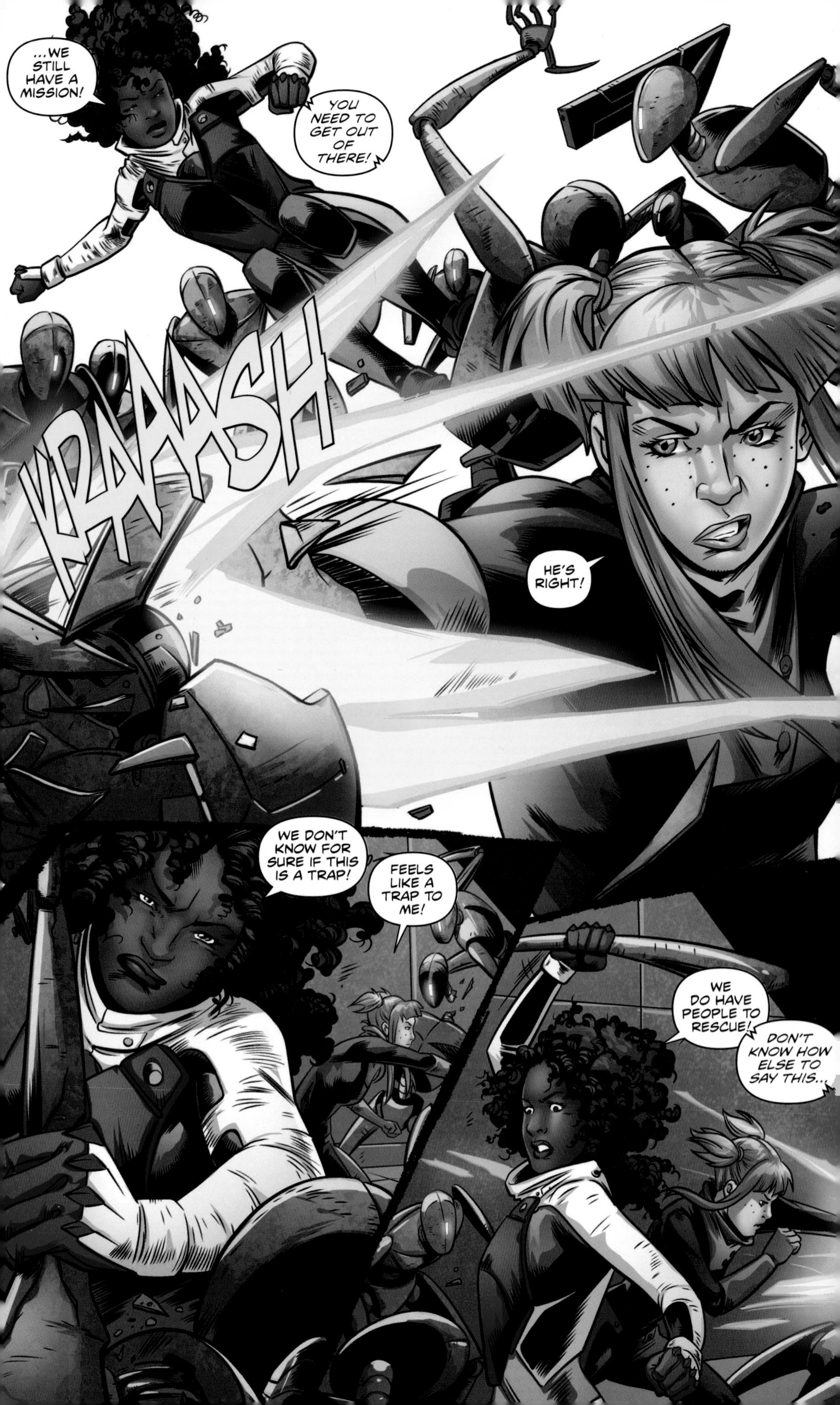
...WE STILL HAVE A MISSION!
YOU NEED TO GET OUT OF THERE!
KRAAASH
HE'S RIGHT!
WE DON'T KNOW FOR SURE IF THIS IS A TRAP!
FEELS LIKE A TRAP TO ME!
WE DO HAVE PEOPLE TO RESCUE!
DON'T KNOW HOW ELSE TO SAY THIS...

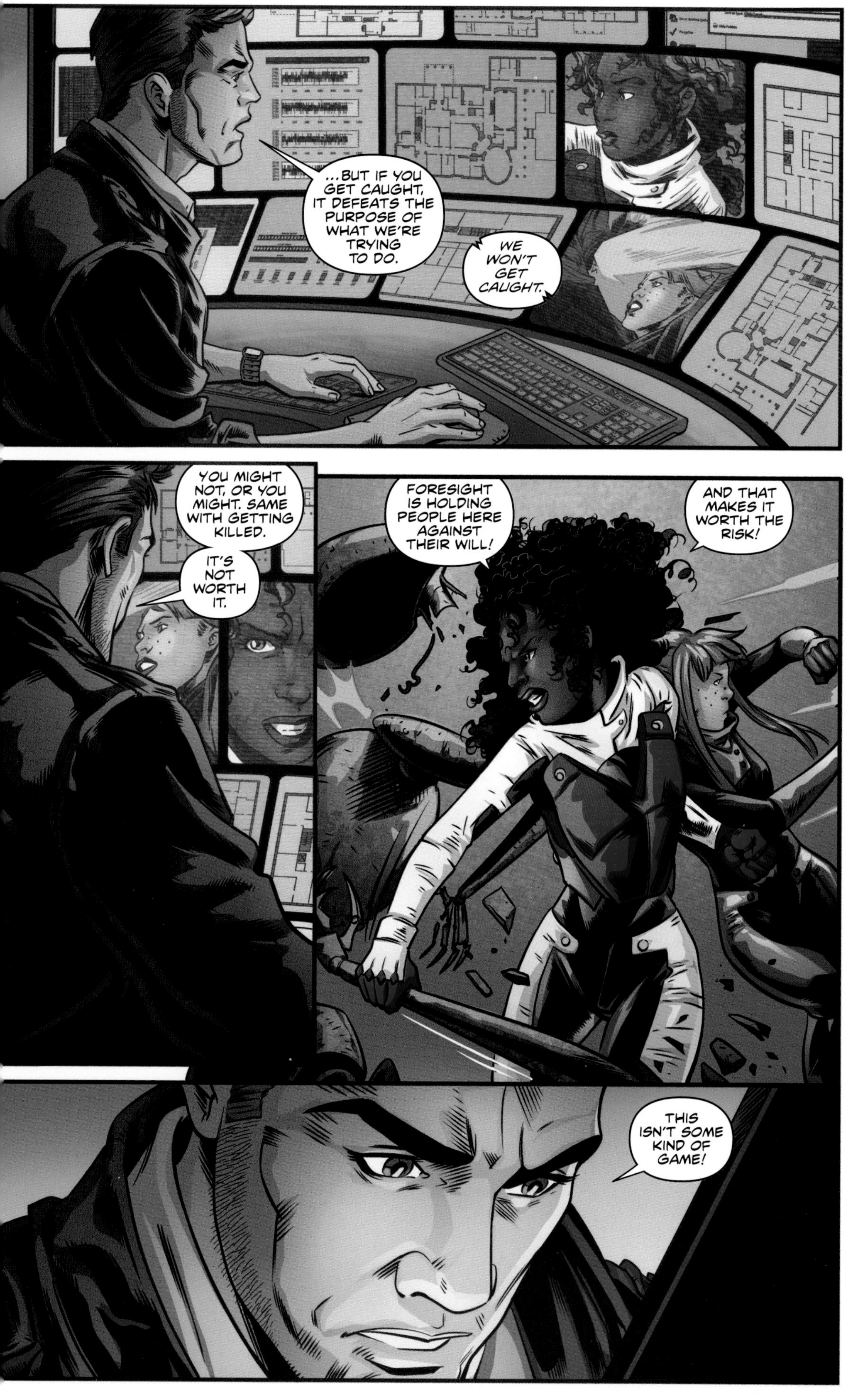
...BUT IF YOU GET CAUGHT, IT DEFEATS THE PURPOSE OF WHAT WE'RE TRYING TO DO.
WE WON'T GET CAUGHT.
YOU MIGHT NOT, OR YOU MIGHT. SAME WITH GETTING KILLED.
IT'S NOT WORTH IT.
FORESIGHT IS HOLDING PEOPLE HERE AGAINST THEIR WILL!
AND THAT MAKES IT WORTH THE RISK!
THIS ISN'T SOME KIND OF GAME!

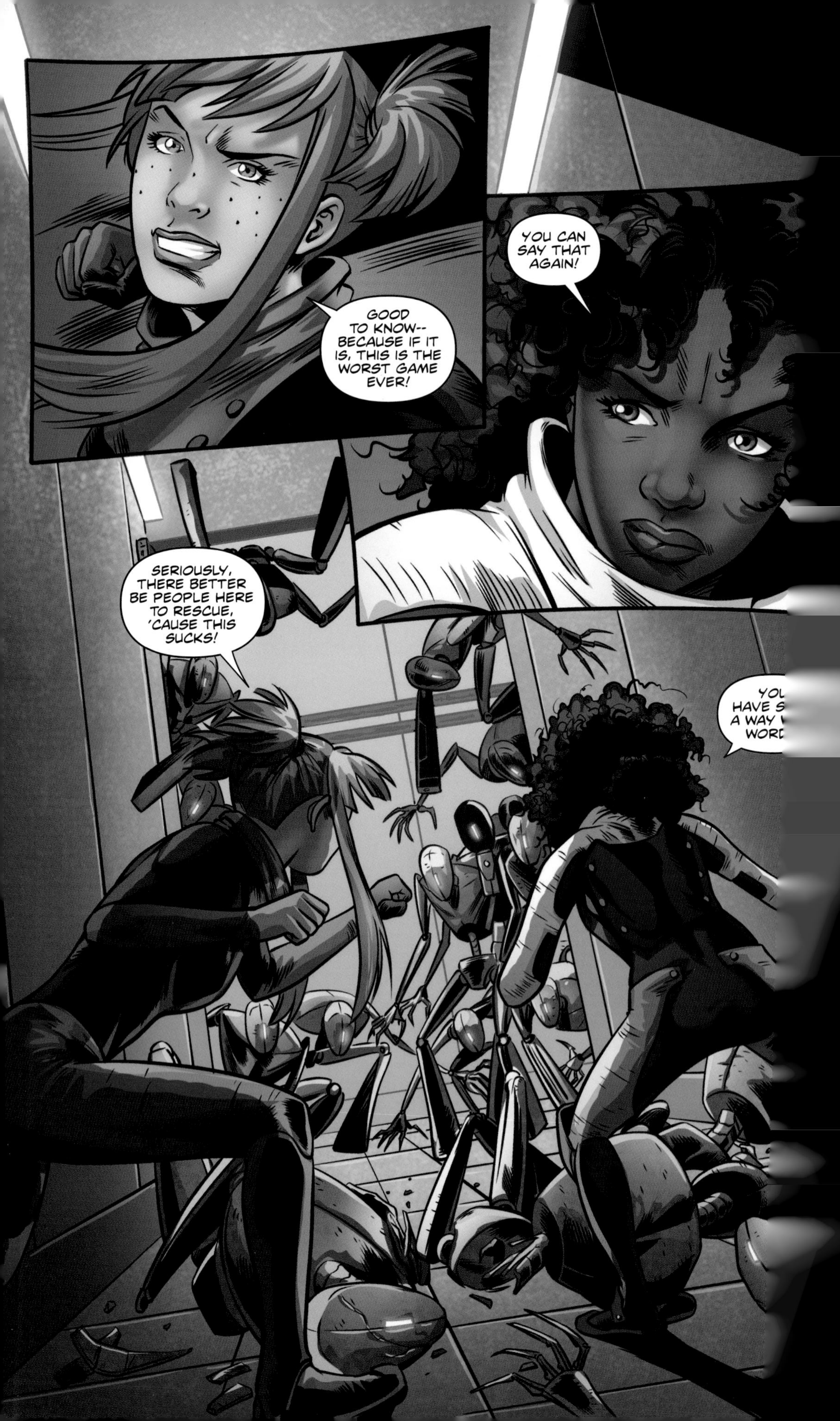
GOOD TO KNOW-- BECAUSE IF IT IS, THIS IS THE WORST GAME EVER!
YOU CAN SAY THAT AGAIN!
SERIOUSLY, THERE BETTER BE PEOPLE HERE TO RESCUE, 'CAUSE THIS SUCKS!

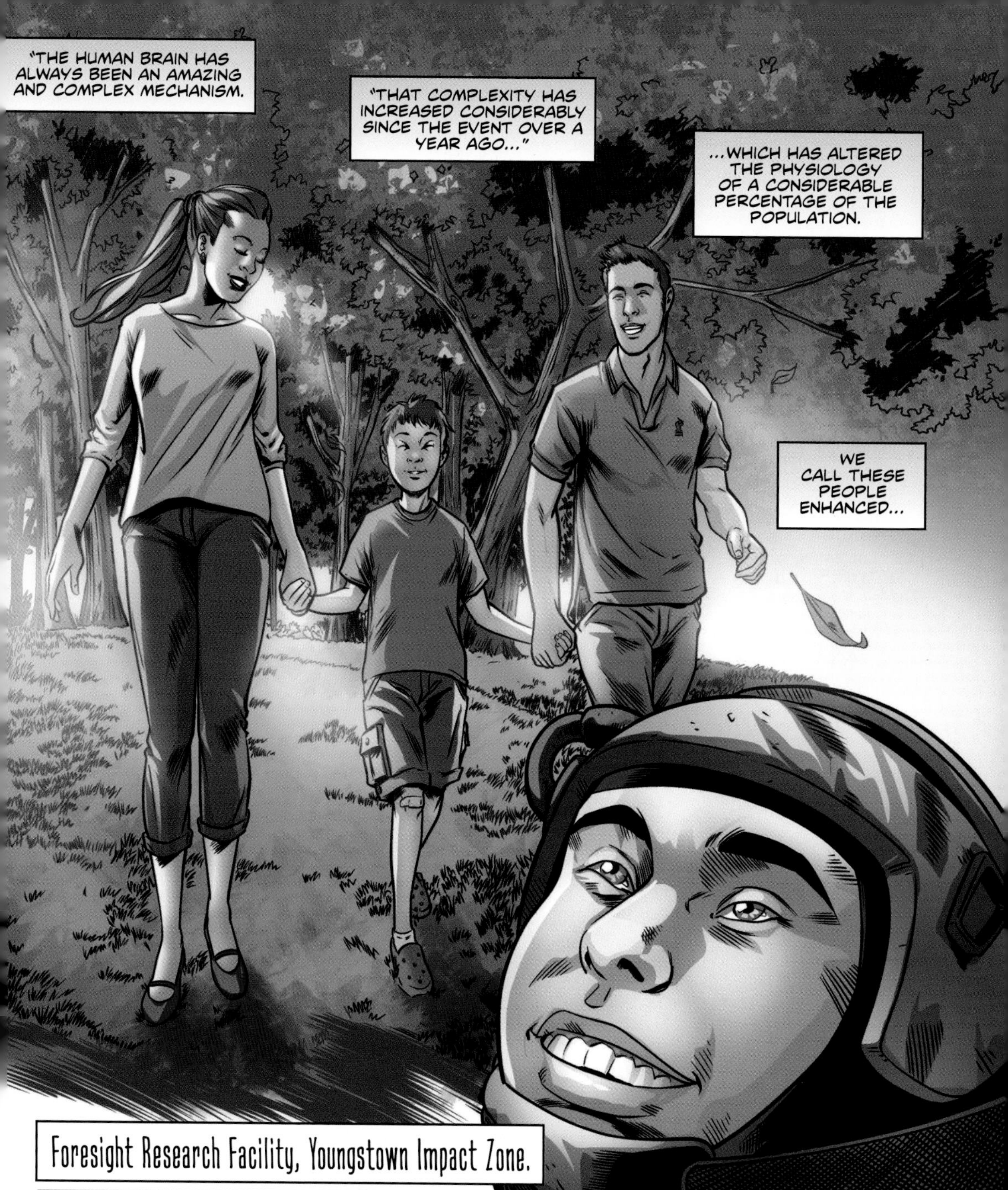
"THE HUMAN BRAIN HAS ALWAYS BEEN AN AMAZING AND COMPLEX MECHANISM.
"THAT COMPLEXITY HAS INCREASED CONSIDERABLY SINCE THE EVENT OVER A YEAR AGO..."
...WHICH HAS ALTERED THE PHYSIOLOGY OF A CONSIDERABLE PERCENTAGE OF THE POPULATION.
WE CALL THESE PEOPLE ENHANCED...
Foresight Research Facility, Youngstown Impact Zone.

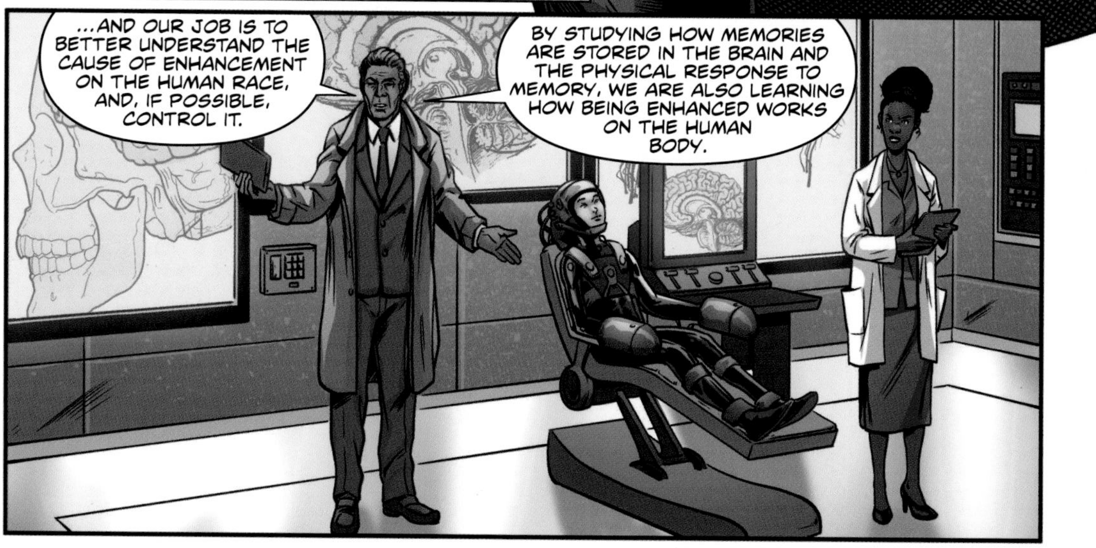
...AND OUR JOB IS TO BETTER UNDERSTAND THE CAUSE OF ENHANCEMENT ON THE HUMAN RACE, AND, IF POSSIBLE, CONTROL IT.
BY STUDYING HOW MEMORIES ARE STORED IN THE BRAIN AND THE PHYSICAL RESPONSE TO MEMORY, WE ARE ALSO LEARNING HOW BEING ENHANCED WORKS ON THE HUMAN BODY.

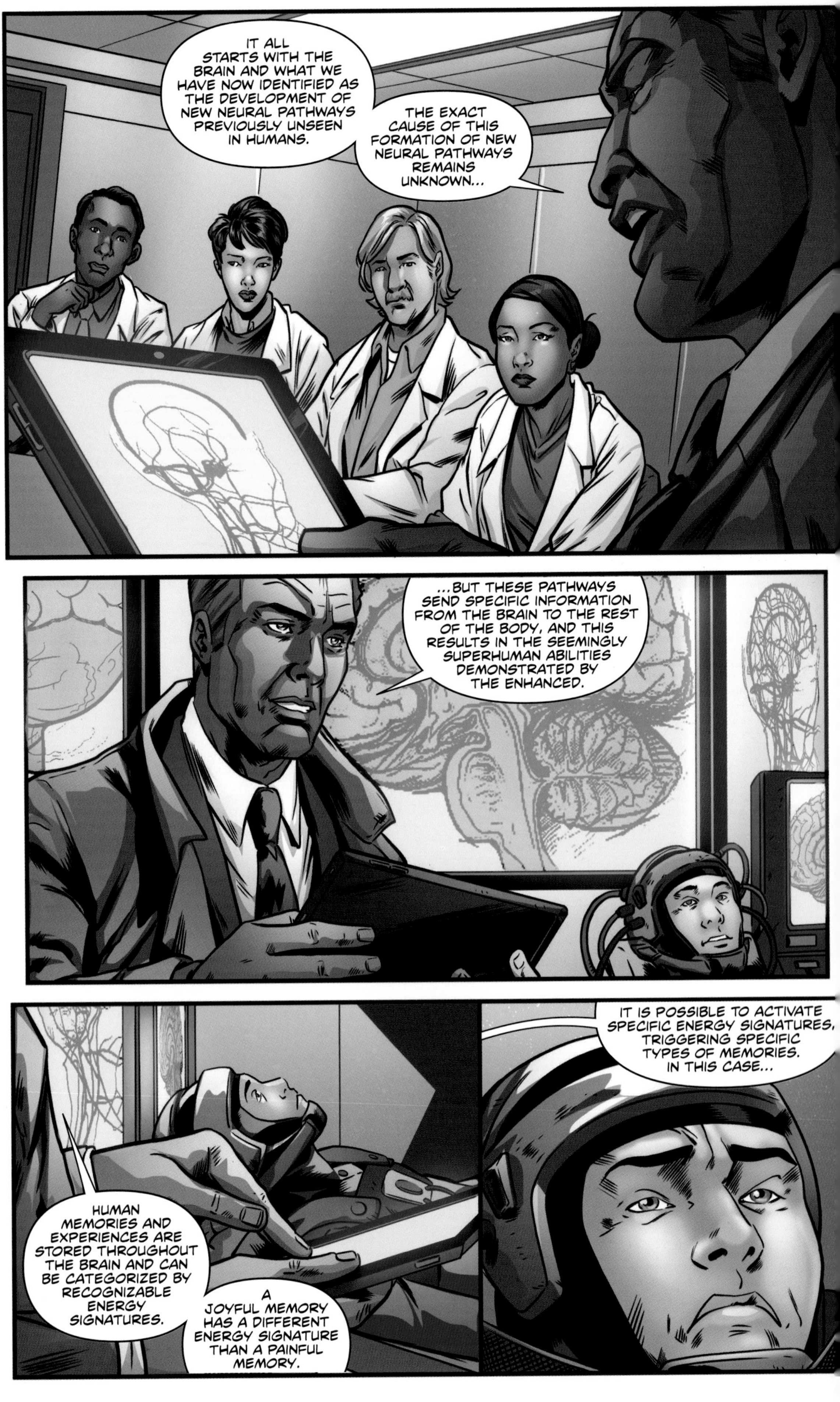
IT ALL STARTS WITH THE BRAIN AND WHAT WE HAVE NOW IDENTIFIED AS THE DEVELOPMENT OF NEW NEURAL PATHWAYS PREVIOUSLY UNSEEN IN HUMANS.
THE EXACT CAUSE OF THIS FORMATION OF NEW NEURAL PATHWAYS REMAINS UNKNOWN...
...BUT THESE PATHWAYS SEND SPECIFIC INFORMATION FROM THE BRAIN TO THE REST OF THE BODY, AND THIS RESULTS IN THE SEEMINGLY SUPERHUMAN ABILITIES DEMONSTRATED BY THE ENHANCED.
HUMAN MEMORIES AND EXPERIENCES ARE STORED THROUGHOUT THE BRAIN AND CAN BE CATEGORIZED BY RECOGNIZABLE ENERGY SIGNATURES.
A JOYFUL MEMORY HAS A DIFFERENT ENERGY SIGNATURE THAN A PAINFUL MEMORY.
IT IS POSSIBLE TO ACTIVATE SPECIFIC ENERGY SIGNATURES, TRIGGERING SPECIFIC TYPES OF MEMORIES. IN THIS CASE...

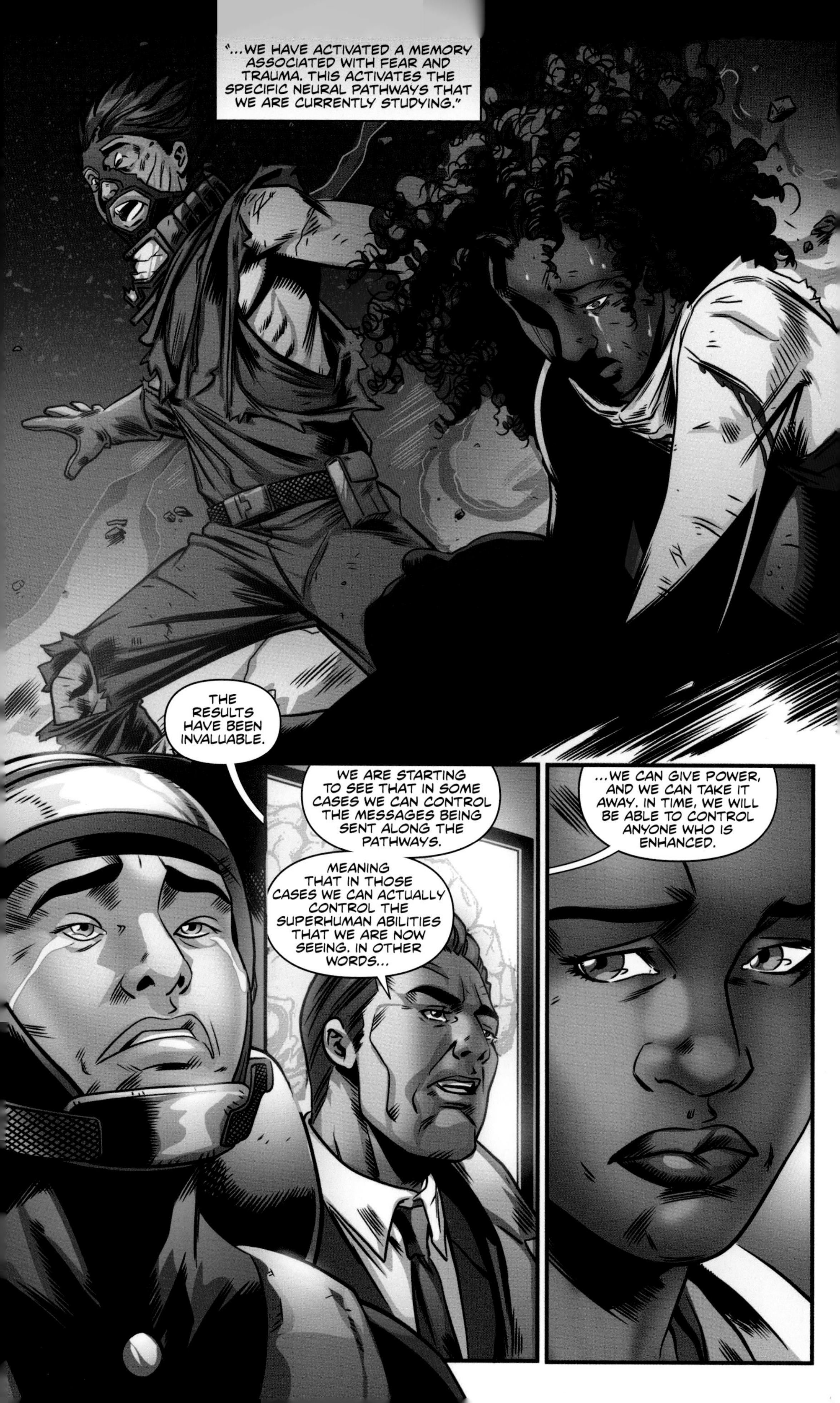
"...WE HAVE ACTIVATED A MEMORY ASSOCIATED WITH FEAR AND TRAUMA. THIS ACTIVATES THE SPECIFIC NEURAL PATHWAYS THAT WE ARE CURRENTLY STUDYING."
THE RESULTS HAVE BEEN INVALUABLE.
WE ARE STARTING TO SEE THAT IN SOME CASES WE CAN CONTROL THE MESSAGES BEING SENT ALONG THE PATHWAYS.
MEANING THAT IN THOSE CASES WE CAN ACTUALLY CONTROL THE SUPERHUMAN ABILITIES THAT WE ARE NOW SEEING. IN OTHER WORDS...
...WE CAN GIVE POWER, AND WE CAN TAKE IT AWAY. IN TIME, WE WILL BE ABLE TO CONTROL ANYONE WHO IS ENHANCED.

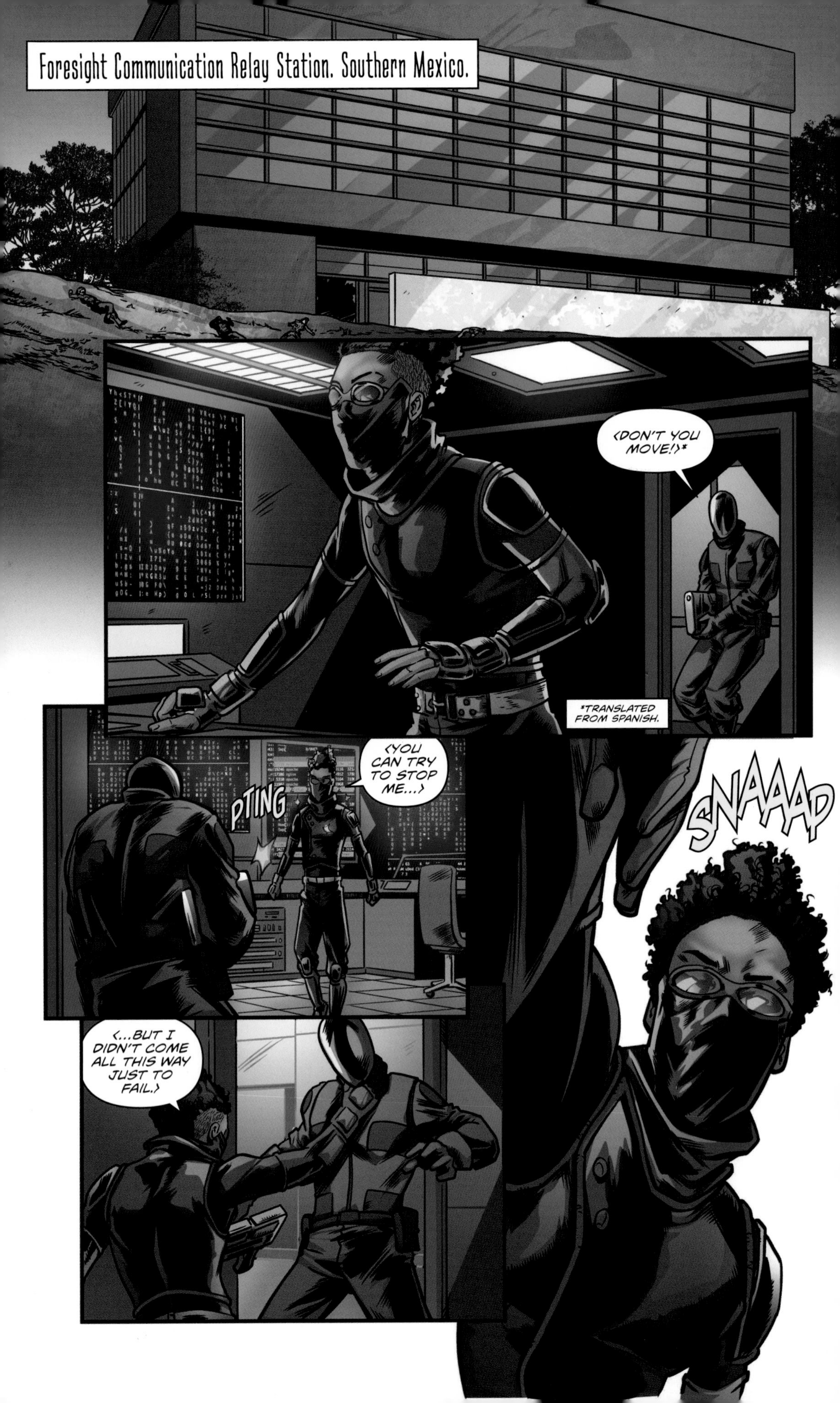
Foresight Communication Relay Station. Southern Mexico.
‹DON'T YOU MOVE!›*
*TRANSLATED FROM SPANISH.
‹YOU CAN TRY TO STOP ME...›
PTING
SNAAAP
‹...BUT I DIDN'T COME ALL THIS WAY JUST TO FAIL.›

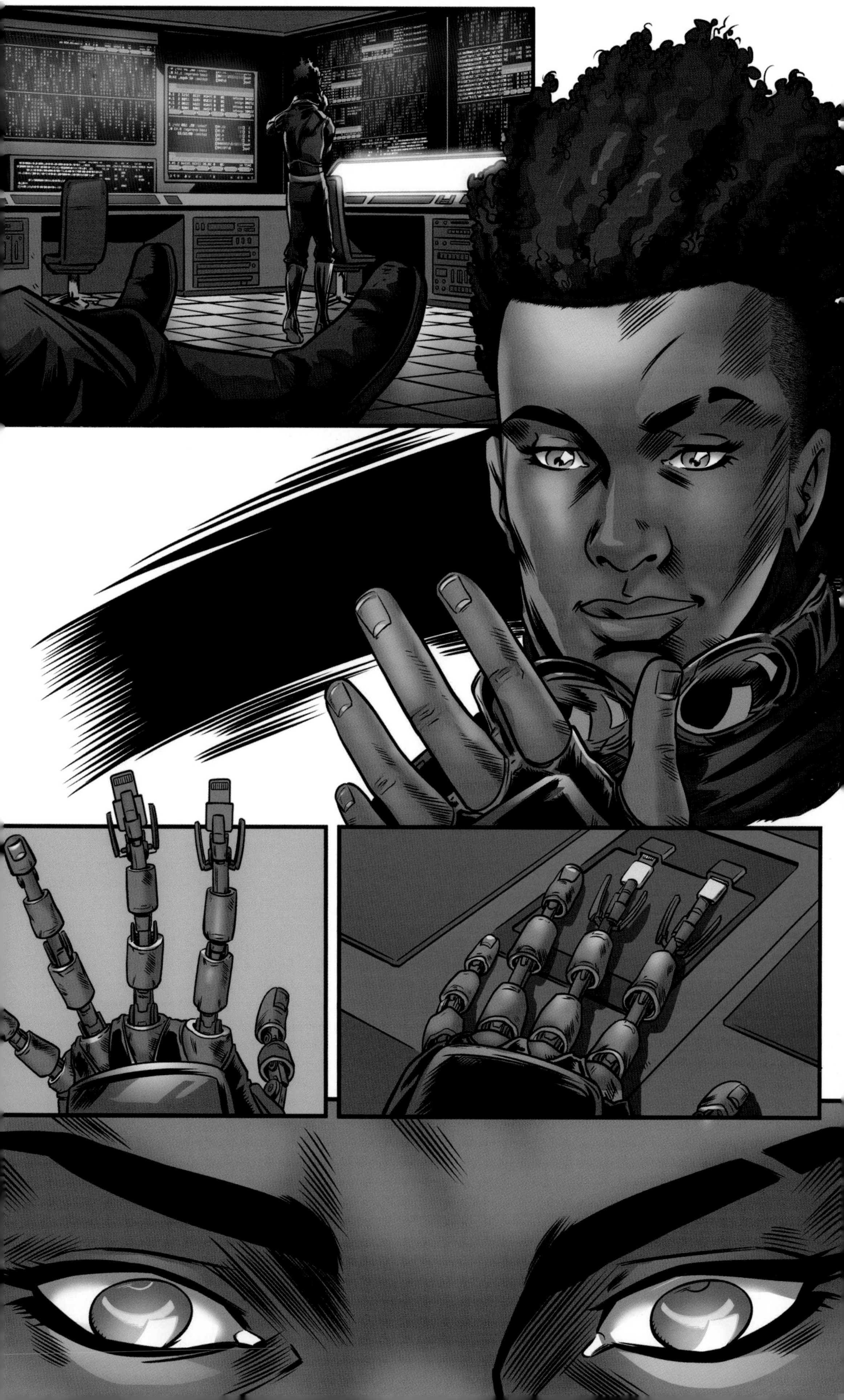

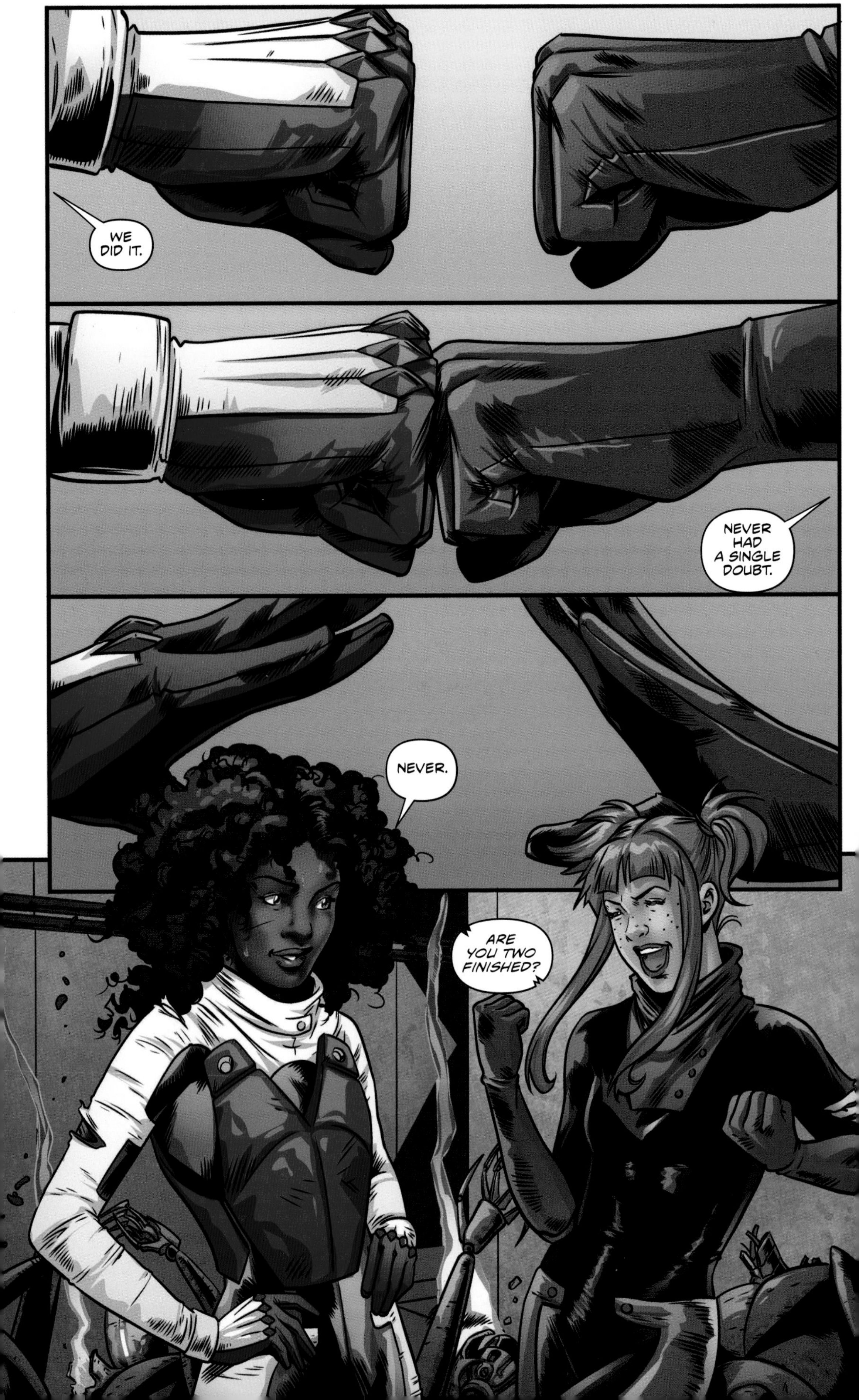
WE DID IT.
NEVER HAD A SINGLE DOUBT.
NEVER.
ARE YOU TWO FINISHED?

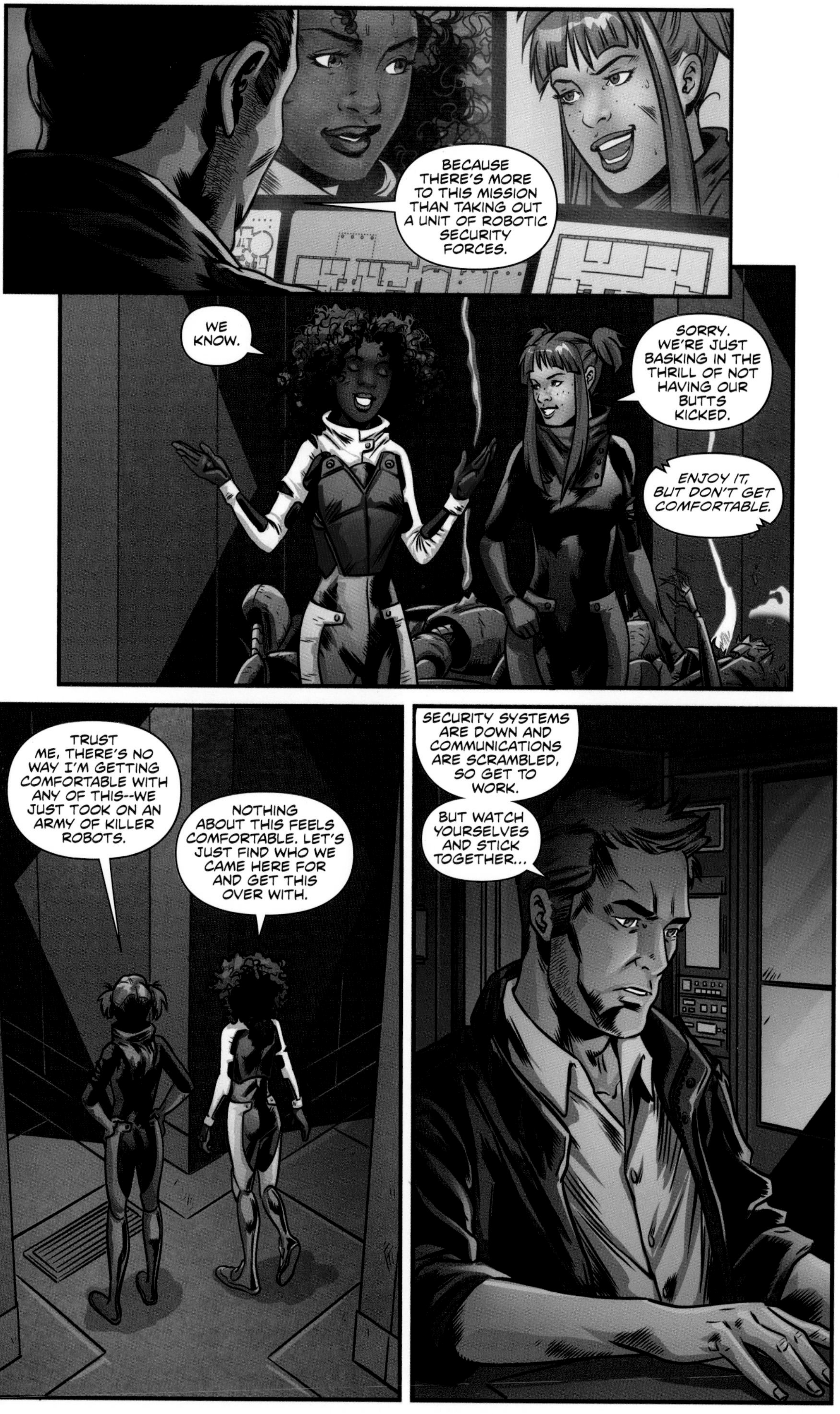

BECAUSE THERE'S MORE TO THIS MISSION THAN TAKING OUT A UNIT OF ROBOTIC SECURITY FORCES.
WE KNOW.
SORRY. WE'RE JUST BASKING IN THE THRILL OF NOT HAVING OUR BUTTS KICKED.
ENJOY IT, BUT DON'T GET COMFORTABLE.
TRUST ME, THERE'S NO WAY I'M GETTING COMFORTABLE WITH ANY OF THIS--WE JUST TOOK ON AN ARMY OF KILLER ROBOTS.
NOTHING ABOUT THIS FEELS COMFORTABLE. LET'S JUST FIND WHO WE CAME HERE FOR AND GET THIS OVER WITH.
SECURITY SYSTEMS ARE DOWN AND COMMUNICATIONS ARE SCRAMBLED, SO GET TO WORK.
BUT WATCH YOURSELVES AND STICK TOGETHER...

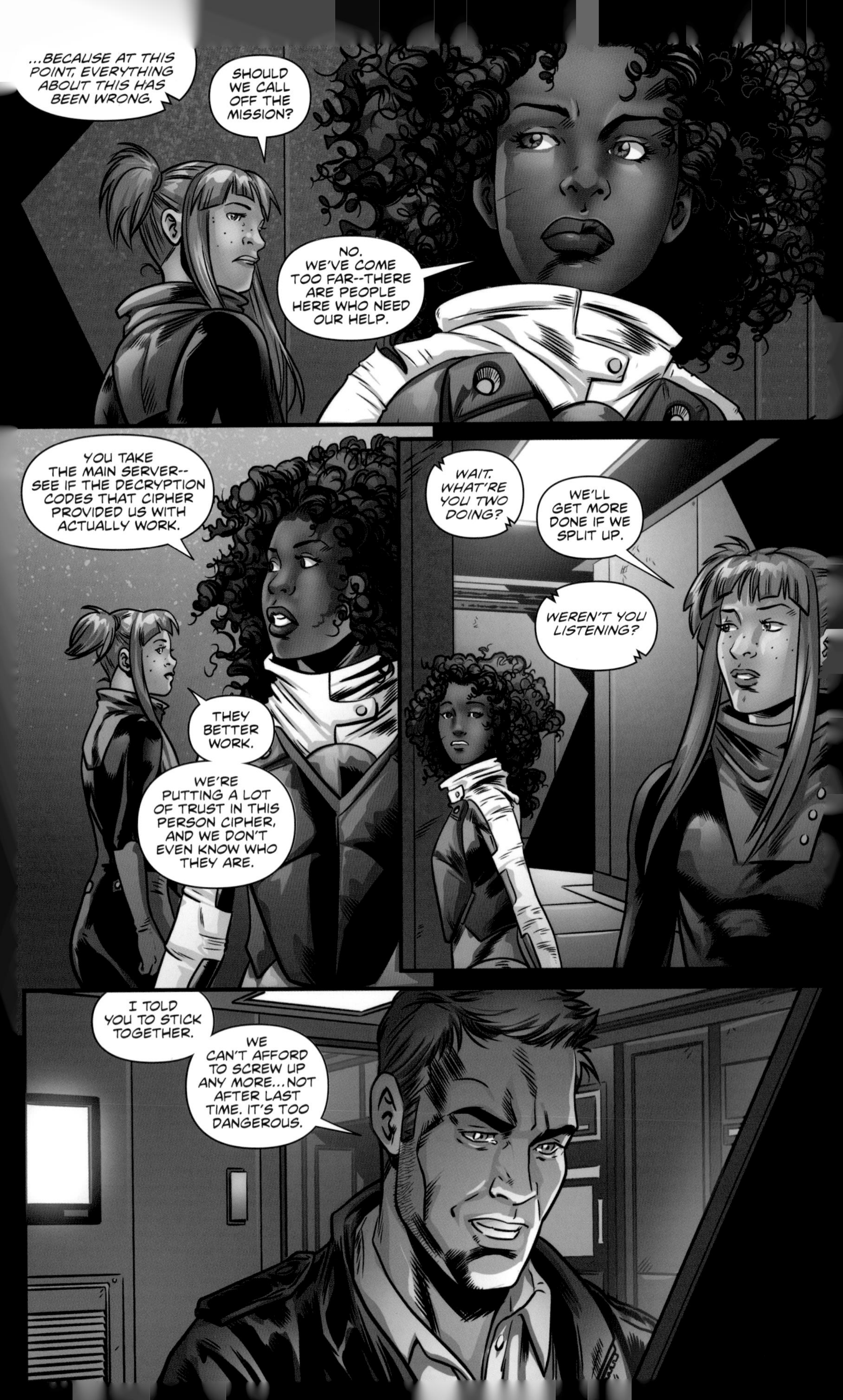
...BECAUSE AT THIS POINT, EVERYTHING ABOUT THIS HAS BEEN WRONG.
SHOULD WE CALL OFF THE MISSION?
NO. WE'VE COME TOO FAR--THERE ARE PEOPLE HERE WHO NEED OUR HELP.
YOU TAKE THE MAIN SERVER--SEE IF THE DECRYPTION CODES THAT CIPHER PROVIDED US WITH ACTUALLY WORK.
THEY BETTER WORK.
WE'RE PUTTING A LOT OF TRUST IN THIS PERSON CIPHER, AND WE DON'T EVEN KNOW WHO THEY ARE.
WAIT. WHAT'RE YOU TWO DOING?
WE'LL GET MORE DONE IF WE SPLIT UP.
WEREN'T YOU LISTENING?
I TOLD YOU TO STICK TOGETHER.
WE CAN'T AFFORD TO SCREW UP ANY MORE...NOT AFTER LAST TIME. IT'S TOO DANGEROUS.

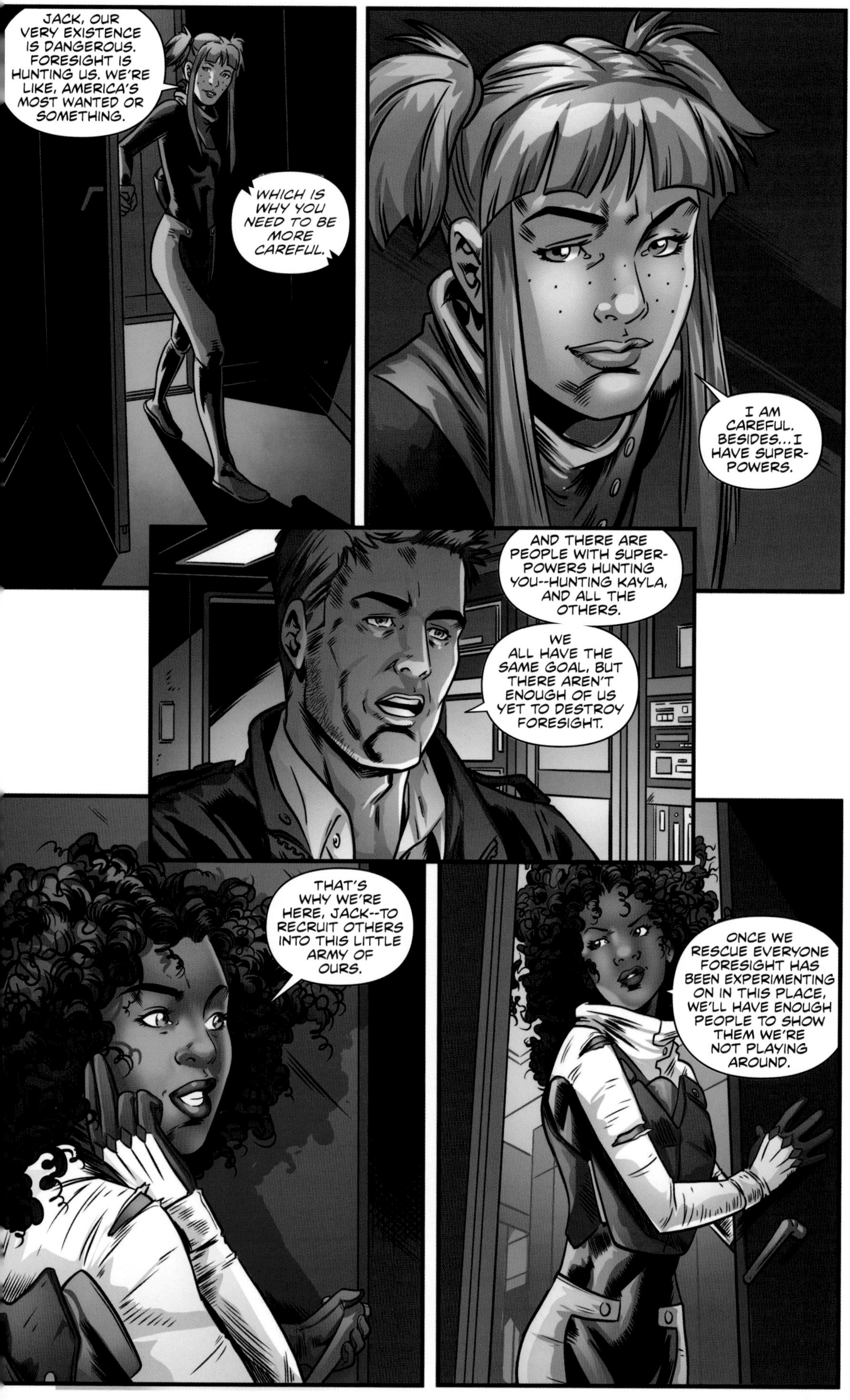
JACK, OUR VERY EXISTENCE IS DANGEROUS. FORESIGHT IS HUNTING US. WE'RE LIKE, AMERICA'S MOST WANTED OR SOMETHING.
WHICH IS WHY YOU NEED TO BE MORE CAREFUL.
I AM CAREFUL. BESIDES... I HAVE SUPER-POWERS.
AND THERE ARE PEOPLE WITH SUPER-POWERS HUNTING YOU--HUNTING KAYLA, AND ALL THE OTHERS.
WE ALL HAVE THE SAME GOAL, BUT THERE AREN'T ENOUGH OF US YET TO DESTROY FORESIGHT.
THAT'S WHY WE'RE HERE, JACK--TO RECRUIT OTHERS INTO THIS LITTLE ARMY OF OURS.
ONCE WE RESCUE EVERYONE FORESIGHT HAS BEEN EXPERIMENTING ON IN THIS PLACE, WE'LL HAVE ENOUGH PEOPLE TO SHOW THEM WE'RE NOT PLAYING AROUND.

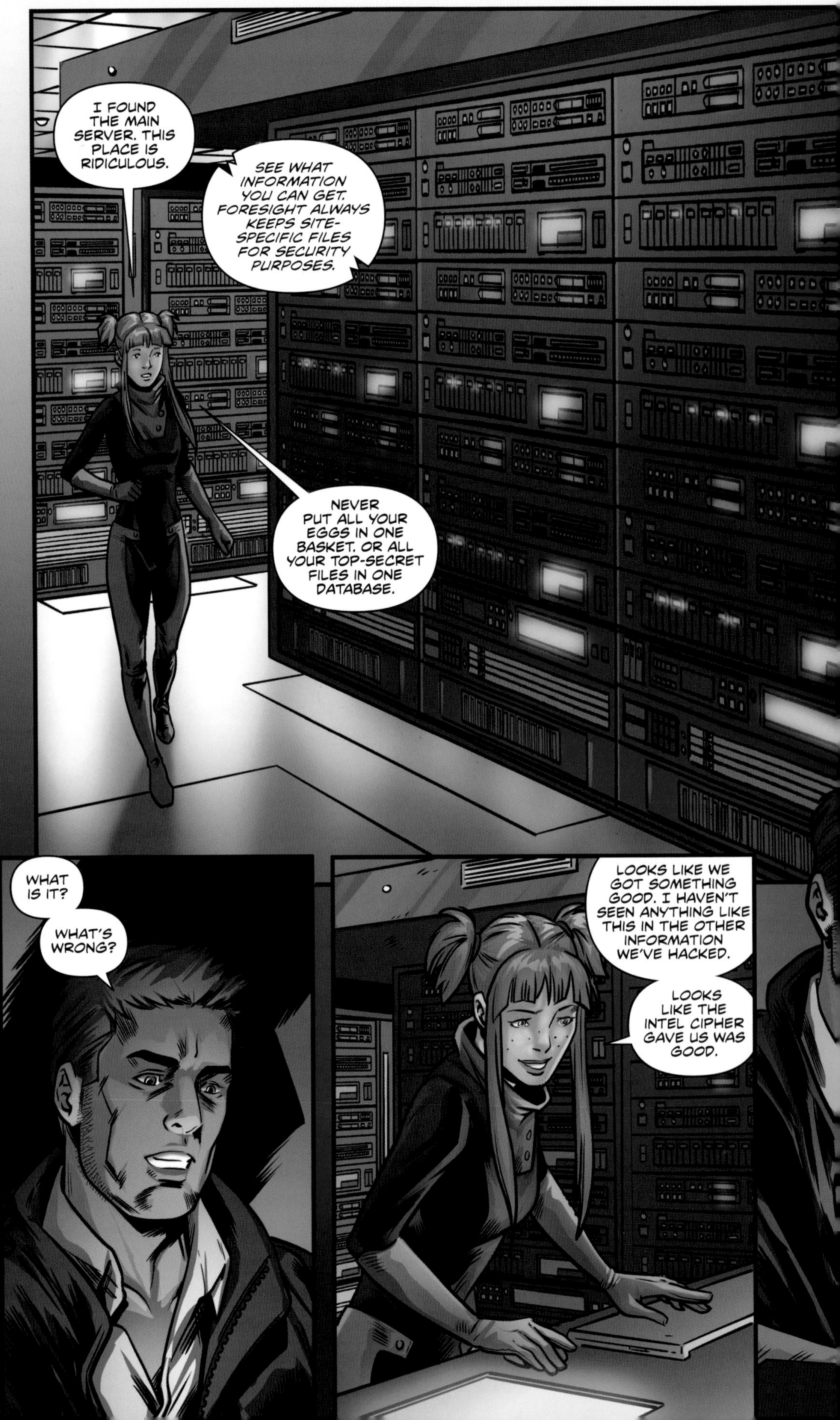
I FOUND THE MAIN SERVER. THIS PLACE IS RIDICULOUS.
SEE WHAT INFORMATION YOU CAN GET. FORESIGHT ALWAYS KEEPS SITE-SPECIFIC FILES FOR SECURITY PURPOSES.
NEVER PUT ALL YOUR EGGS IN ONE BASKET. OR ALL YOUR TOP-SECRET FILES IN ONE DATABASE.
WHAT IS IT?
WHAT'S WRONG?
LOOKS LIKE WE GOT SOMETHING GOOD. I HAVEN'T SEEN ANYTHING LIKE THIS IN THE OTHER INFORMATION WE'VE HACKED.
LOOKS LIKE THE INTEL CIPHER GAVE US WAS GOOD.

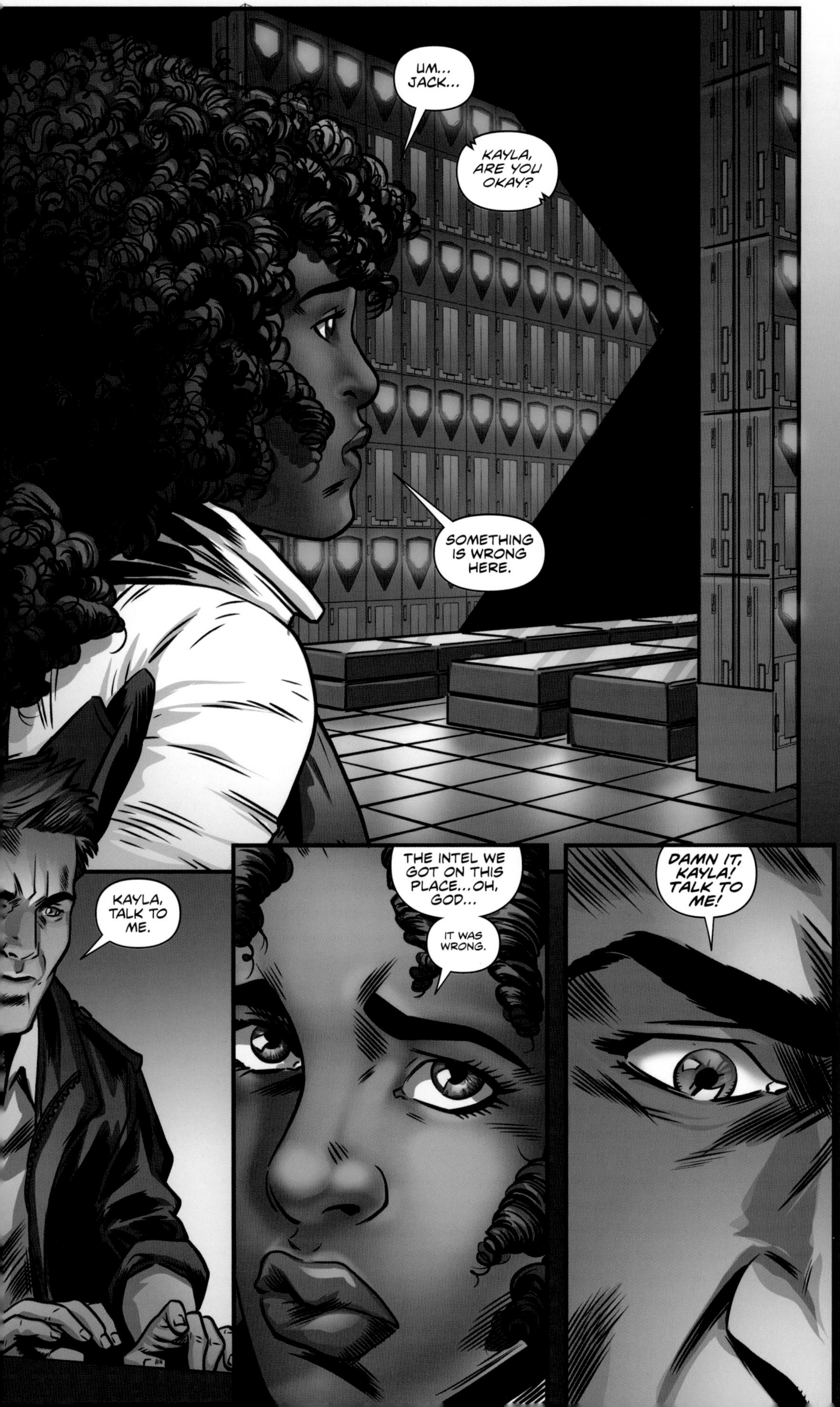
UM... JACK...
KAYLA, ARE YOU OKAY?
SOMETHING IS WRONG HERE.
KAYLA, TALK TO ME.
THE INTEL WE GOT ON THIS PLACE...OH, GOD...
IT WAS WRONG.
DAMN IT, KAYLA! TALK TO ME!

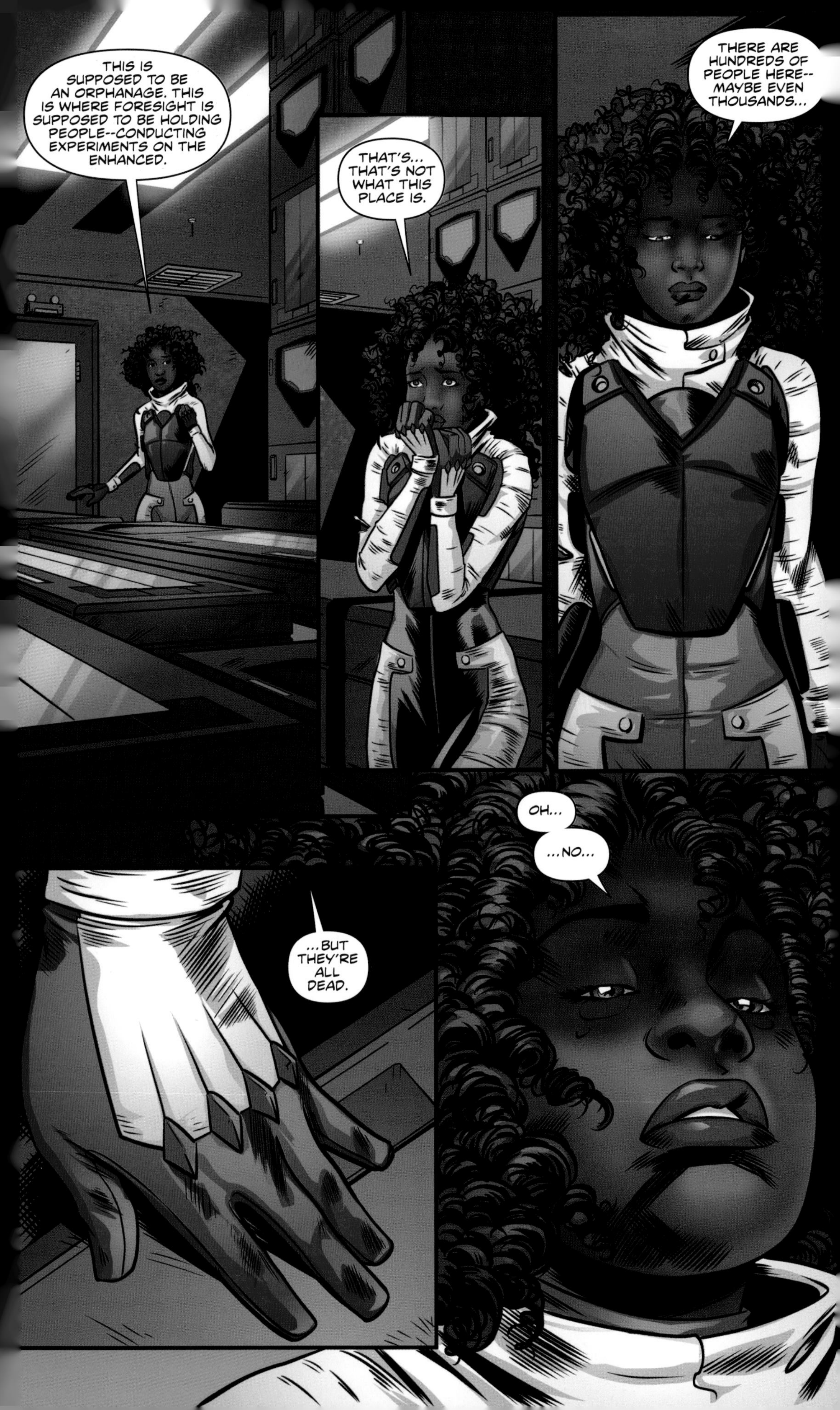
THIS IS SUPPOSED TO BE AN ORPHANAGE. THIS IS WHERE FORESIGHT IS SUPPOSED TO BE HOLDING PEOPLE--CONDUCTING EXPERIMENTS ON THE ENHANCED.
THAT'S... THAT'S NOT WHAT THIS PLACE IS.
THERE ARE HUNDREDS OF PEOPLE HERE-- MAYBE EVEN THOUSANDS...
OH...
...NO...
...BUT THEY'RE ALL DEAD.

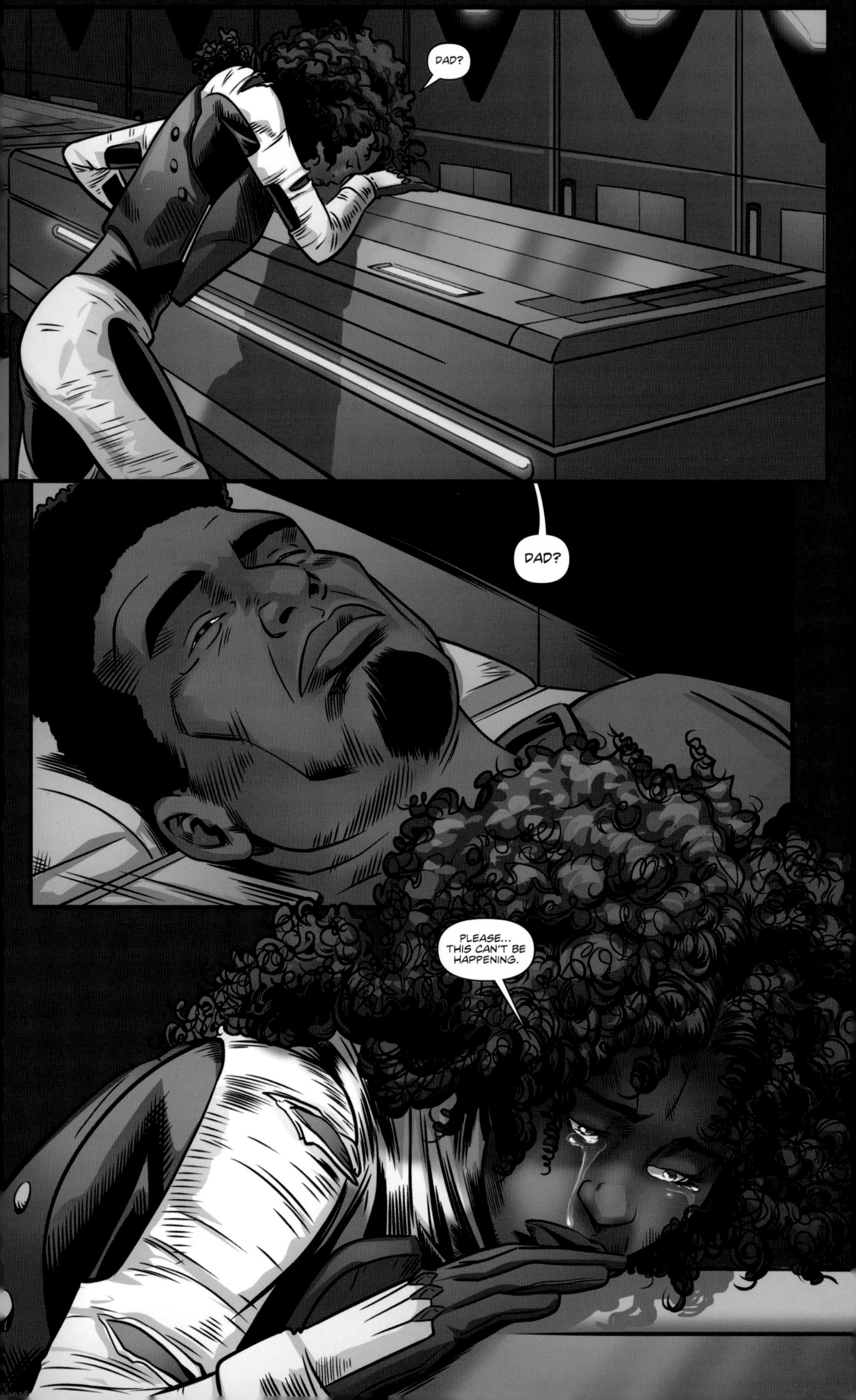

DAD?
DAD?
PLEASE... THIS CAN'T BE HAPPENING.

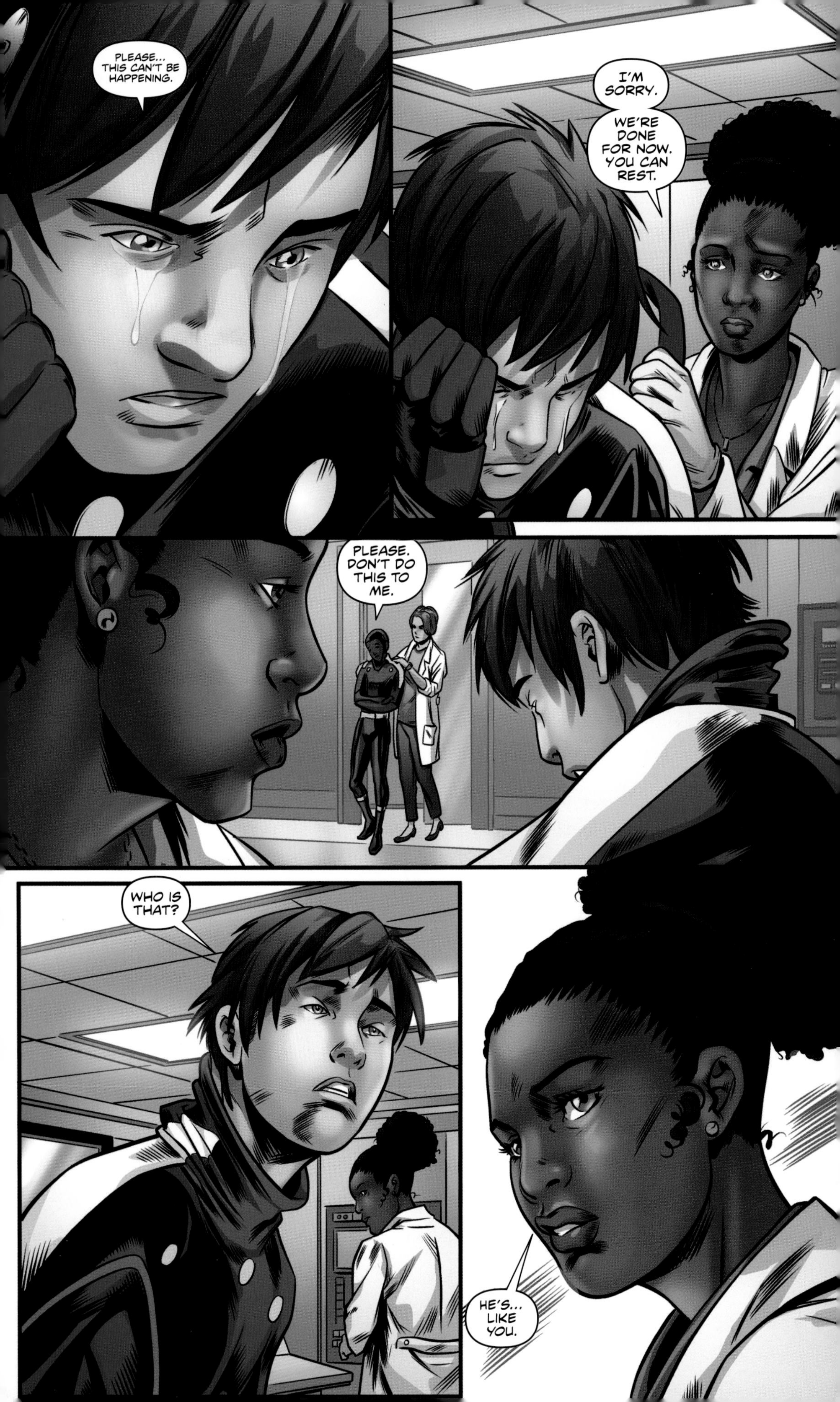
PLEASE... THIS CAN'T BE HAPPENING.
I'M SORRY.
WE'RE DONE FOR NOW. YOU CAN REST.
PLEASE. DON'T DO THIS TO ME.
WHO IS THAT?
HE'S... LIKE YOU.

LIKE ME?

HE'S A TEST SUBJECT. HE'S HELPING US LEARN MORE ABOUT THE ENHANCED.

ARE THEY HURTING HIM LIKE THEY'RE HURTING ME?

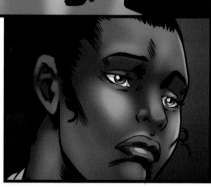

I CAN'T DO THIS ANYMORE.

THEY... THEY CAN'T DO THIS TO US.

LET'S GO, JONAH. YOU NEED SOME REST.

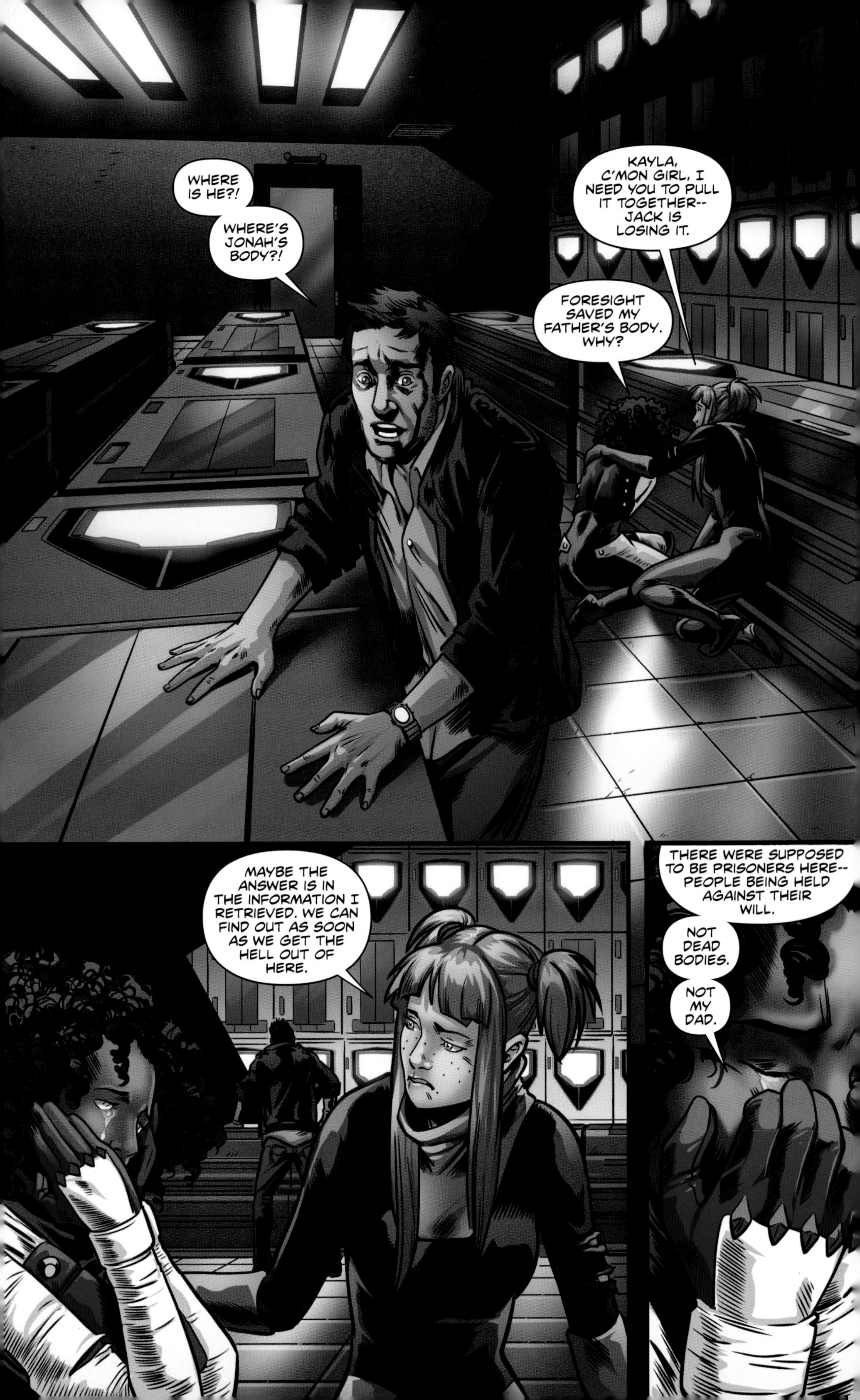

WHERE IS HE?!
WHERE'S JONAH'S BODY?!
KAYLA, C'MON GIRL, I NEED YOU TO PULL IT TOGETHER-- JACK IS LOSING IT.
FORESIGHT SAVED MY FATHER'S BODY. WHY?
MAYBE THE ANSWER IS IN THE INFORMATION I RETRIEVED. WE CAN FIND OUT AS SOON AS WE GET THE HELL OUT OF HERE.
THERE WERE SUPPOSED TO BE PRISONERS HERE-- PEOPLE BEING HELD AGAINST THEIR WILL.
NOT DEAD BODIES.
NOT MY DAD.

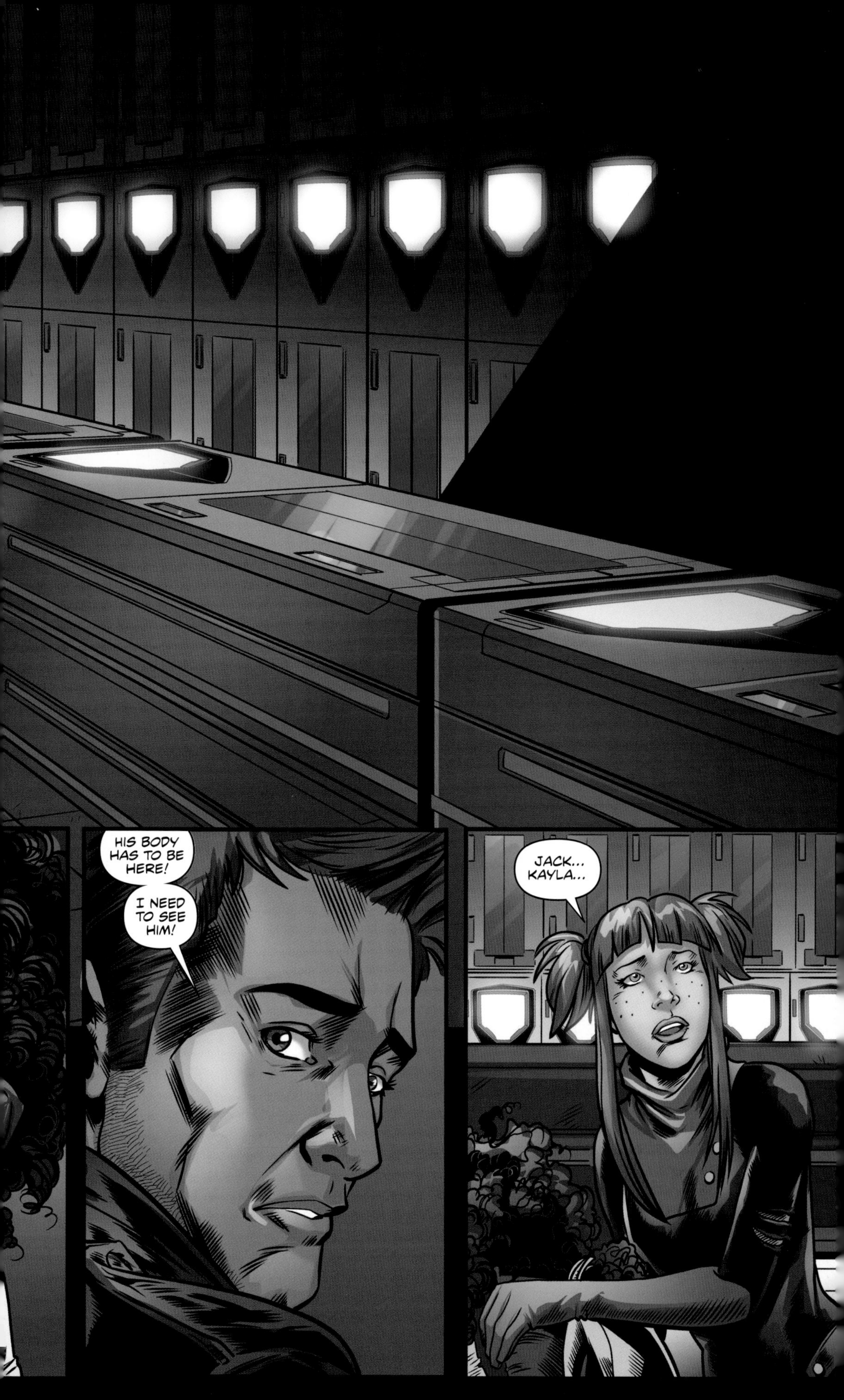
HIS BODY HAS TO BE HERE!
I NEED TO SEE HIM!
JACK... KAYLA...

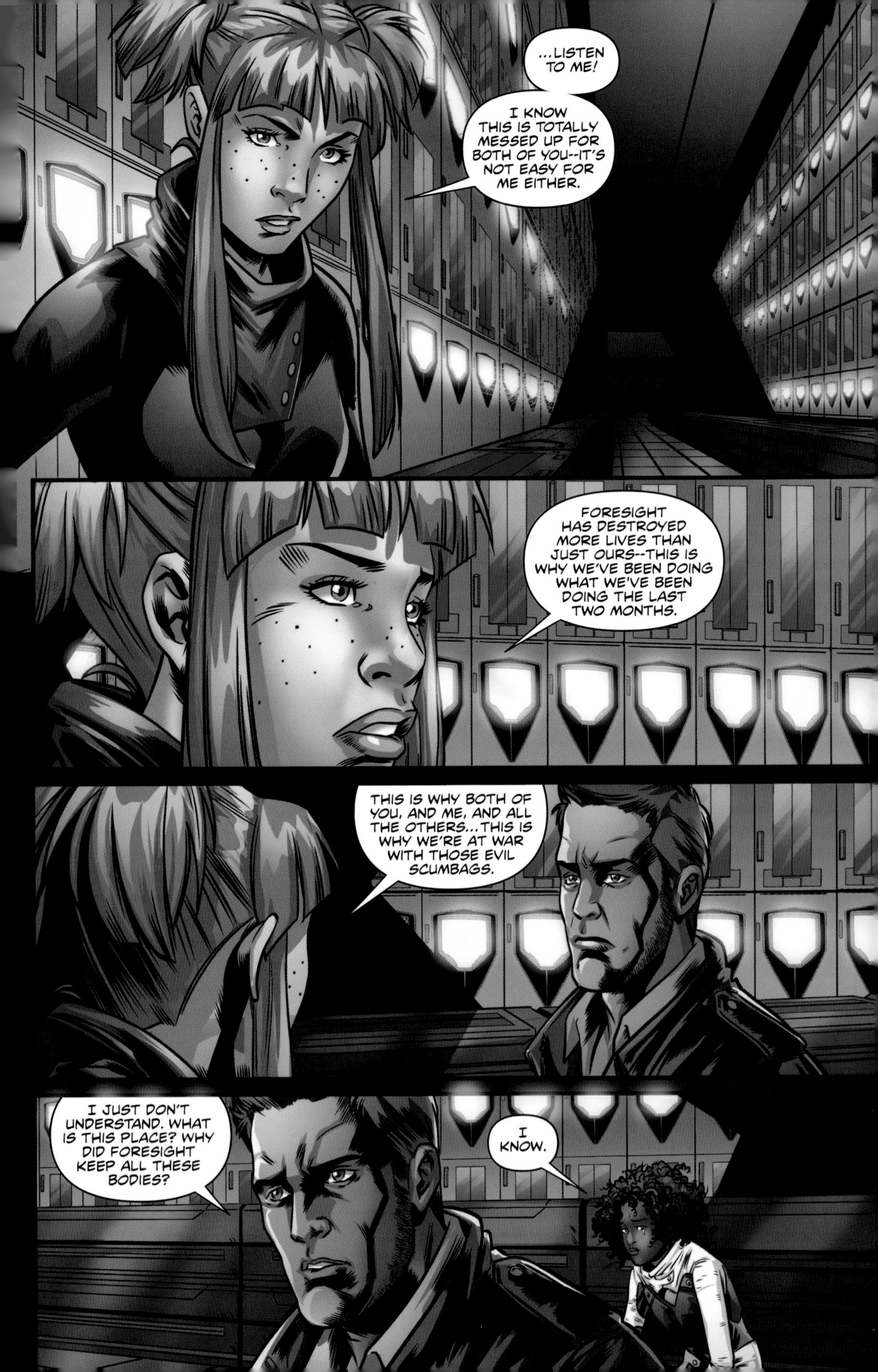
...LISTEN TO ME!
I KNOW THIS IS TOTALLY MESSED UP FOR BOTH OF YOU--IT'S NOT EASY FOR ME EITHER.
FORESIGHT HAS DESTROYED MORE LIVES THAN JUST OURS--THIS IS WHY WE'VE BEEN DOING WHAT WE'VE BEEN DOING THE LAST TWO MONTHS.
THIS IS WHY BOTH OF YOU, AND ME, AND ALL THE OTHERS...THIS IS WHY WE'RE AT WAR WITH THOSE EVIL SCUMBAGS.
I JUST DON'T UNDERSTAND. WHAT IS THIS PLACE? WHY DID FORESIGHT KEEP ALL THESE BODIES?
I KNOW.

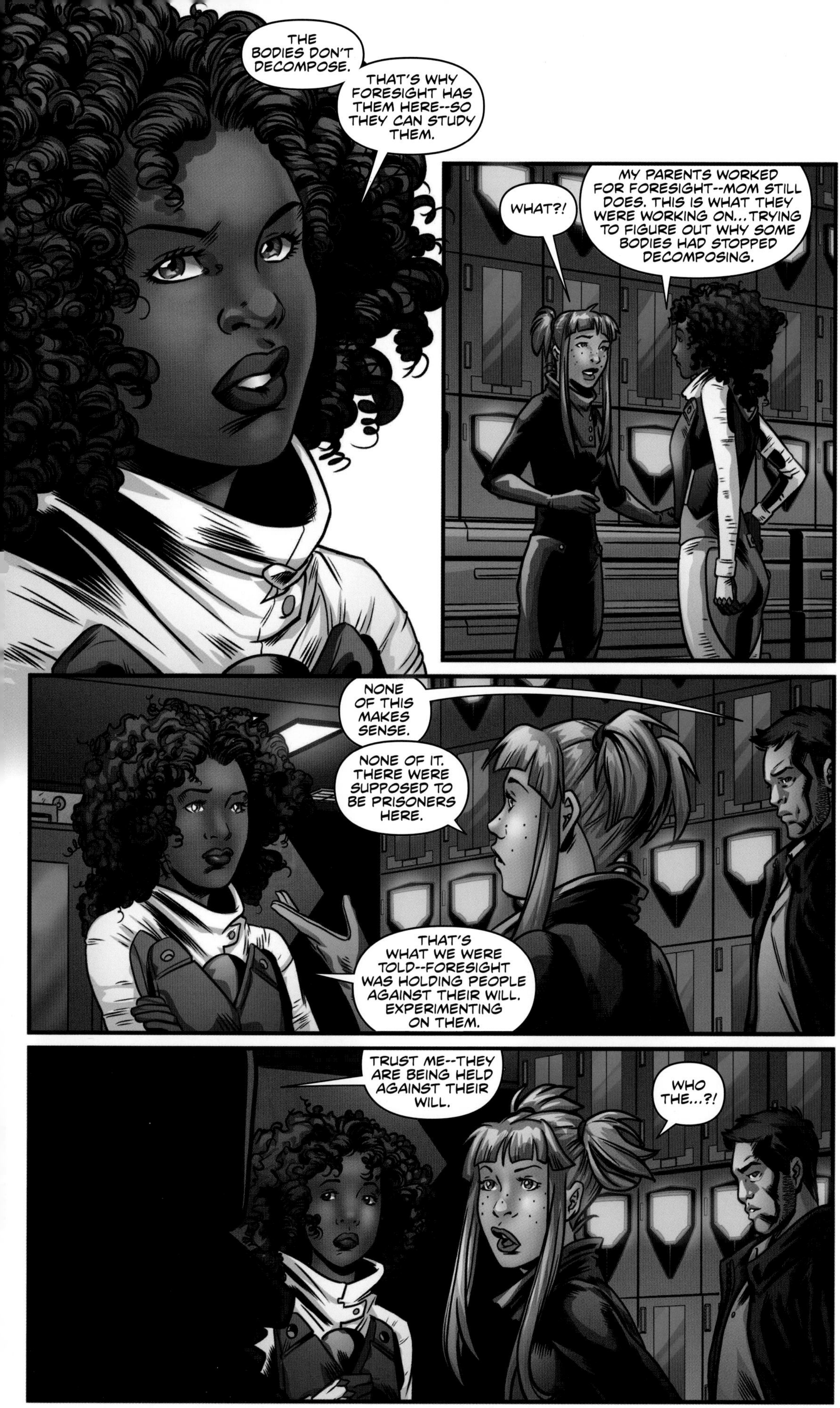
THE BODIES DON'T DECOMPOSE.
THAT'S WHY FORESIGHT HAS THEM HERE--SO THEY CAN STUDY THEM.
WHAT?!
MY PARENTS WORKED FOR FORESIGHT--MOM STILL DOES. THIS IS WHAT THEY WERE WORKING ON... TRYING TO FIGURE OUT WHY SOME BODIES HAD STOPPED DECOMPOSING.
NONE OF THIS MAKES SENSE.
NONE OF IT. THERE WERE SUPPOSED TO BE PRISONERS HERE.
THAT'S WHAT WE WERE TOLD--FORESIGHT WAS HOLDING PEOPLE AGAINST THEIR WILL. EXPERIMENTING ON THEM.
TRUST ME--THEY ARE BEING HELD AGAINST THEIR WILL.
WHO THE...?!

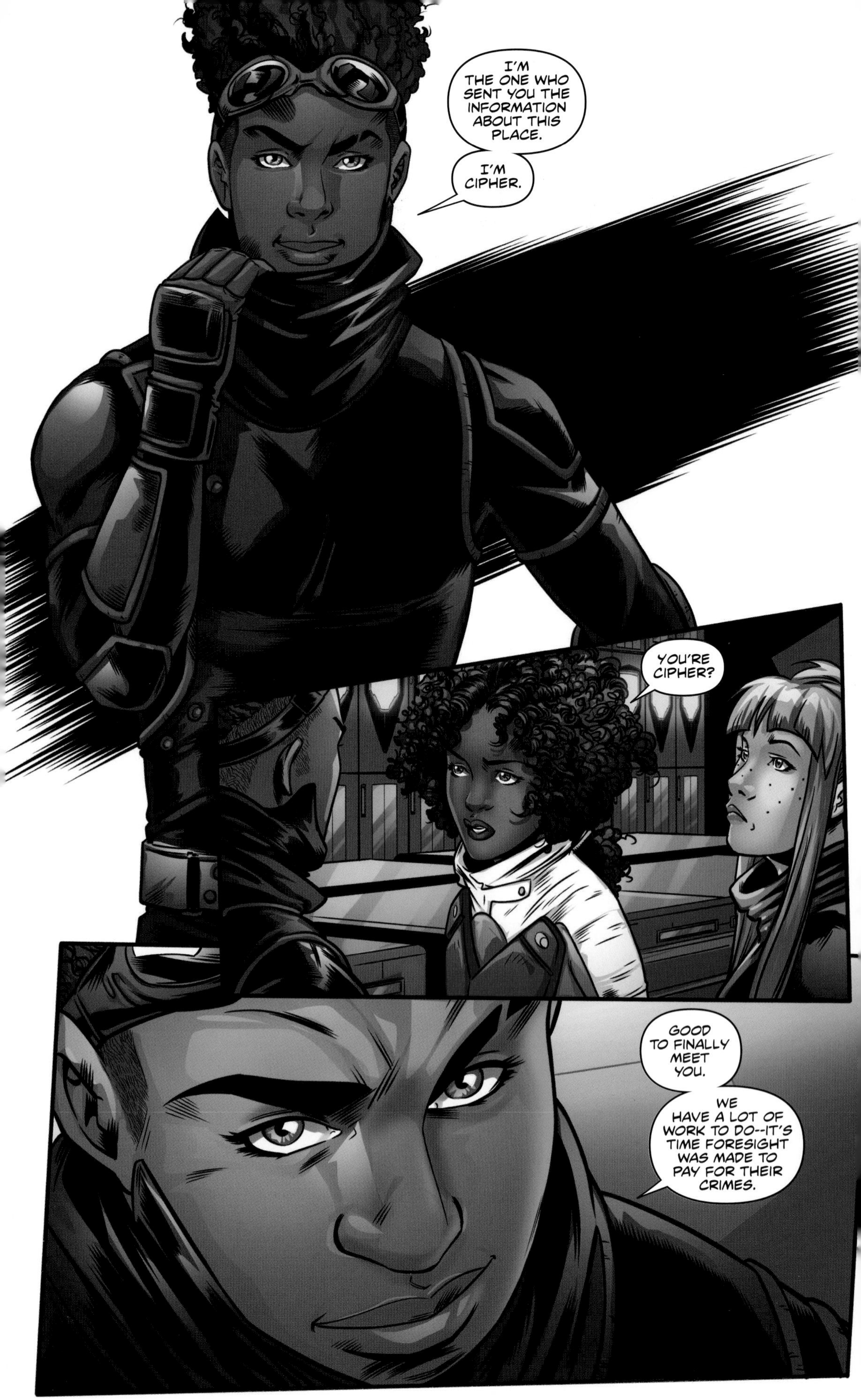
I'M THE ONE WHO SENT YOU THE INFORMATION ABOUT THIS PLACE.
I'M CIPHER.
YOU'RE CIPHER?
GOOD TO FINALLY MEET YOU.
WE HAVE A LOT OF WORK TO DO--IT'S TIME FORESIGHT WAS MADE TO PAY FOR THEIR CRIMES.

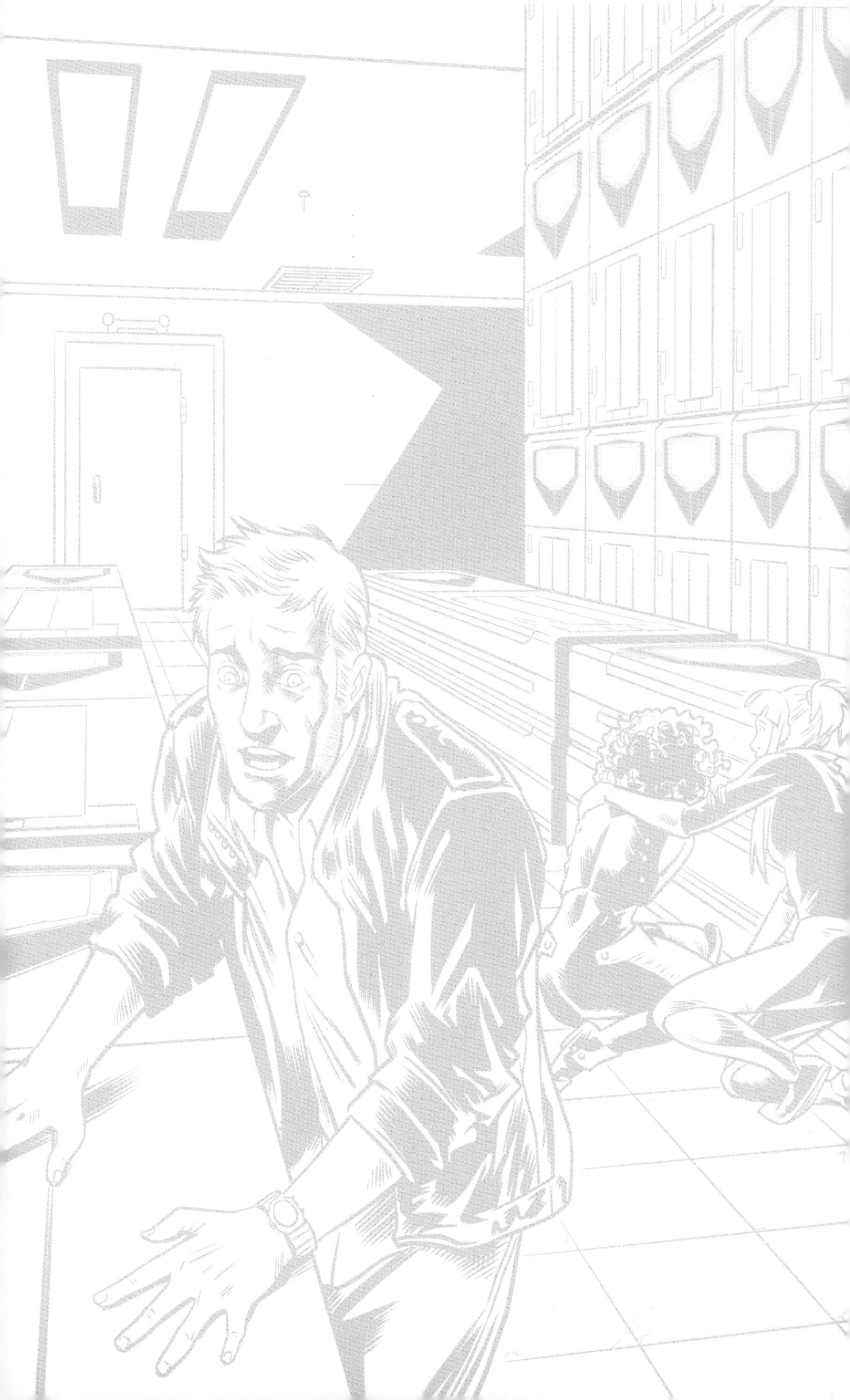

CHAPTER THREE

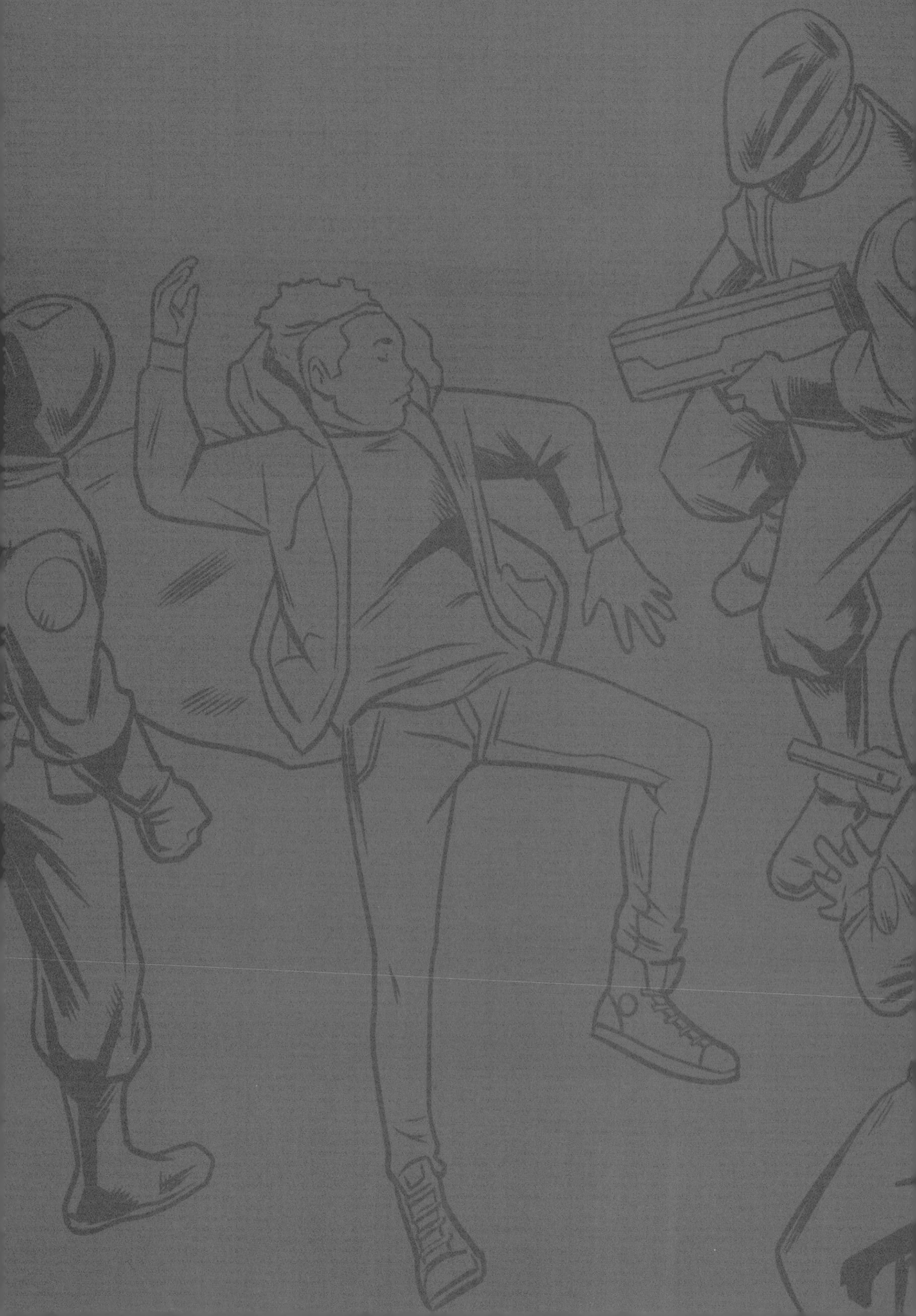

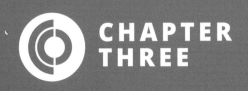

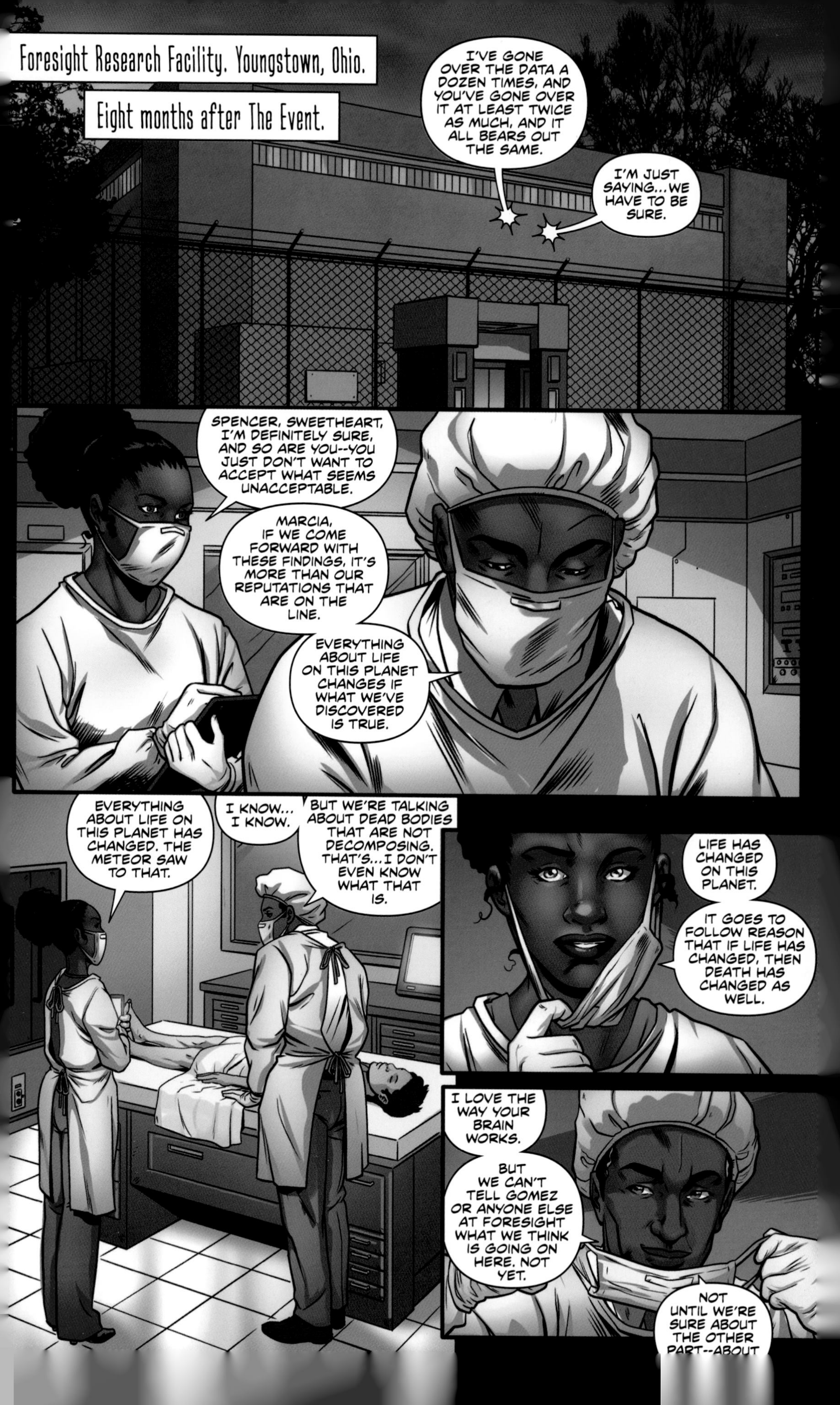
Foresight Research Facility. Youngstown, Ohio.
Eight months after The Event.
I'VE GONE OVER THE DATA A DOZEN TIMES, AND YOU'VE GONE OVER IT AT LEAST TWICE AS MUCH, AND IT ALL BEARS OUT THE SAME.
I'M JUST SAYING...WE HAVE TO BE SURE.
SPENCER, SWEETHEART, I'M DEFINITELY SURE, AND SO ARE YOU--YOU JUST DON'T WANT TO ACCEPT WHAT SEEMS UNACCEPTABLE.
MARCIA, IF WE COME FORWARD WITH THESE FINDINGS, IT'S MORE THAN OUR REPUTATIONS THAT ARE ON THE LINE.
EVERYTHING ABOUT LIFE ON THIS PLANET CHANGES IF WHAT WE'VE DISCOVERED IS TRUE.
EVERYTHING ABOUT LIFE ON THIS PLANET HAS CHANGED. THE METEOR SAW TO THAT.
I KNOW... I KNOW.
BUT WE'RE TALKING ABOUT DEAD BODIES THAT ARE NOT DECOMPOSING. THAT'S...I DON'T EVEN KNOW WHAT THAT IS.
LIFE HAS CHANGED ON THIS PLANET.
IT GOES TO FOLLOW REASON THAT IF LIFE HAS CHANGED, THEN DEATH HAS CHANGED AS WELL.
I LOVE THE WAY YOUR BRAIN WORKS.
BUT WE CAN'T TELL GOMEZ OR ANYONE ELSE AT FORESIGHT WHAT WE THINK IS GOING ON HERE. NOT YET.
NOT UNTIL WE'RE SURE ABOUT THE OTHER PART--ABOUT

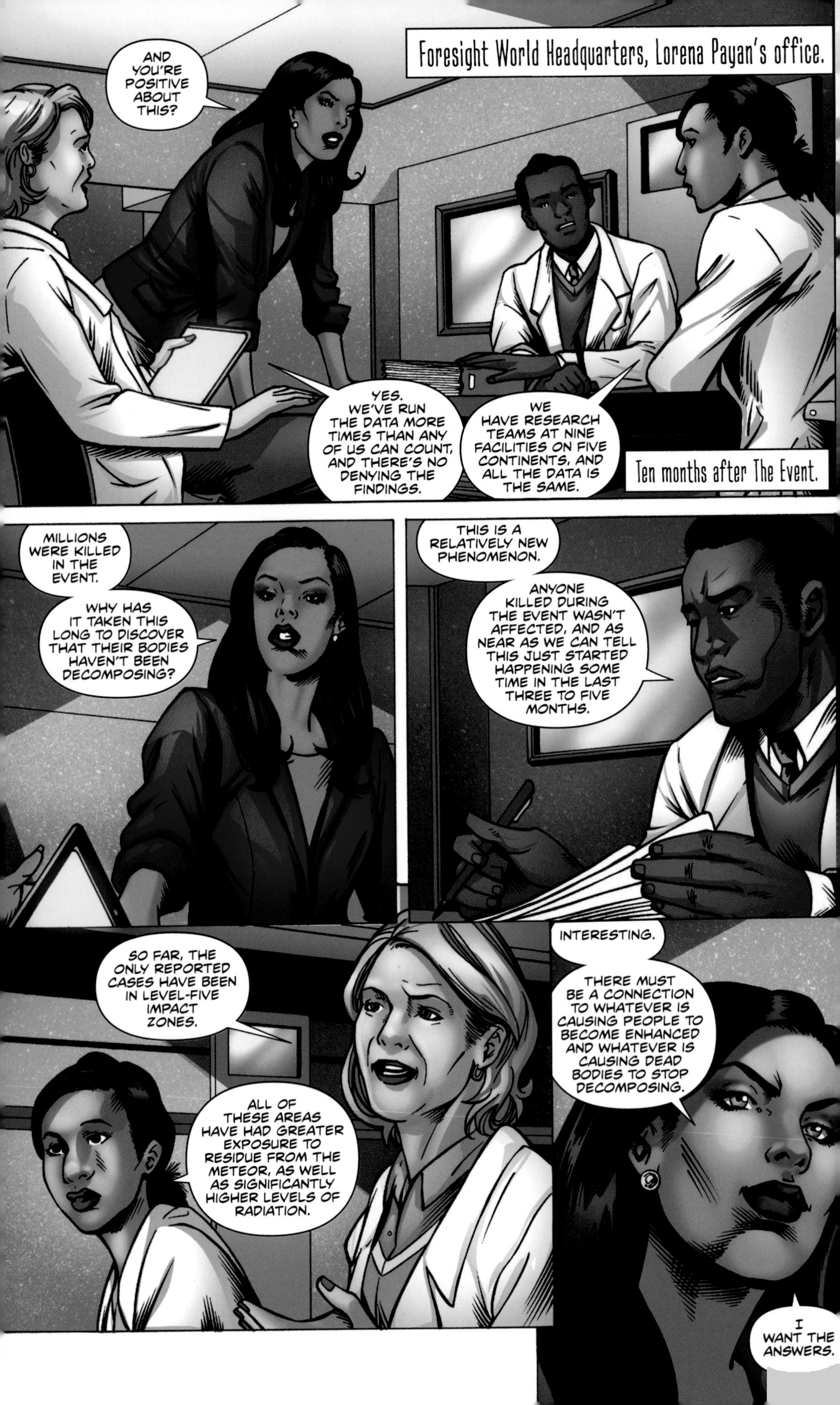
Foresight World Headquarters, Lorena Payan's office.
AND YOU'RE POSITIVE ABOUT THIS?
YES. WE'VE RUN THE DATA MORE TIMES THAN ANY OF US CAN COUNT, AND THERE'S NO DENYING THE FINDINGS.
WE HAVE RESEARCH TEAMS AT NINE FACILITIES ON FIVE CONTINENTS, AND ALL THE DATA IS THE SAME.
Ten months after The Event.
MILLIONS WERE KILLED IN THE EVENT.
WHY HAS IT TAKEN THIS LONG TO DISCOVER THAT THEIR BODIES HAVEN'T BEEN DECOMPOSING?
THIS IS A RELATIVELY NEW PHENOMENON.
ANYONE KILLED DURING THE EVENT WASN'T AFFECTED, AND AS NEAR AS WE CAN TELL THIS JUST STARTED HAPPENING SOME TIME IN THE LAST THREE TO FIVE MONTHS.
SO FAR, THE ONLY REPORTED CASES HAVE BEEN IN LEVEL-FIVE IMPACT ZONES.
ALL OF THESE AREAS HAVE HAD GREATER EXPOSURE TO RESIDUE FROM THE METEOR, AS WELL AS SIGNIFICANTLY HIGHER LEVELS OF RADIATION.
INTERESTING.
THERE MUST BE A CONNECTION TO WHATEVER IS CAUSING PEOPLE TO BECOME ENHANCED AND WHATEVER IS CAUSING DEAD BODIES TO STOP DECOMPOSING.
I WANT THE ANSWERS.

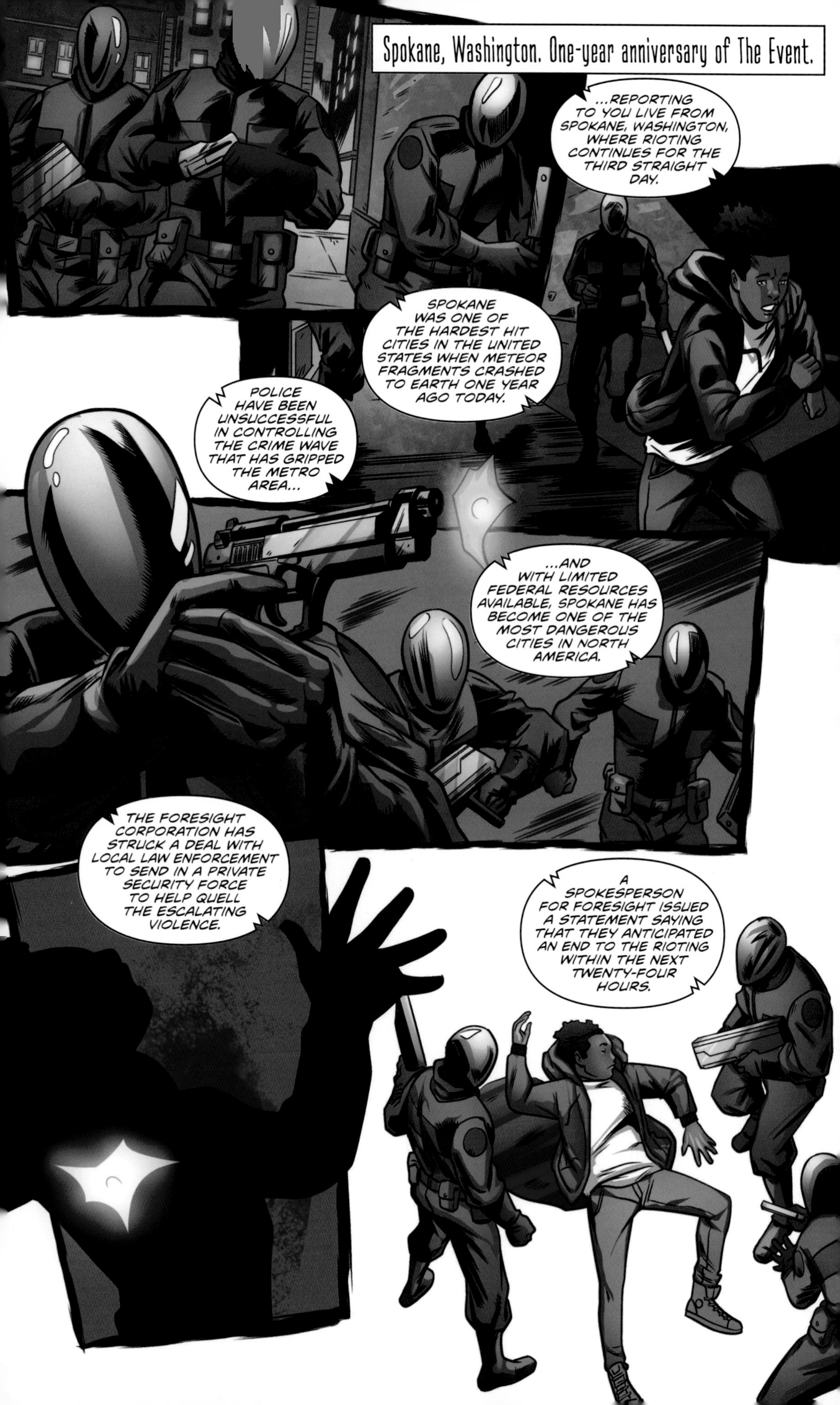

Spokane, Washington. One-year anniversary of The Event.
...REPORTING TO YOU LIVE FROM SPOKANE, WASHINGTON, WHERE RIOTING CONTINUES FOR THE THIRD STRAIGHT DAY.
SPOKANE WAS ONE OF THE HARDEST HIT CITIES IN THE UNITED STATES WHEN METEOR FRAGMENTS CRASHED TO EARTH ONE YEAR AGO TODAY.
POLICE HAVE BEEN UNSUCCESSFUL IN CONTROLLING THE CRIME WAVE THAT HAS GRIPPED THE METRO AREA...
...AND WITH LIMITED FEDERAL RESOURCES AVAILABLE, SPOKANE HAS BECOME ONE OF THE MOST DANGEROUS CITIES IN NORTH AMERICA.
THE FORESIGHT CORPORATION HAS STRUCK A DEAL WITH LOCAL LAW ENFORCEMENT TO SEND IN A PRIVATE SECURITY FORCE TO HELP QUELL THE ESCALATING VIOLENCE.
A SPOKESPERSON FOR FORESIGHT ISSUED A STATEMENT SAYING THAT THEY ANTICIPATED AN END TO THE RIOTING WITHIN THE NEXT TWENTY-FOUR HOURS.

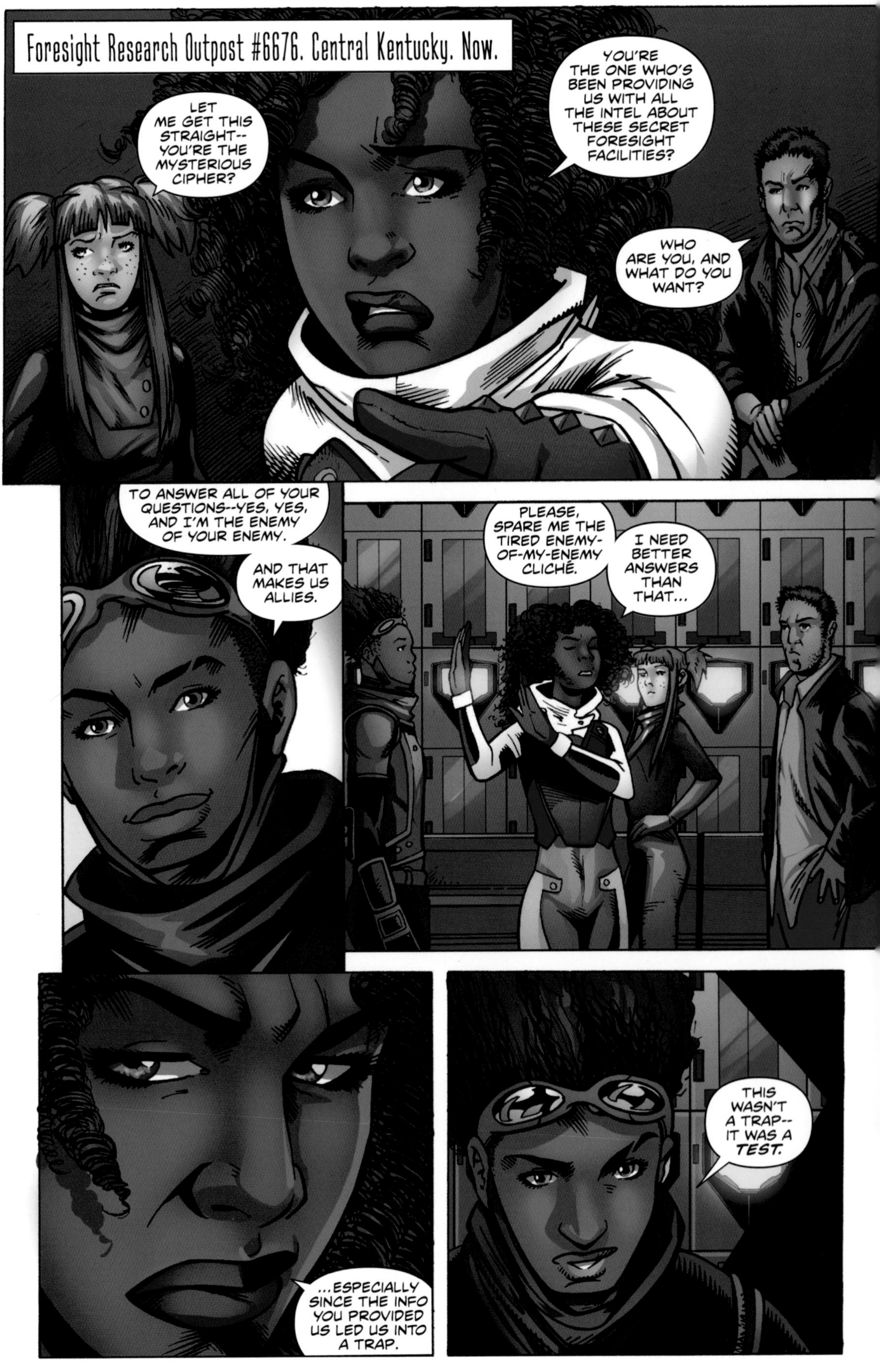

Foresight Research Outpost #6676. Central Kentucky. Now.
LET ME GET THIS STRAIGHT--YOU'RE THE MYSTERIOUS CIPHER?
YOU'RE THE ONE WHO'S BEEN PROVIDING US WITH ALL THE INTEL ABOUT THESE SECRET FORESIGHT FACILITIES?
WHO ARE YOU, AND WHAT DO YOU WANT?
TO ANSWER ALL OF YOUR QUESTIONS--YES, YES, AND I'M THE ENEMY OF YOUR ENEMY.
AND THAT MAKES US ALLIES.
PLEASE, SPARE ME THE TIRED ENEMY-OF-MY-ENEMY CLICHÉ.
I NEED BETTER ANSWERS THAN THAT...
...ESPECIALLY SINCE THE INFO YOU PROVIDED US LED US INTO A TRAP.
THIS WASN'T A TRAP--IT WAS A *TEST.*

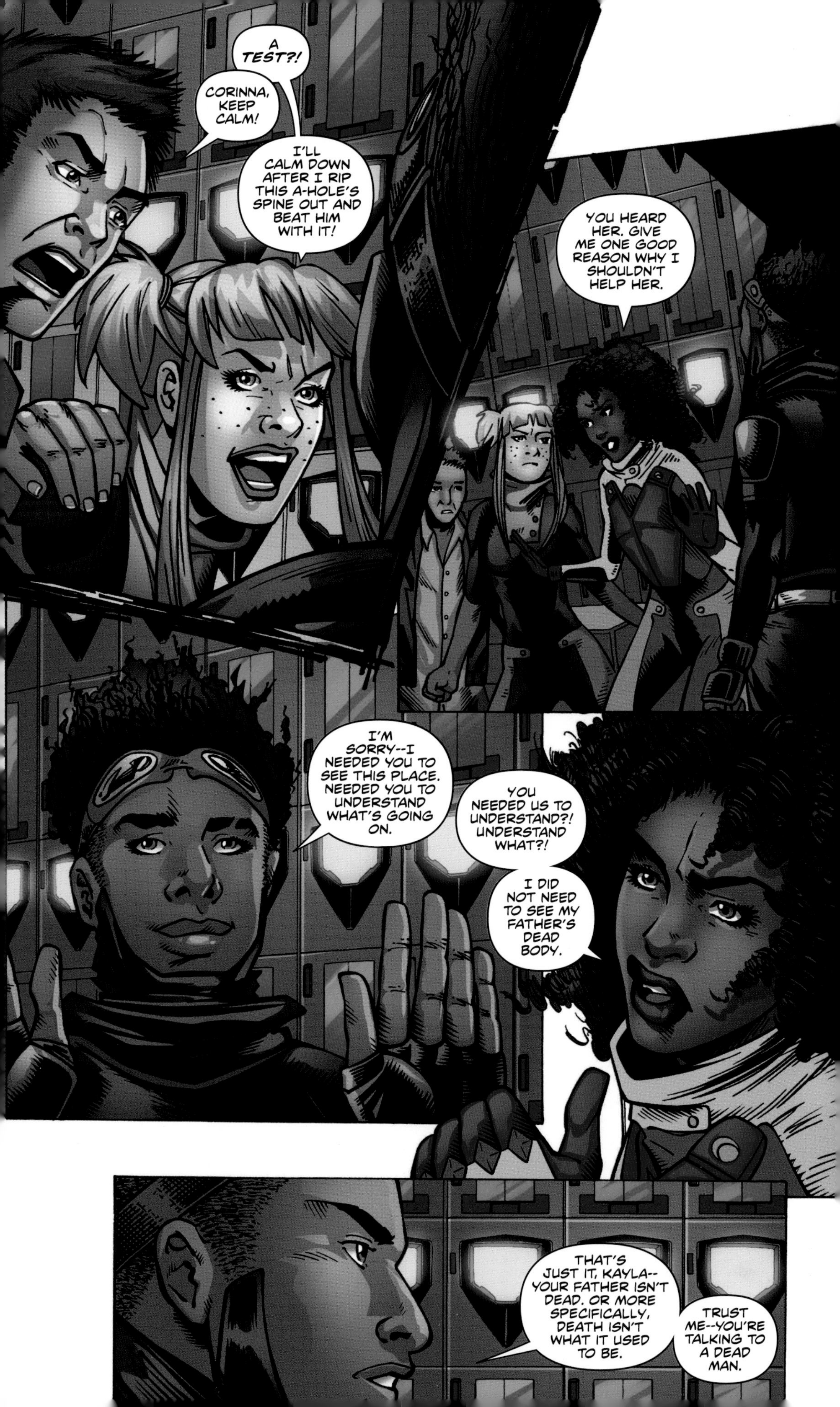
A TEST?!
CORINNA, KEEP CALM!
I'LL CALM DOWN AFTER I RIP THIS A-HOLE'S SPINE OUT AND BEAT HIM WITH IT!
YOU HEARD HER. GIVE ME ONE GOOD REASON WHY I SHOULDN'T HELP HER.
I'M SORRY--I NEEDED YOU TO SEE THIS PLACE. NEEDED YOU TO UNDERSTAND WHAT'S GOING ON.
YOU NEEDED US TO UNDERSTAND?! UNDERSTAND WHAT?!
I DID NOT NEED TO SEE MY FATHER'S DEAD BODY.
THAT'S JUST IT, KAYLA-- YOUR FATHER ISN'T DEAD. OR MORE SPECIFICALLY, DEATH ISN'T WHAT IT USED TO BE.
TRUST ME--YOU'RE TALKING TO A DEAD MAN.

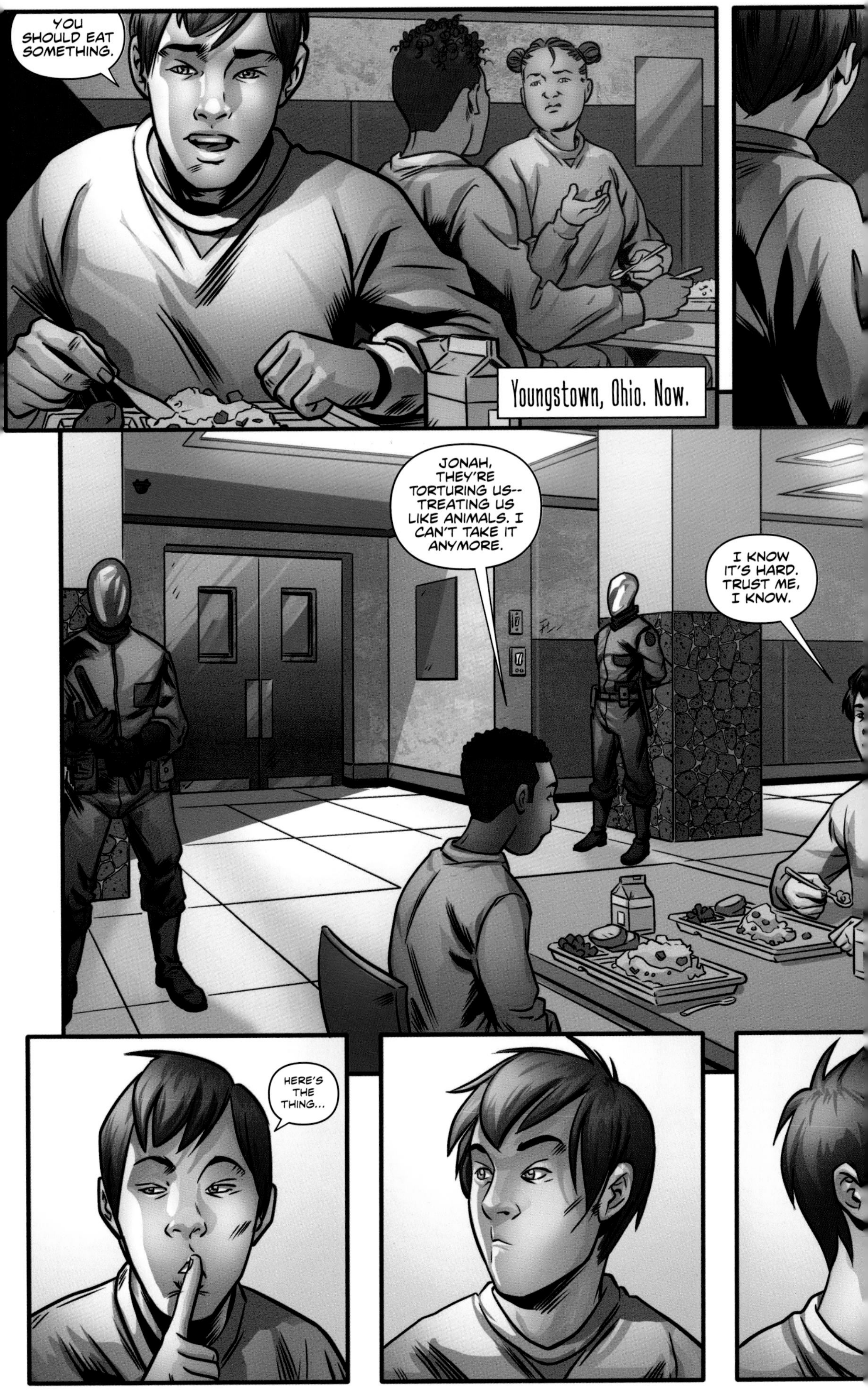

YOU SHOULD EAT SOMETHING.
Youngstown, Ohio. Now.
JONAH, THEY'RE TORTURING US-- TREATING US LIKE ANIMALS. I CAN'T TAKE IT ANYMORE.
I KNOW IT'S HARD. TRUST ME, I KNOW.
HERE'S THE THING...

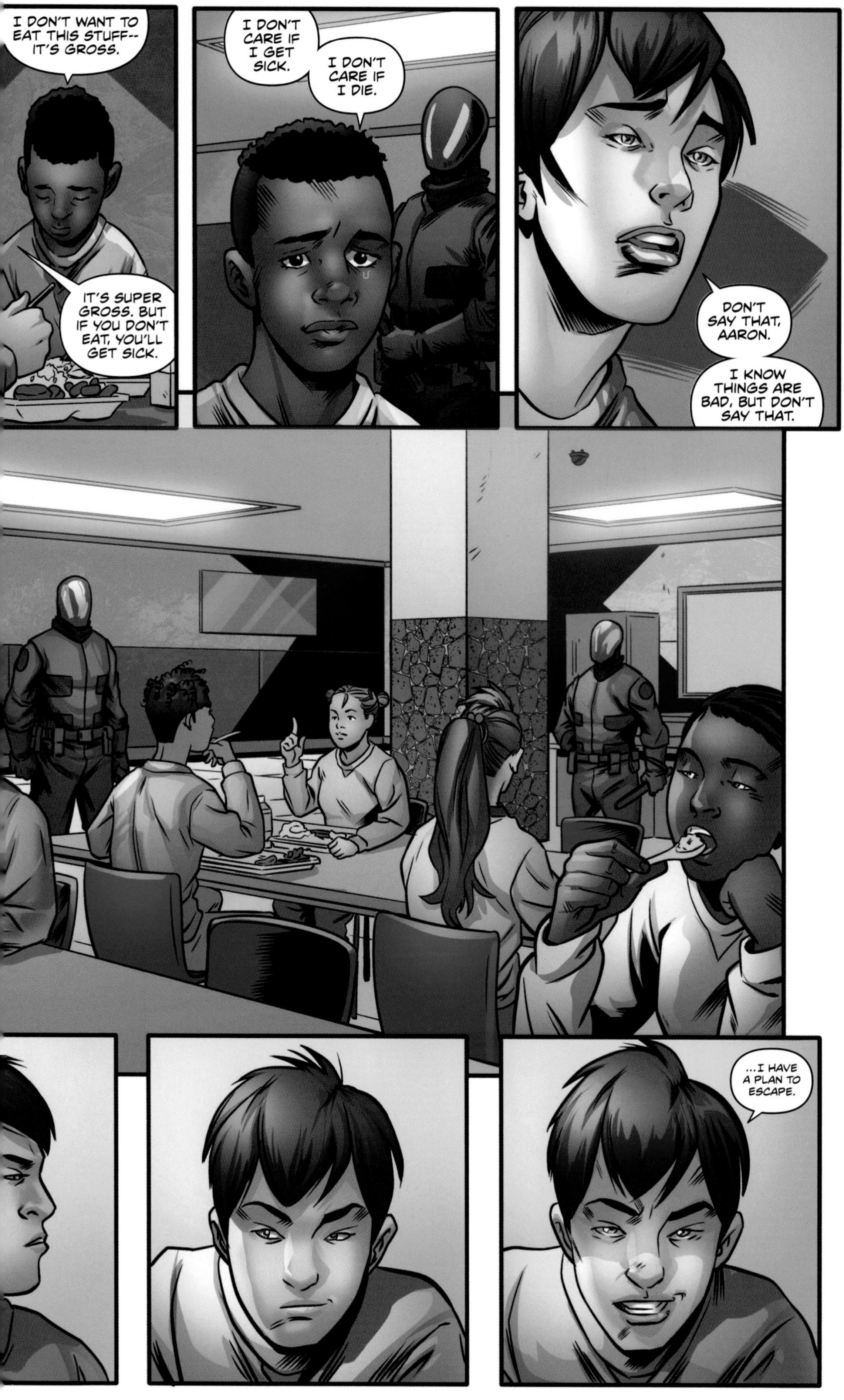
I DON'T WANT TO EAT THIS STUFF-- IT'S GROSS.
IT'S SUPER GROSS. BUT IF YOU DON'T EAT, YOU'LL GET SICK.
I DON'T CARE IF I GET SICK.
I DON'T CARE IF I DIE.
DON'T SAY THAT, AARON.
I KNOW THINGS ARE BAD, BUT DON'T SAY THAT.
...I HAVE A PLAN TO ESCAPE.

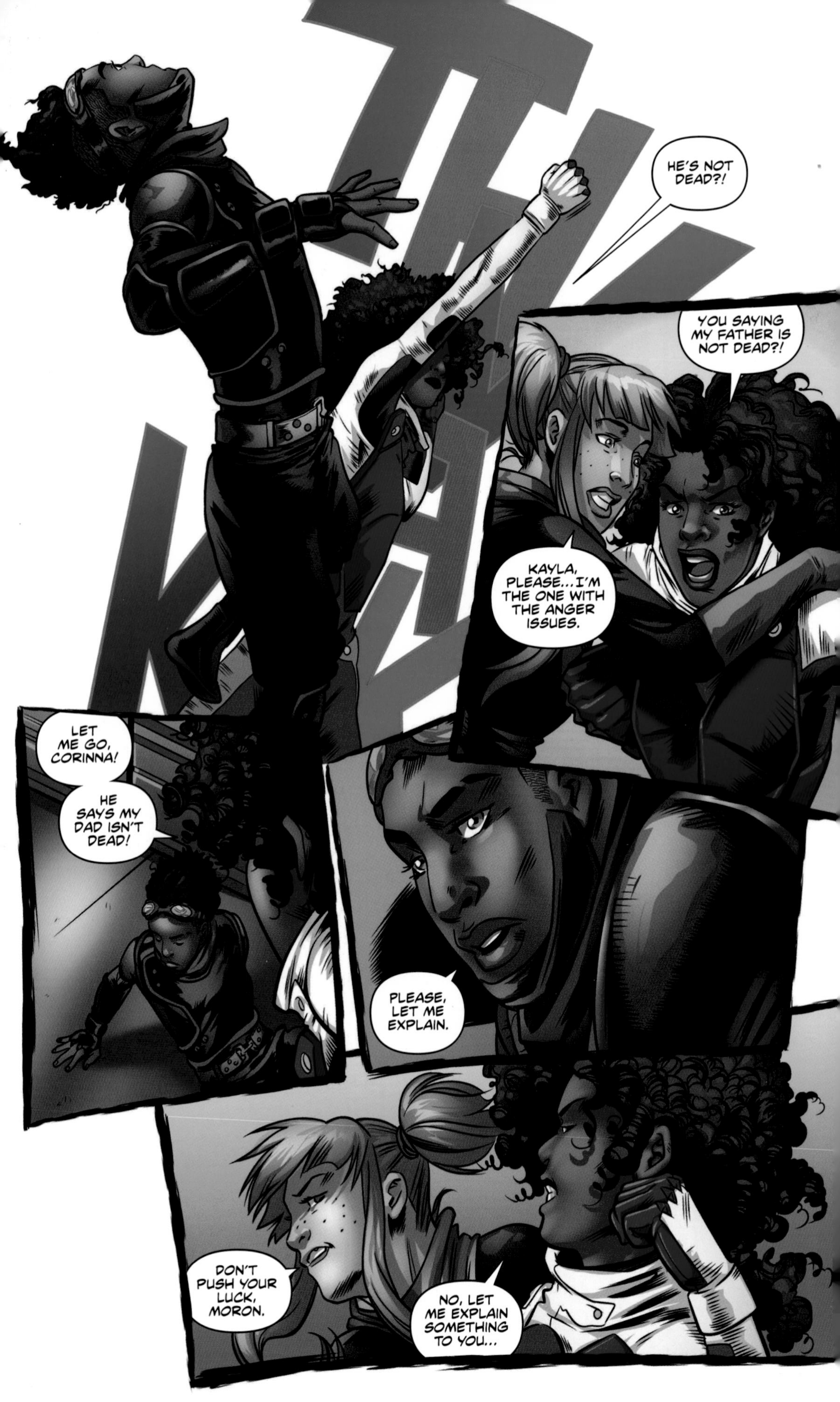
THK
HE'S NOT DEAD?!
YOU SAYING MY FATHER IS NOT DEAD?!
KAYLA, PLEASE...I'M THE ONE WITH THE ANGER ISSUES.
LET ME GO, CORINNA!
HE SAYS MY DAD ISN'T DEAD!
PLEASE, LET ME EXPLAIN.
DON'T PUSH YOUR LUCK, MORON.
NO, LET ME EXPLAIN SOMETHING TO YOU...

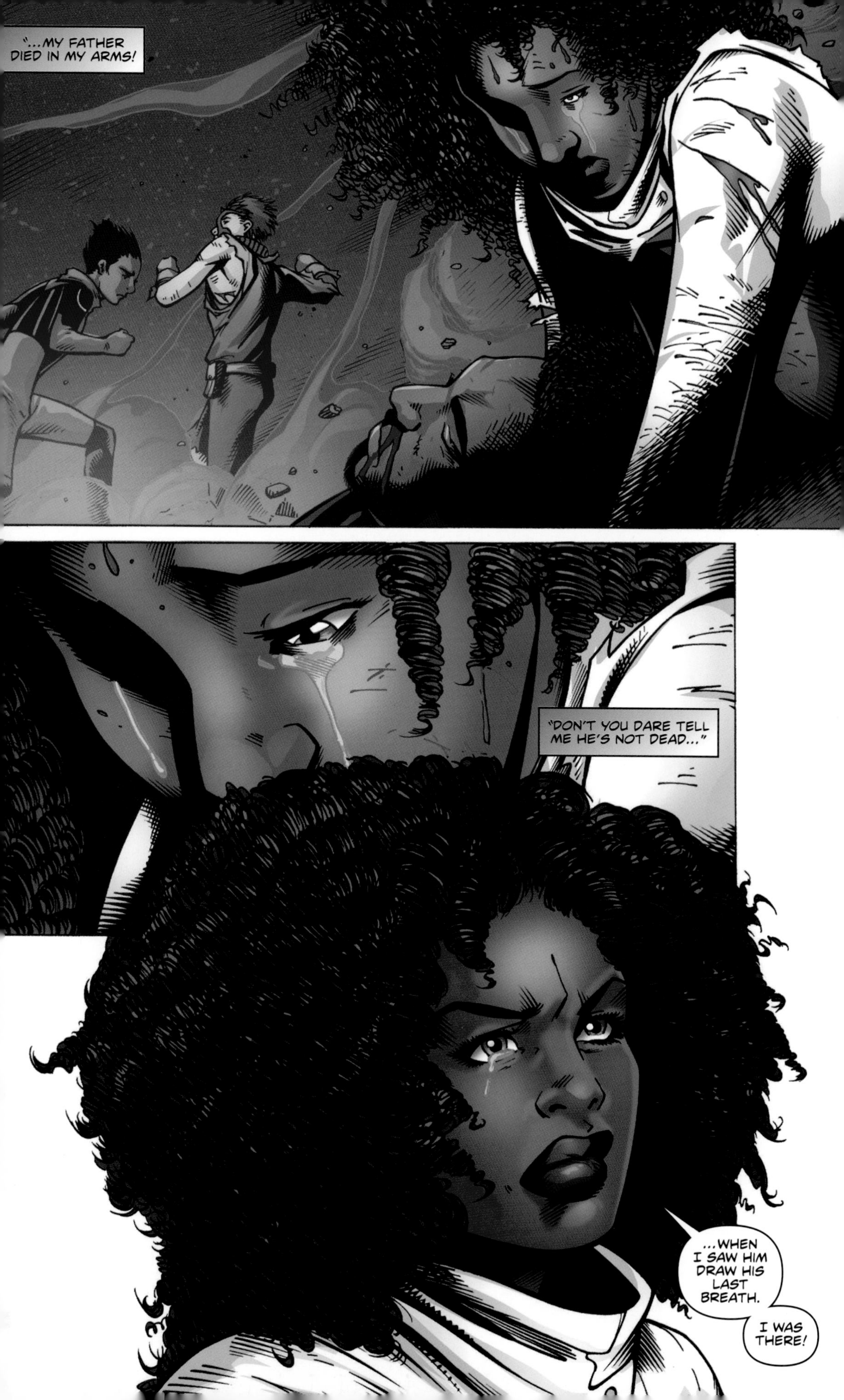
"...MY FATHER DIED IN MY ARMS!
"DON'T YOU DARE TELL ME HE'S NOT DEAD..."
...WHEN I SAW HIM DRAW HIS LAST BREATH.
I WAS THERE!

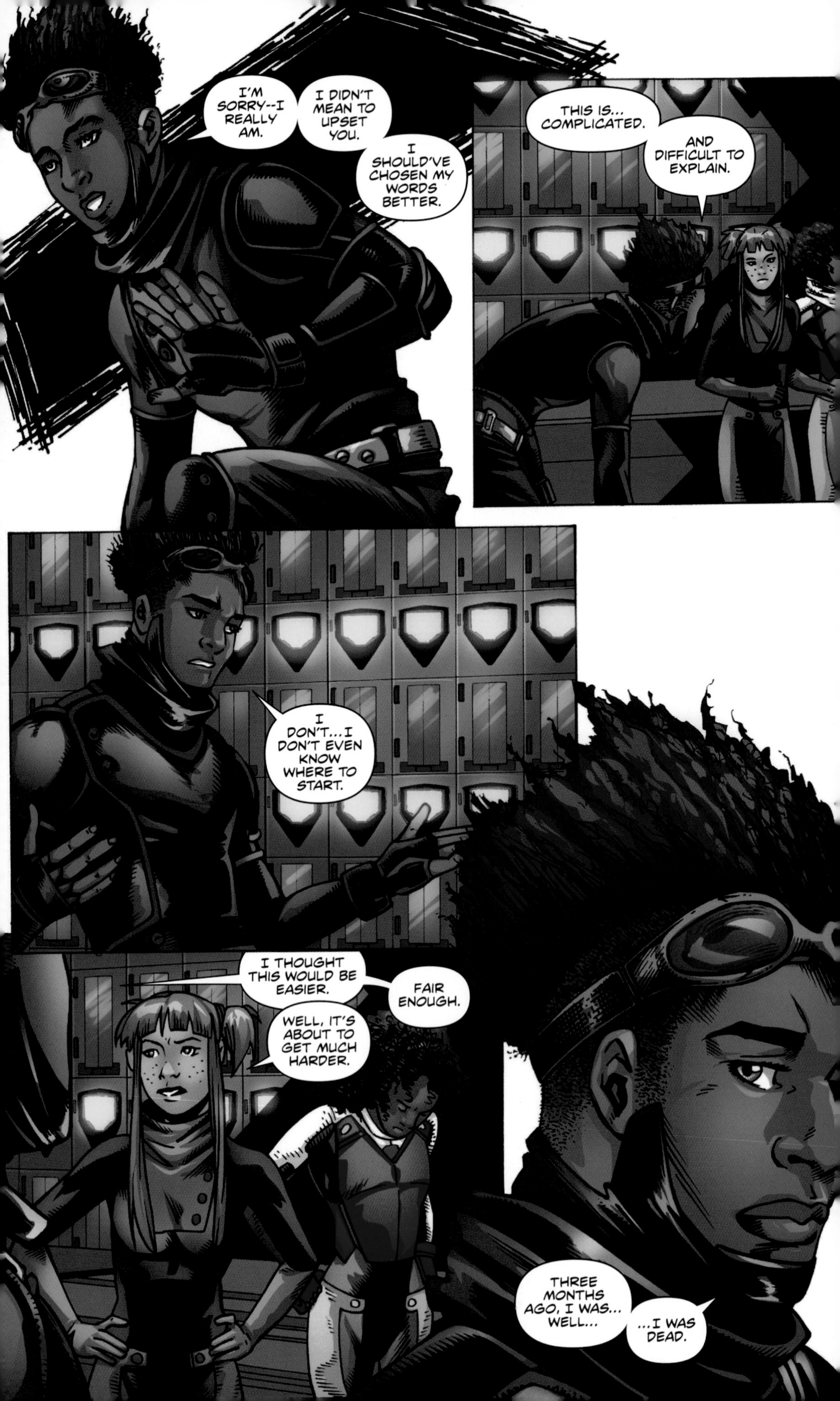
I'M SORRY--I REALLY AM.
I DIDN'T MEAN TO UPSET YOU.
I SHOULD'VE CHOSEN MY WORDS BETTER.
THIS IS... COMPLICATED.
AND DIFFICULT TO EXPLAIN.
I DON'T... I DON'T EVEN KNOW WHERE TO START.
I THOUGHT THIS WOULD BE EASIER.
FAIR ENOUGH.
WELL, IT'S ABOUT TO GET MUCH HARDER.
THREE MONTHS AGO, I WAS... WELL...
...I WAS DEAD.

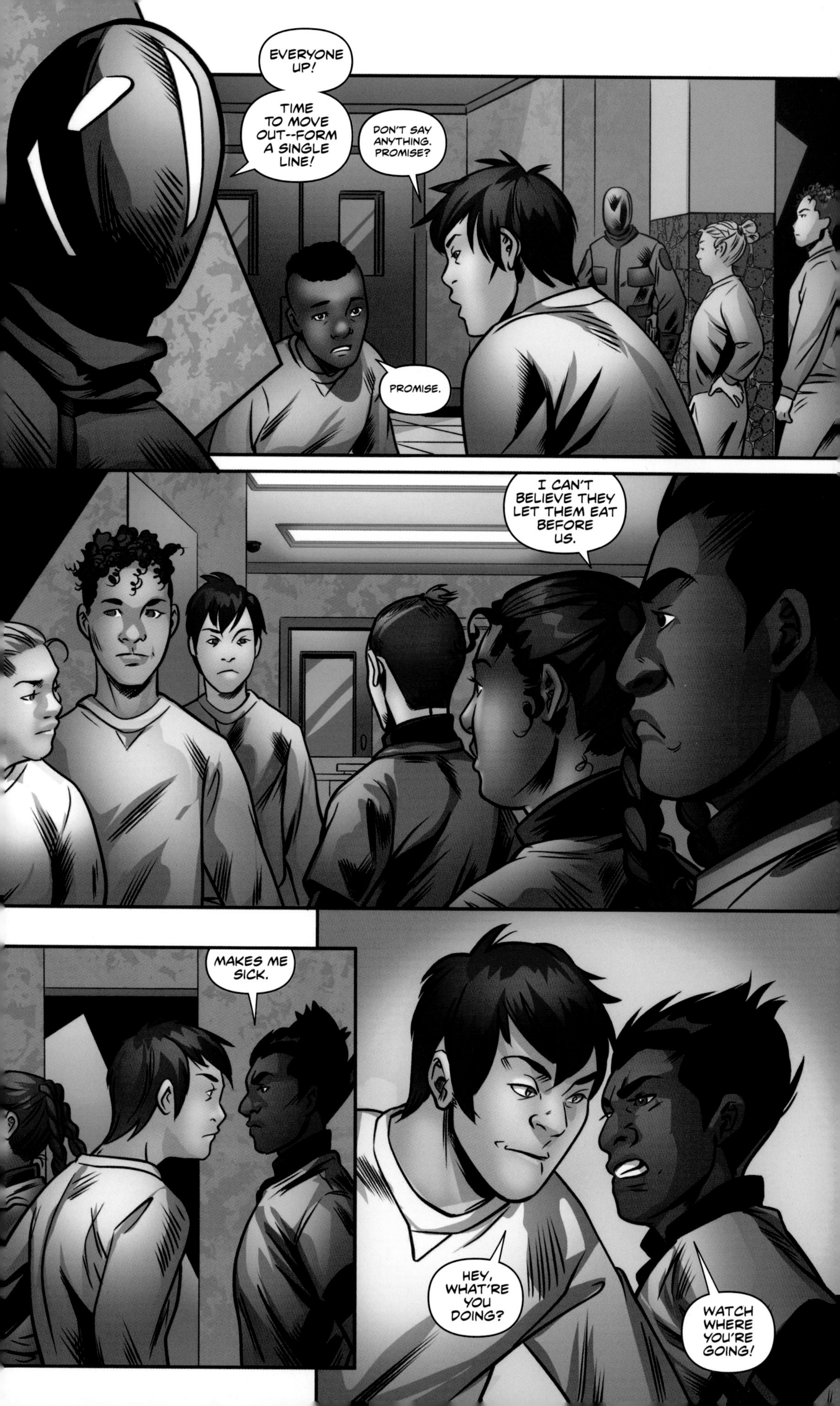
EVERYONE UP!
TIME TO MOVE OUT--FORM A SINGLE LINE!
DON'T SAY ANYTHING. PROMISE?
PROMISE.
I CAN'T BELIEVE THEY LET THEM EAT BEFORE US.
MAKES ME SICK.
HEY, WHAT'RE YOU DOING?
WATCH WHERE YOU'RE GOING!

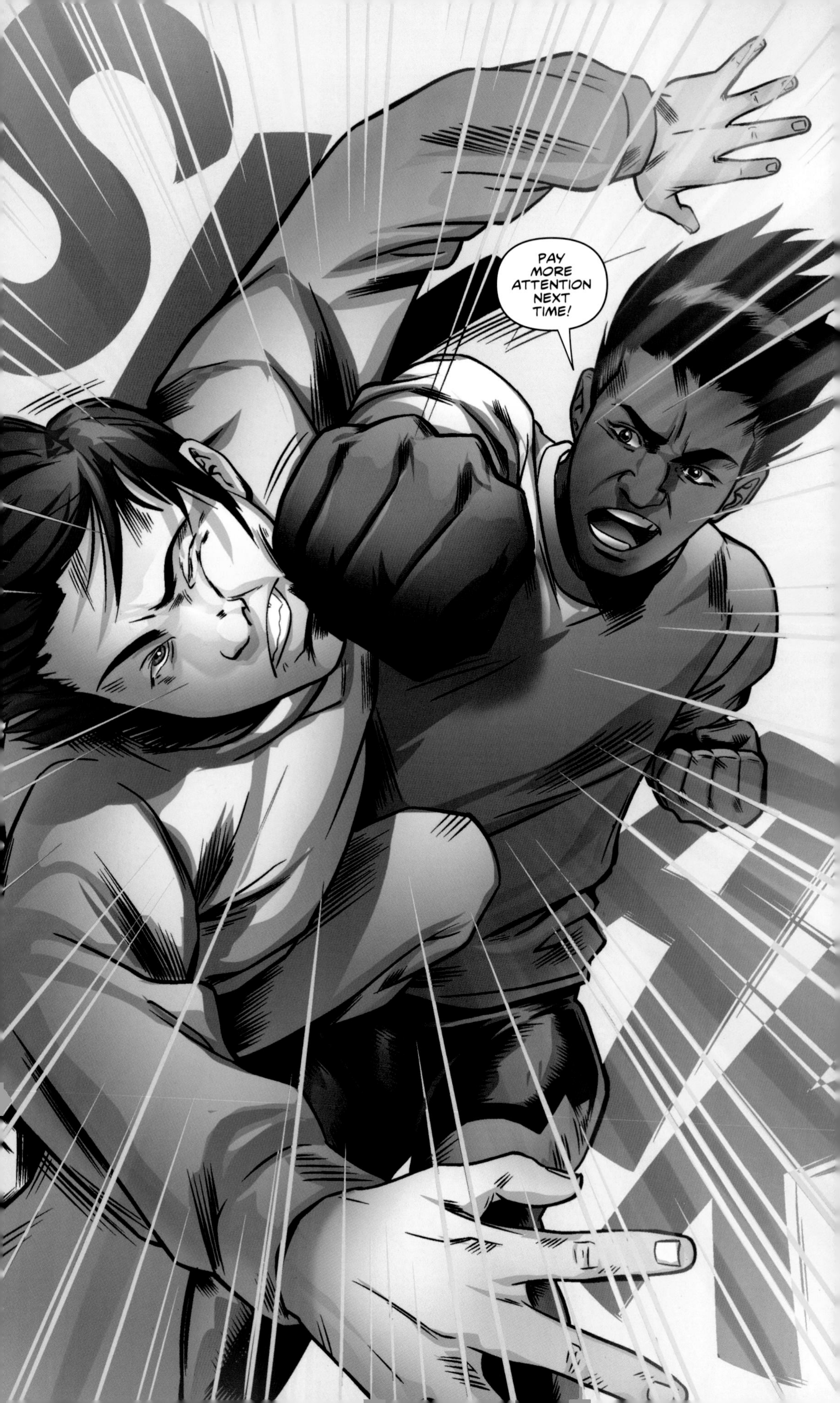
PAY MORE ATTENTION NEXT TIME!

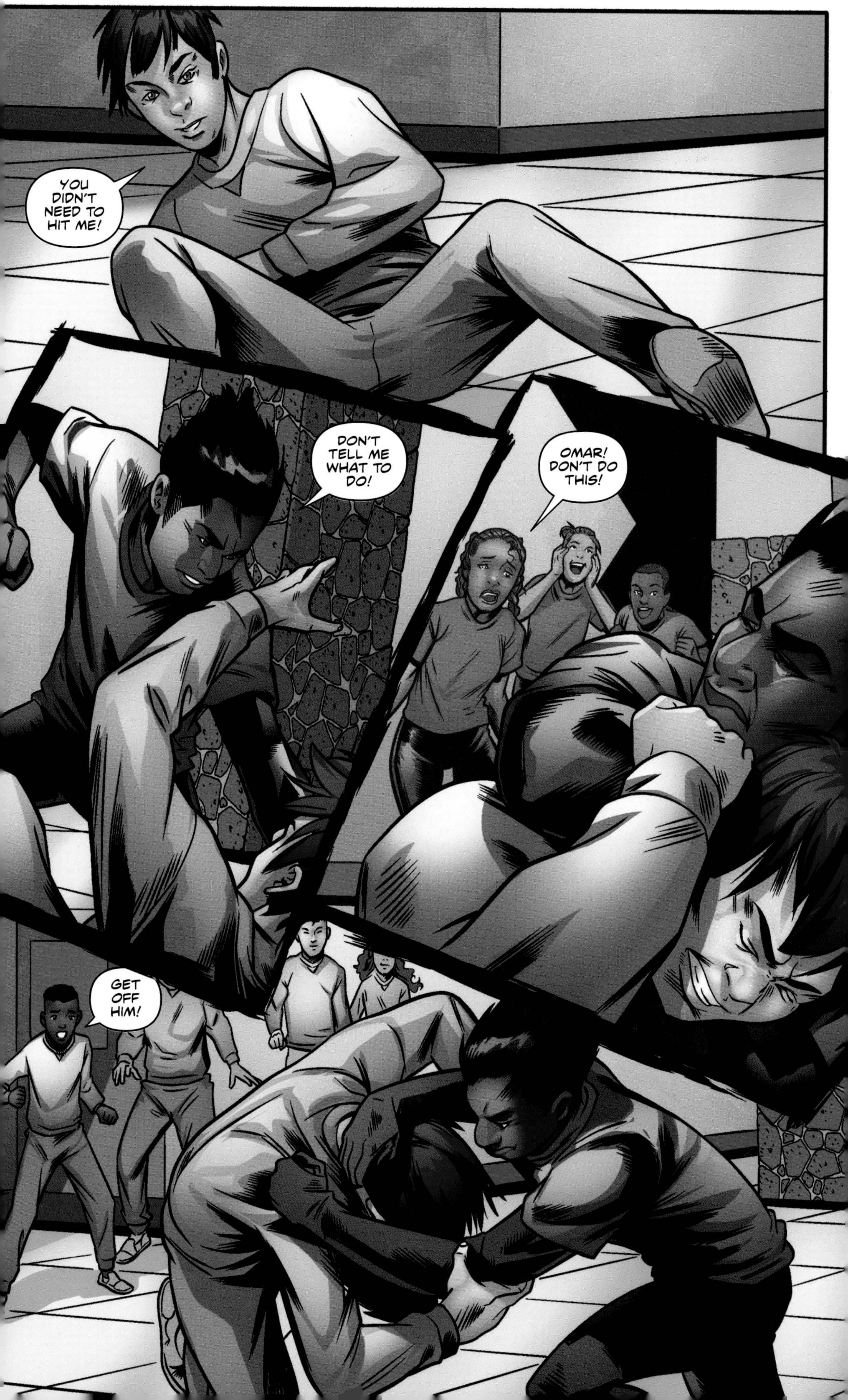
YOU DIDN'T NEED TO HIT ME!
DON'T TELL ME WHAT TO DO!
OMAR! DON'T DO THIS!
GET OFF HIM!

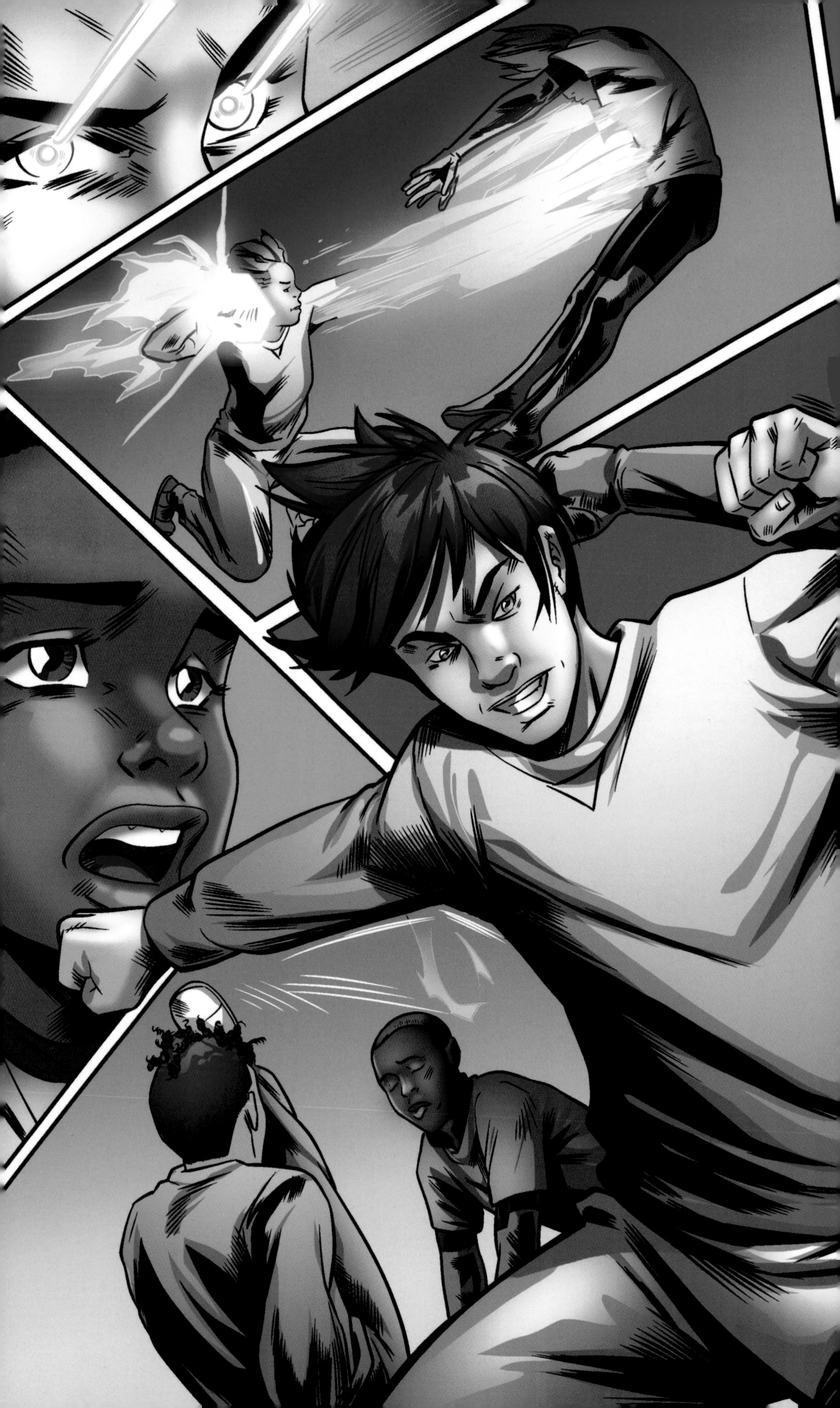

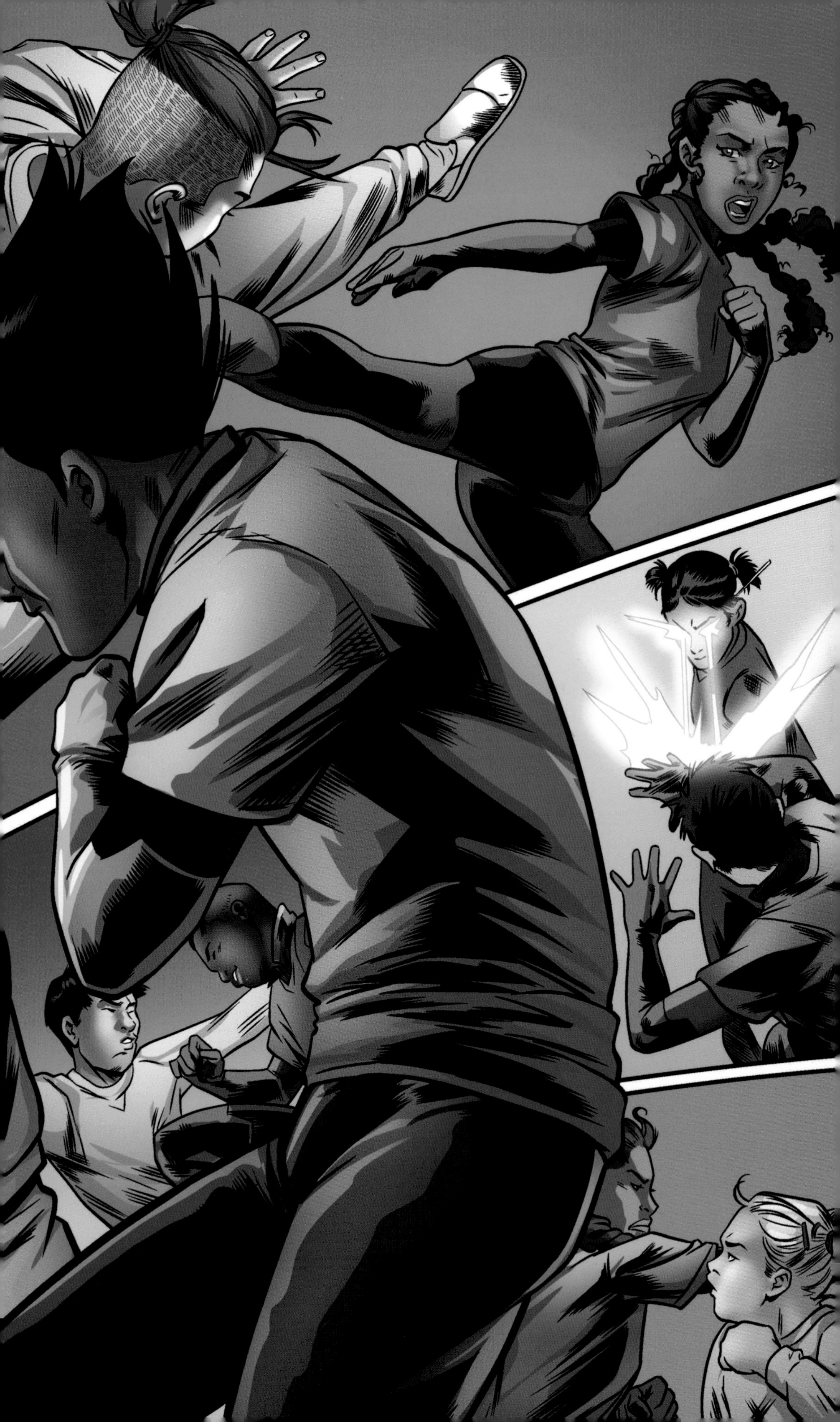

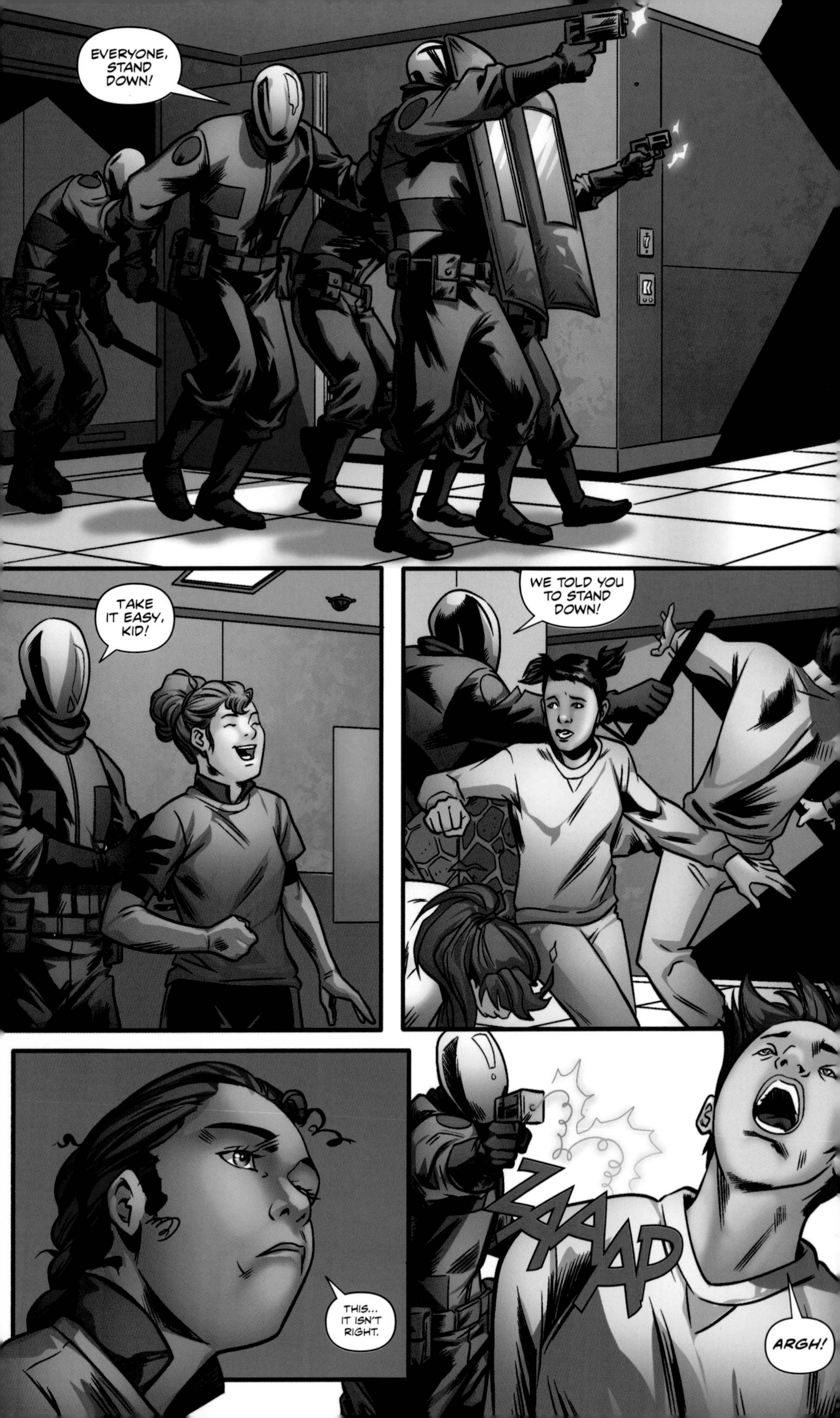
EVERYONE, STAND DOWN!
TAKE IT EASY, KID!
WE TOLD YOU TO STAND DOWN!
THIS... IT ISN'T RIGHT.
ZAAAP
ARGH!

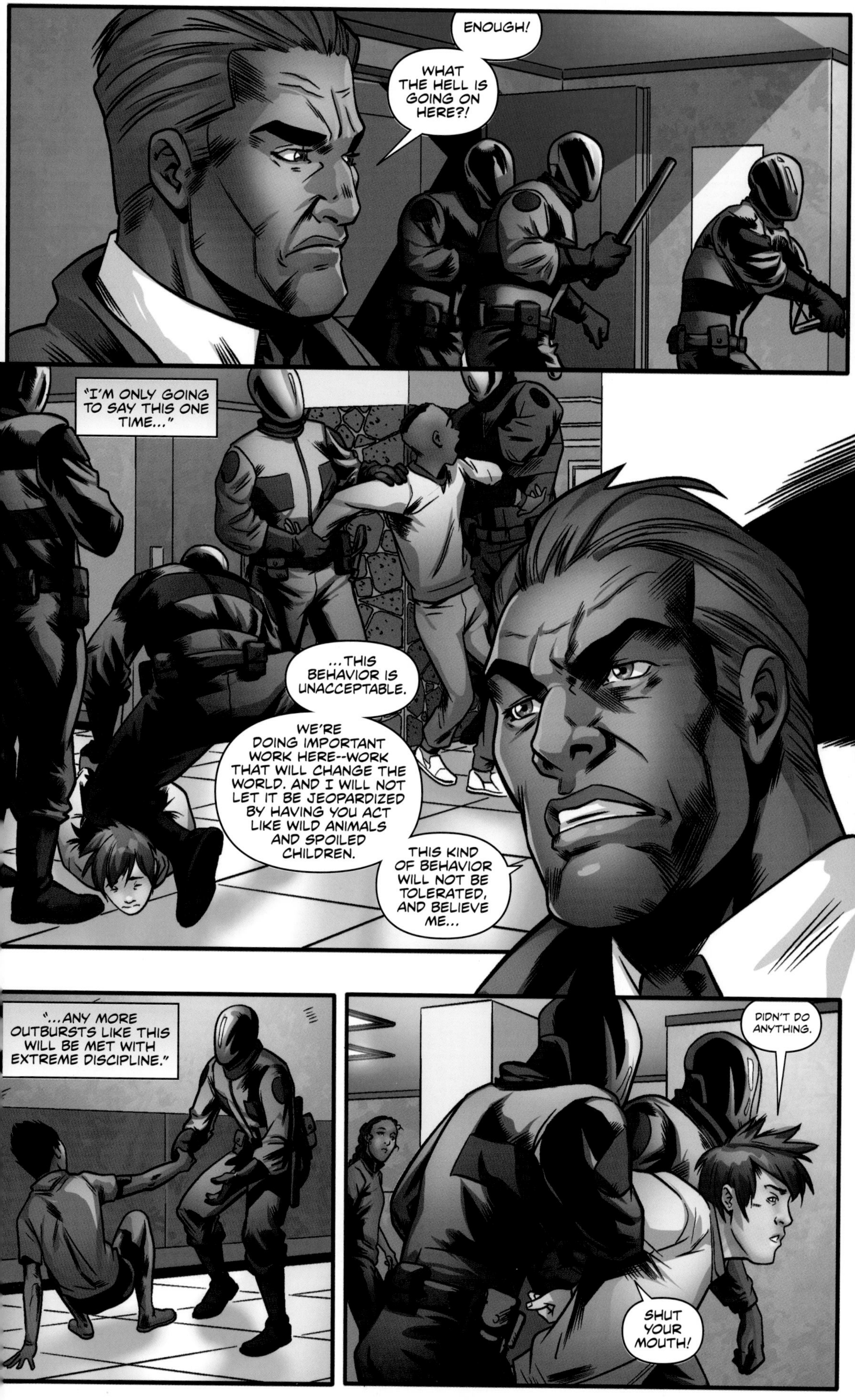
ENOUGH!
WHAT THE HELL IS GOING ON HERE?!
"I'M ONLY GOING TO SAY THIS ONE TIME..."
...THIS BEHAVIOR IS UNACCEPTABLE.
WE'RE DOING IMPORTANT WORK HERE--WORK THAT WILL CHANGE THE WORLD. AND I WILL NOT LET IT BE JEOPARDIZED BY HAVING YOU ACT LIKE WILD ANIMALS AND SPOILED CHILDREN.
THIS KIND OF BEHAVIOR WILL NOT BE TOLERATED, AND BELIEVE ME...
"...ANY MORE OUTBURSTS LIKE THIS WILL BE MET WITH EXTREME DISCIPLINE."
DIDN'T DO ANYTHING.
SHUT YOUR MOUTH!

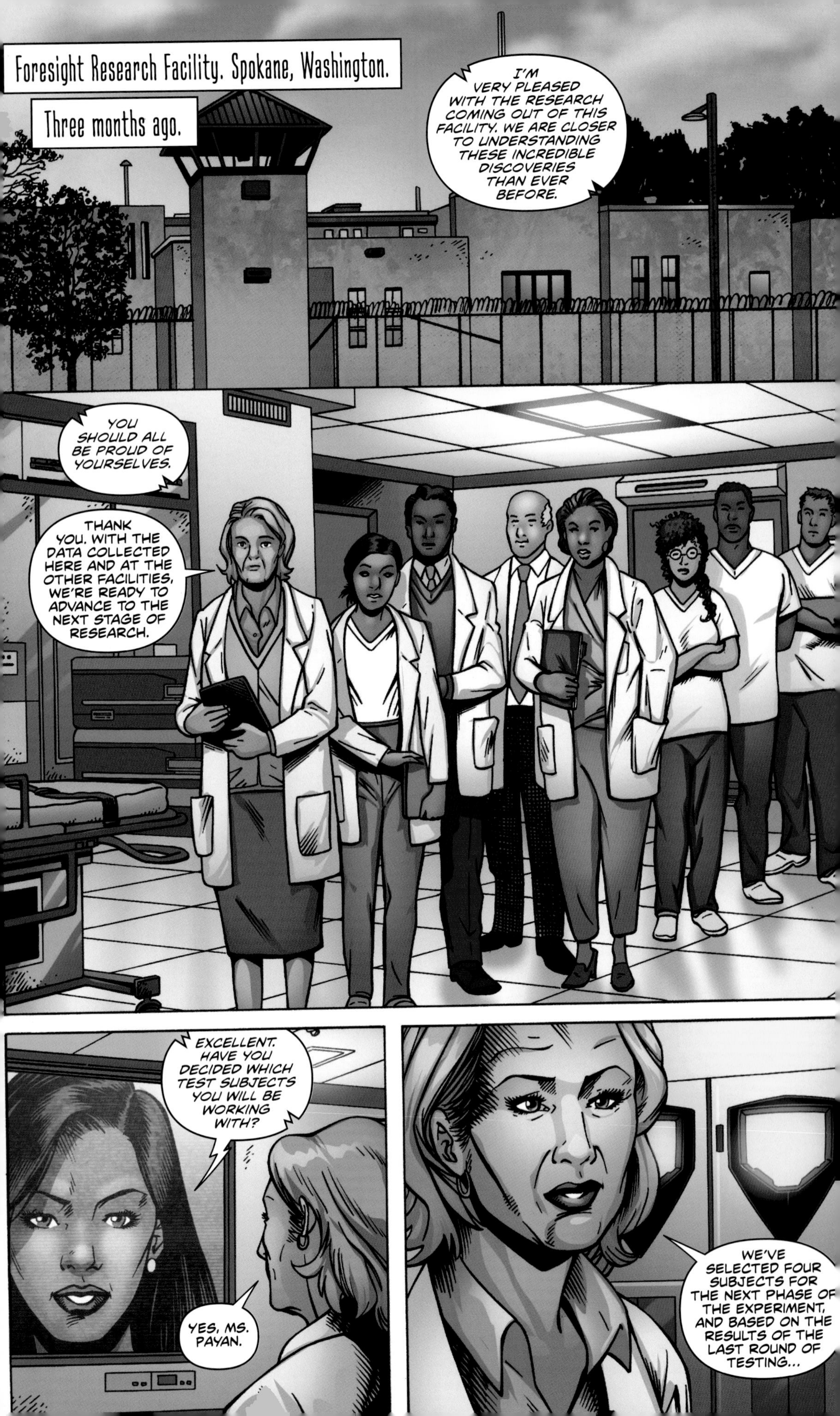
Foresight Research Facility. Spokane, Washington.
Three months ago.
I'M VERY PLEASED WITH THE RESEARCH COMING OUT OF THIS FACILITY. WE ARE CLOSER TO UNDERSTANDING THESE INCREDIBLE DISCOVERIES THAN EVER BEFORE.
YOU SHOULD ALL BE PROUD OF YOURSELVES.
THANK YOU. WITH THE DATA COLLECTED HERE AND AT THE OTHER FACILITIES, WE'RE READY TO ADVANCE TO THE NEXT STAGE OF RESEARCH.
EXCELLENT. HAVE YOU DECIDED WHICH TEST SUBJECTS YOU WILL BE WORKING WITH?
YES, MS. PAYAN.
WE'VE SELECTED FOUR SUBJECTS FOR THE NEXT PHASE OF THE EXPERIMENT, AND BASED ON THE RESULTS OF THE LAST ROUND OF TESTING...

"...WE'RE POSITIVE THAT WE CAN AVOID THE PREVIOUS SETBACKS THAT HAVE BEEN ENCOUNTERED.

"WITH EACH REVIVAL WE'VE ATTEMPTED, THERE HAVE BEEN FEWER AND FEWER ADVERSE REACTIONS--FEWER AND FEWER TEST SUBJECTS LOST.

"NOW THAT WE HAVE FINALLY FIGURED OUT WHY THESE DEAD BODIES HAVE NOT BEEN DECOMPOSING AND THE CHANGES THAT HAVE OCCURRED TO THEIR PHYSIOLOGY...

"...WE ARE THAT MUCH CLOSER TO...WELL...IT STILL SOUNDS ODD SAYING IT OUT LOUD...

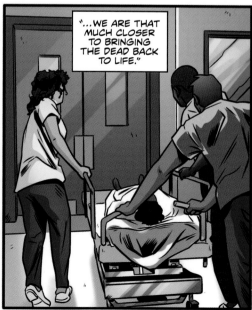

"...WE ARE THAT MUCH CLOSER TO BRINGING THE DEAD BACK TO LIFE."

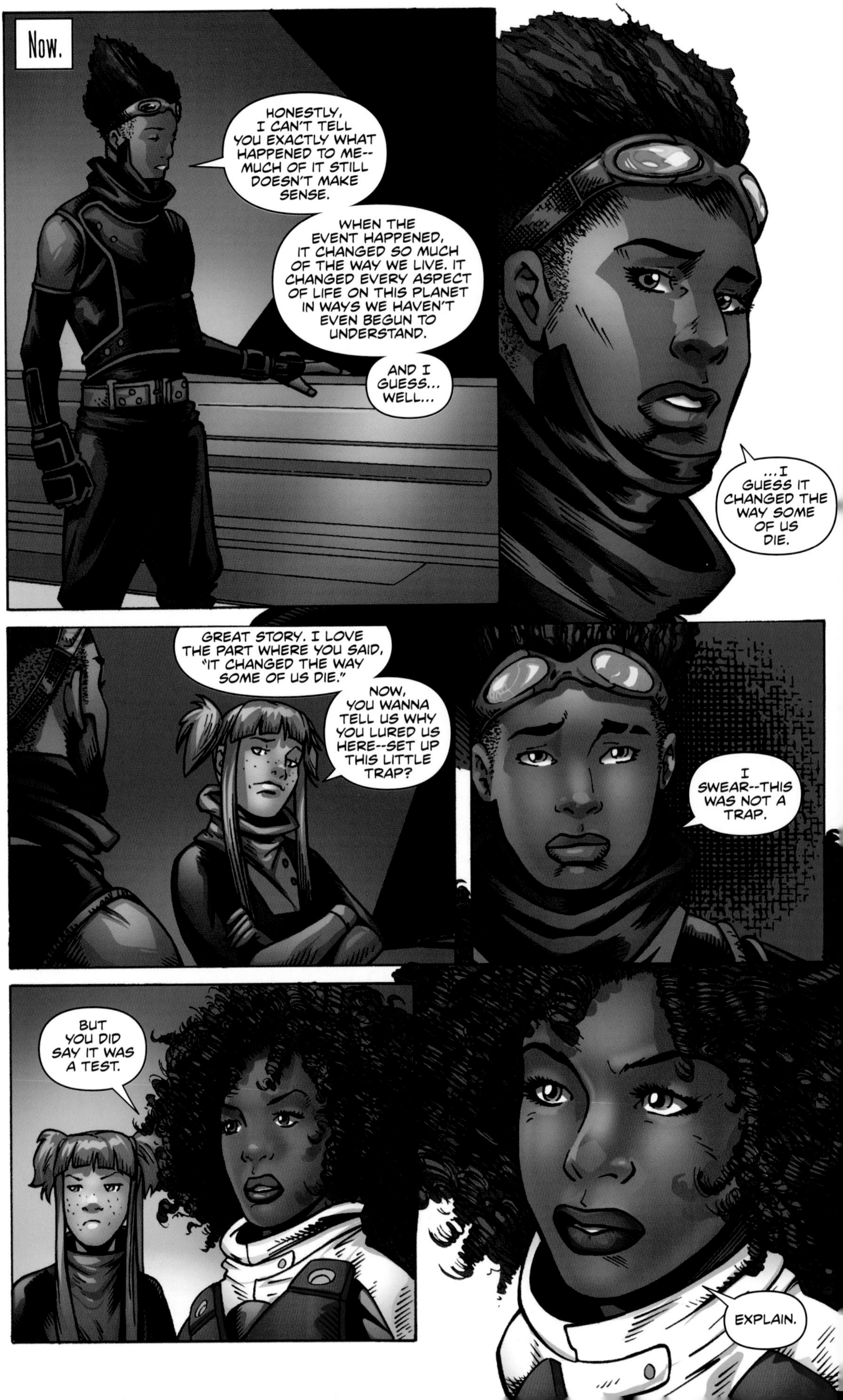
Now.
HONESTLY, I CAN'T TELL YOU EXACTLY WHAT HAPPENED TO ME--MUCH OF IT STILL DOESN'T MAKE SENSE.
WHEN THE EVENT HAPPENED, IT CHANGED SO MUCH OF THE WAY WE LIVE. IT CHANGED EVERY ASPECT OF LIFE ON THIS PLANET IN WAYS WE HAVEN'T EVEN BEGUN TO UNDERSTAND.
AND I GUESS... WELL...
...I GUESS IT CHANGED THE WAY SOME OF US DIE.
GREAT STORY. I LOVE THE PART WHERE YOU SAID, "IT CHANGED THE WAY SOME OF US DIE."
NOW, YOU WANNA TELL US WHY YOU LURED US HERE--SET UP THIS LITTLE TRAP?
I SWEAR--THIS WAS NOT A TRAP.
BUT YOU DID SAY IT WAS A TEST.
EXPLAIN.

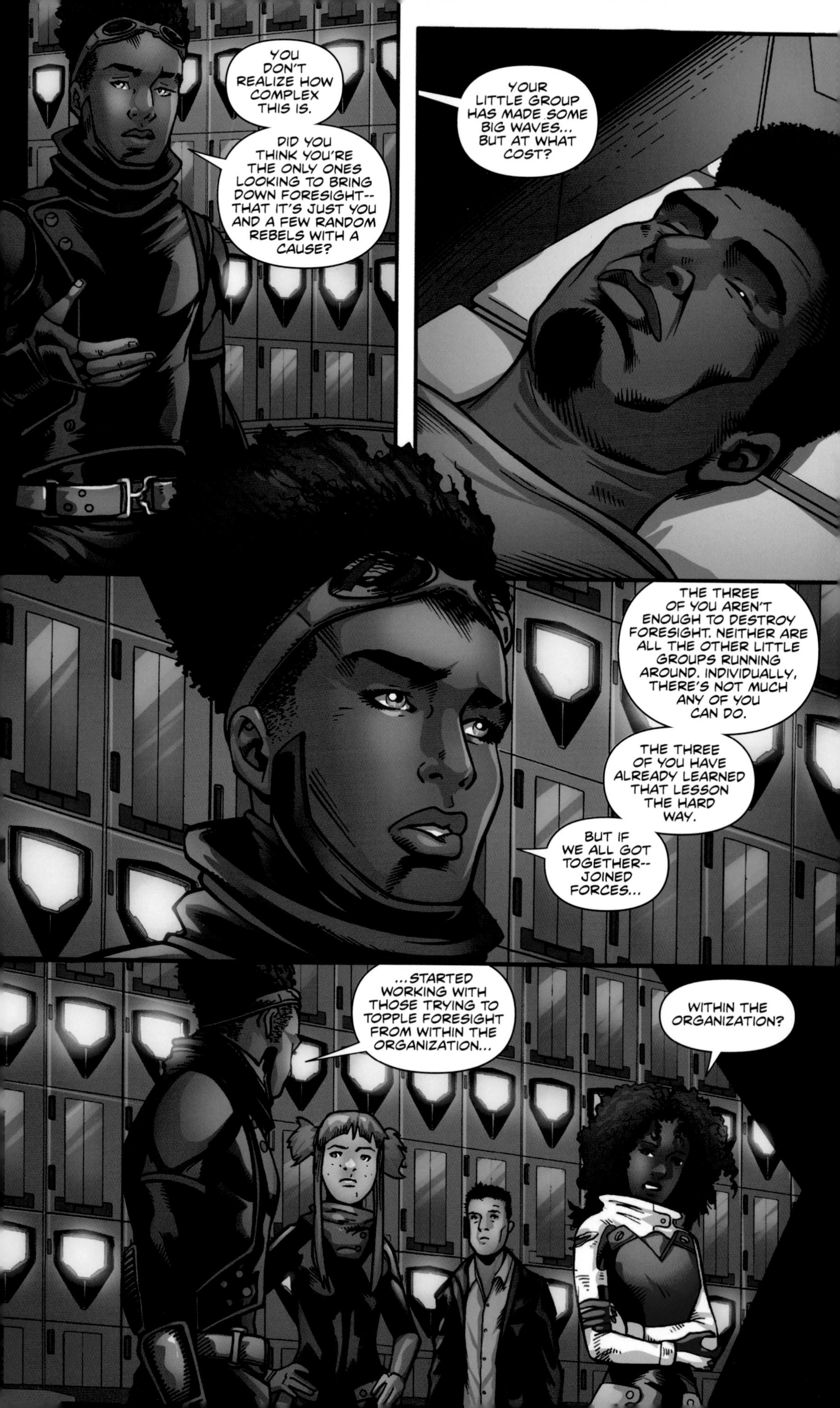
YOU DON'T REALIZE HOW COMPLEX THIS IS.
DID YOU THINK YOU'RE THE ONLY ONES LOOKING TO BRING DOWN FORESIGHT-- THAT IT'S JUST YOU AND A FEW RANDOM REBELS WITH A CAUSE?
YOUR LITTLE GROUP HAS MADE SOME BIG WAVES... BUT AT WHAT COST?
THE THREE OF YOU AREN'T ENOUGH TO DESTROY FORESIGHT. NEITHER ARE ALL THE OTHER LITTLE GROUPS RUNNING AROUND. INDIVIDUALLY, THERE'S NOT MUCH ANY OF YOU CAN DO.
THE THREE OF YOU HAVE ALREADY LEARNED THAT LESSON THE HARD WAY.
BUT IF WE ALL GOT TOGETHER-- JOINED FORCES...
...STARTED WORKING WITH THOSE TRYING TO TOPPLE FORESIGHT FROM WITHIN THE ORGANIZATION...
WITHIN THE ORGANIZATION?

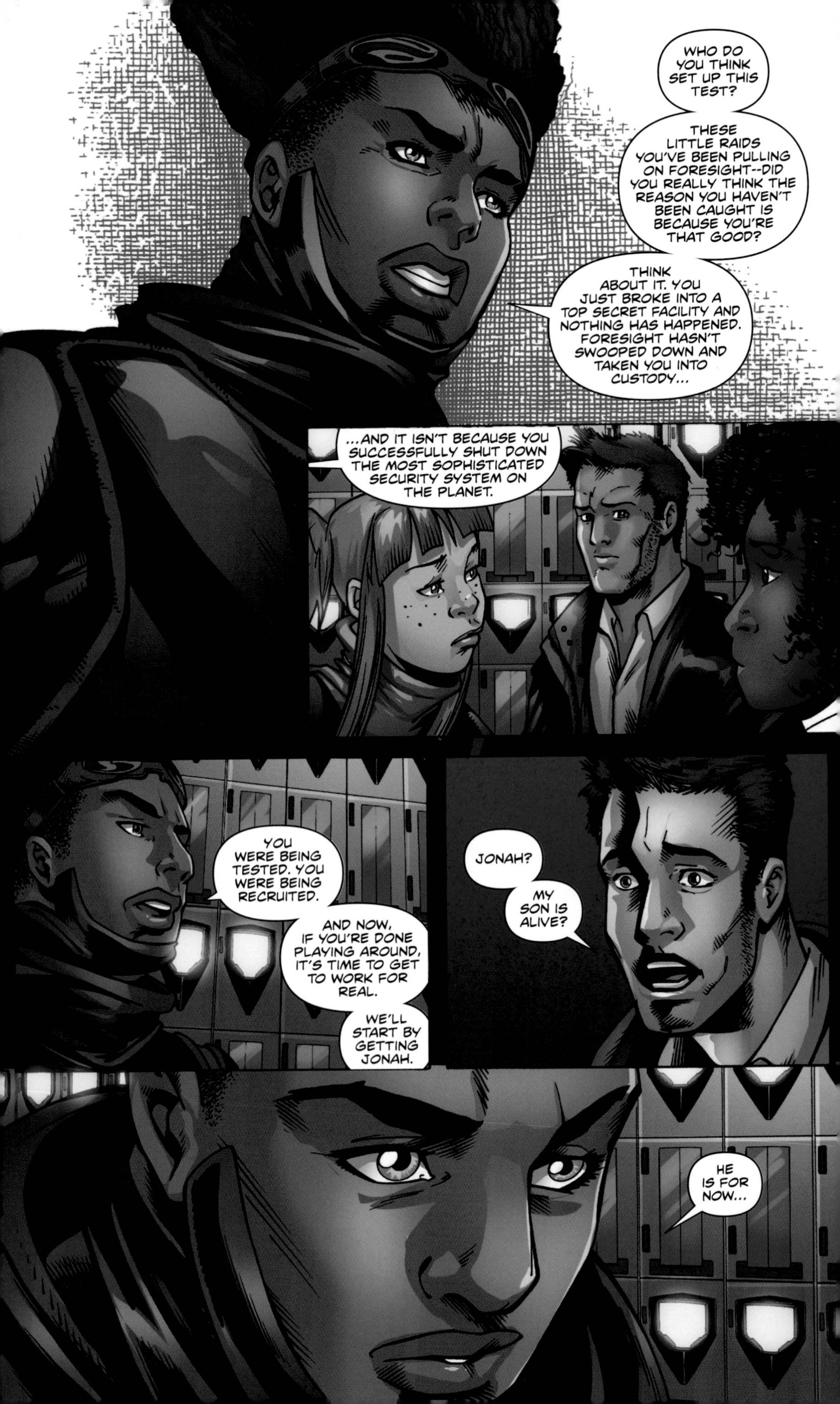
WHO DO YOU THINK SET UP THIS TEST?
THESE LITTLE RAIDS YOU'VE BEEN PULLING ON FORESIGHT--DID YOU REALLY THINK THE REASON YOU HAVEN'T BEEN CAUGHT IS BECAUSE YOU'RE THAT GOOD?
THINK ABOUT IT. YOU JUST BROKE INTO A TOP SECRET FACILITY AND NOTHING HAS HAPPENED. FORESIGHT HASN'T SWOOPED DOWN AND TAKEN YOU INTO CUSTODY...
...AND IT ISN'T BECAUSE YOU SUCCESSFULLY SHUT DOWN THE MOST SOPHISTICATED SECURITY SYSTEM ON THE PLANET.
YOU WERE BEING TESTED. YOU WERE BEING RECRUITED.
AND NOW, IF YOU'RE DONE PLAYING AROUND, IT'S TIME TO GET TO WORK FOR REAL.
WE'LL START BY GETTING JONAH.
JONAH?
MY SON IS ALIVE?
HE IS FOR NOW...

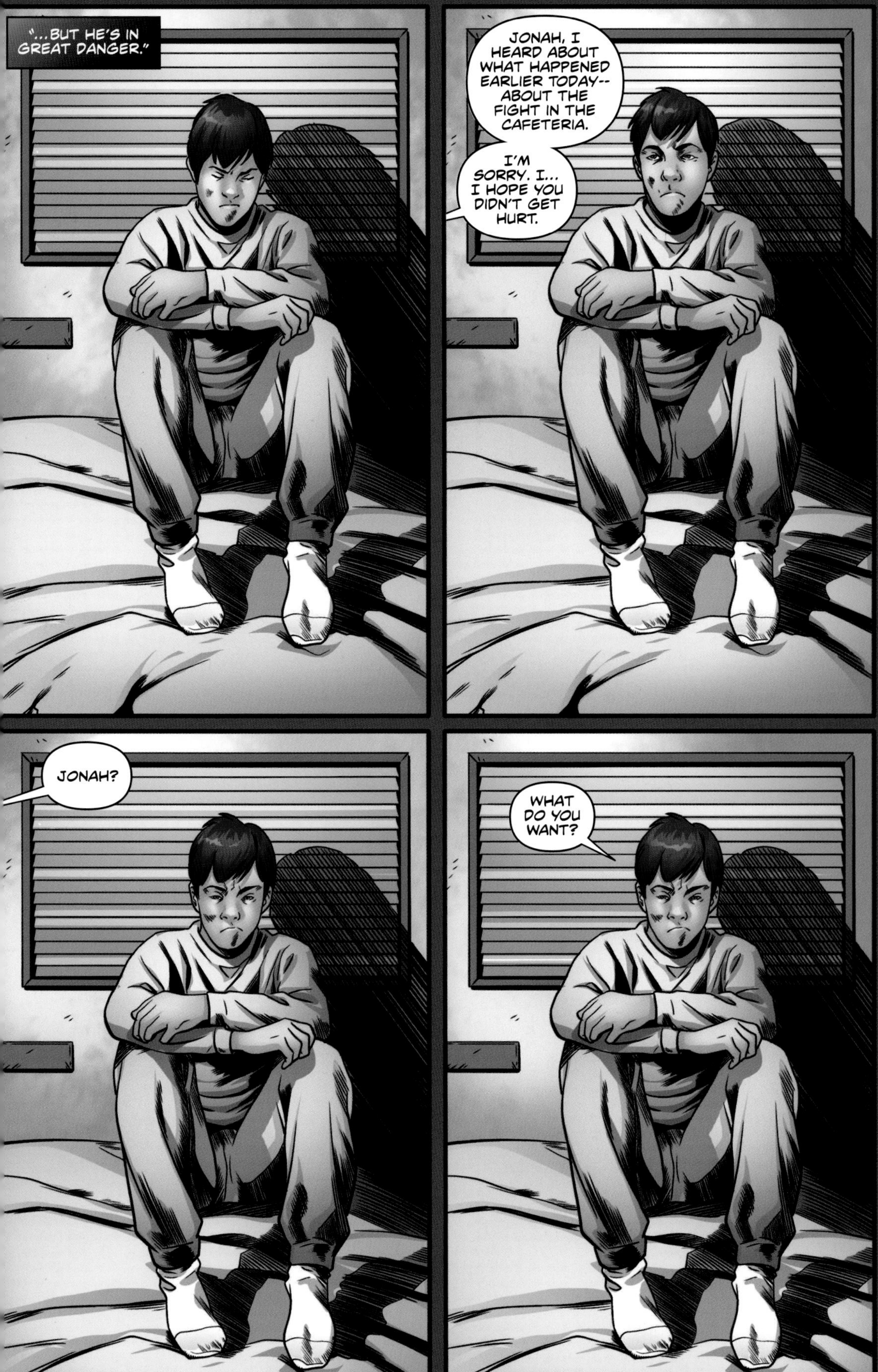
"...BUT HE'S IN GREAT DANGER."
JONAH, I HEARD ABOUT WHAT HAPPENED EARLIER TODAY-- ABOUT THE FIGHT IN THE CAFETERIA.
I'M SORRY. I... I HOPE YOU DIDN'T GET HURT.
JONAH?
WHAT DO YOU WANT?

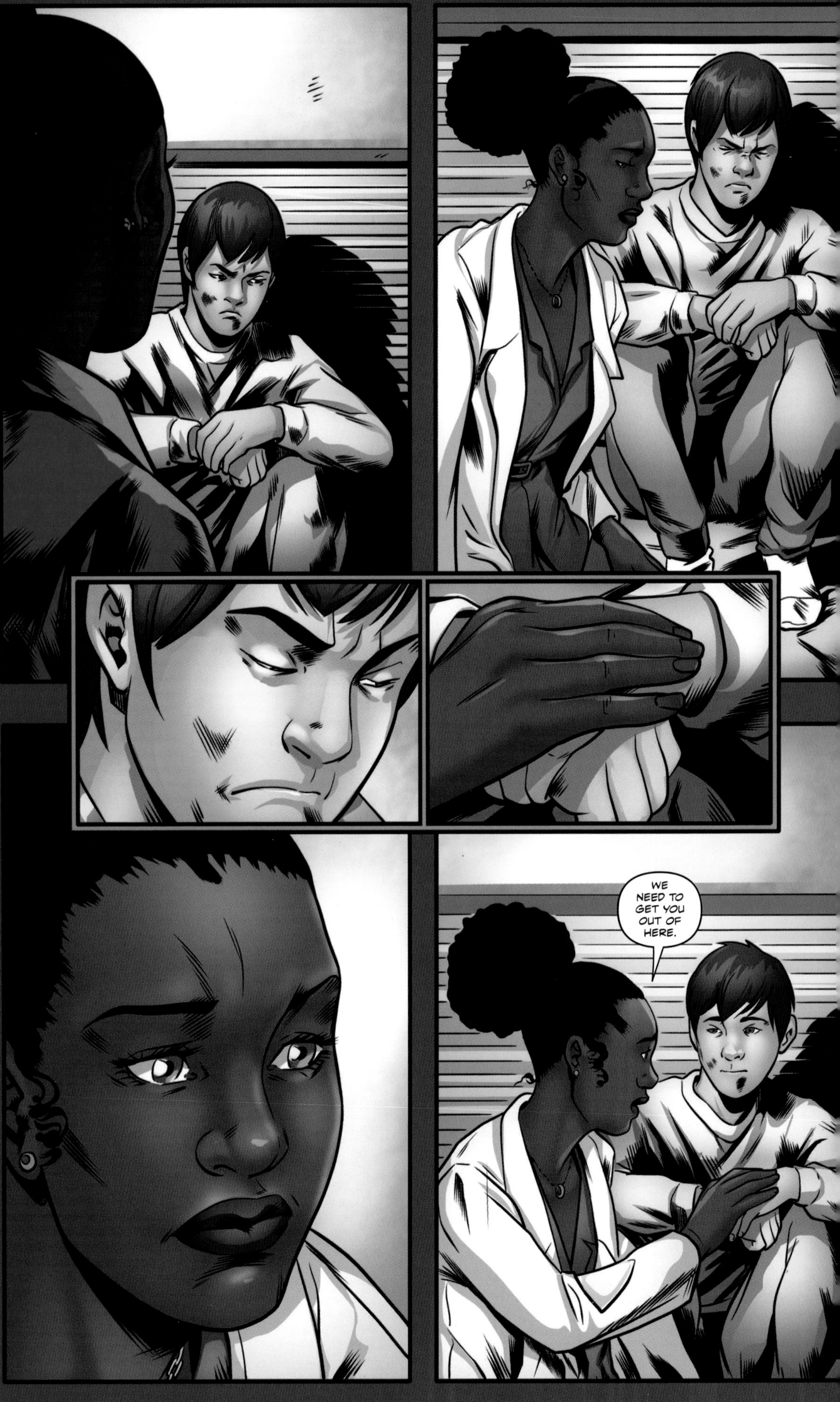
WE NEED TO GET YOU OUT OF HERE.

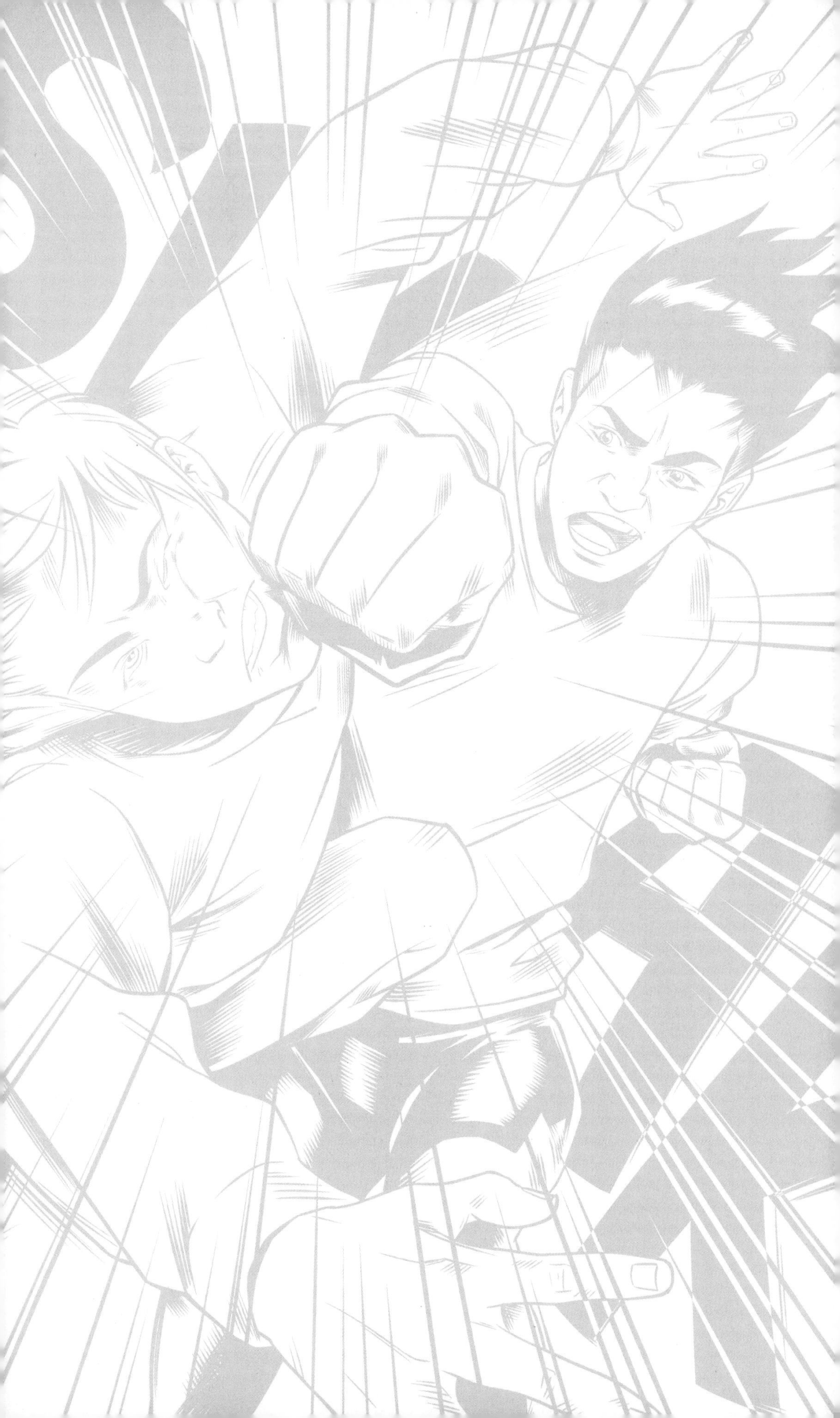

CHAPTER FOUR

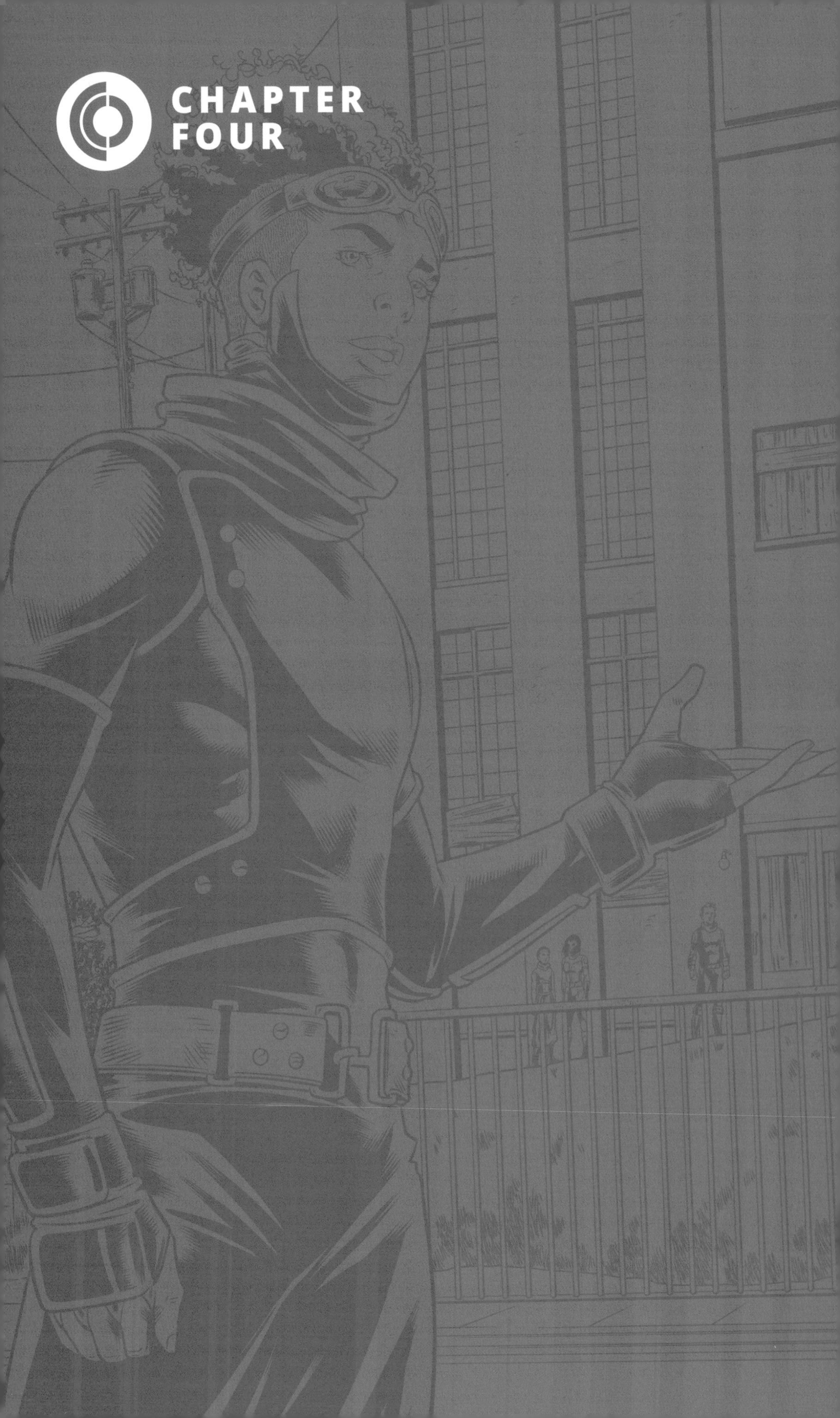

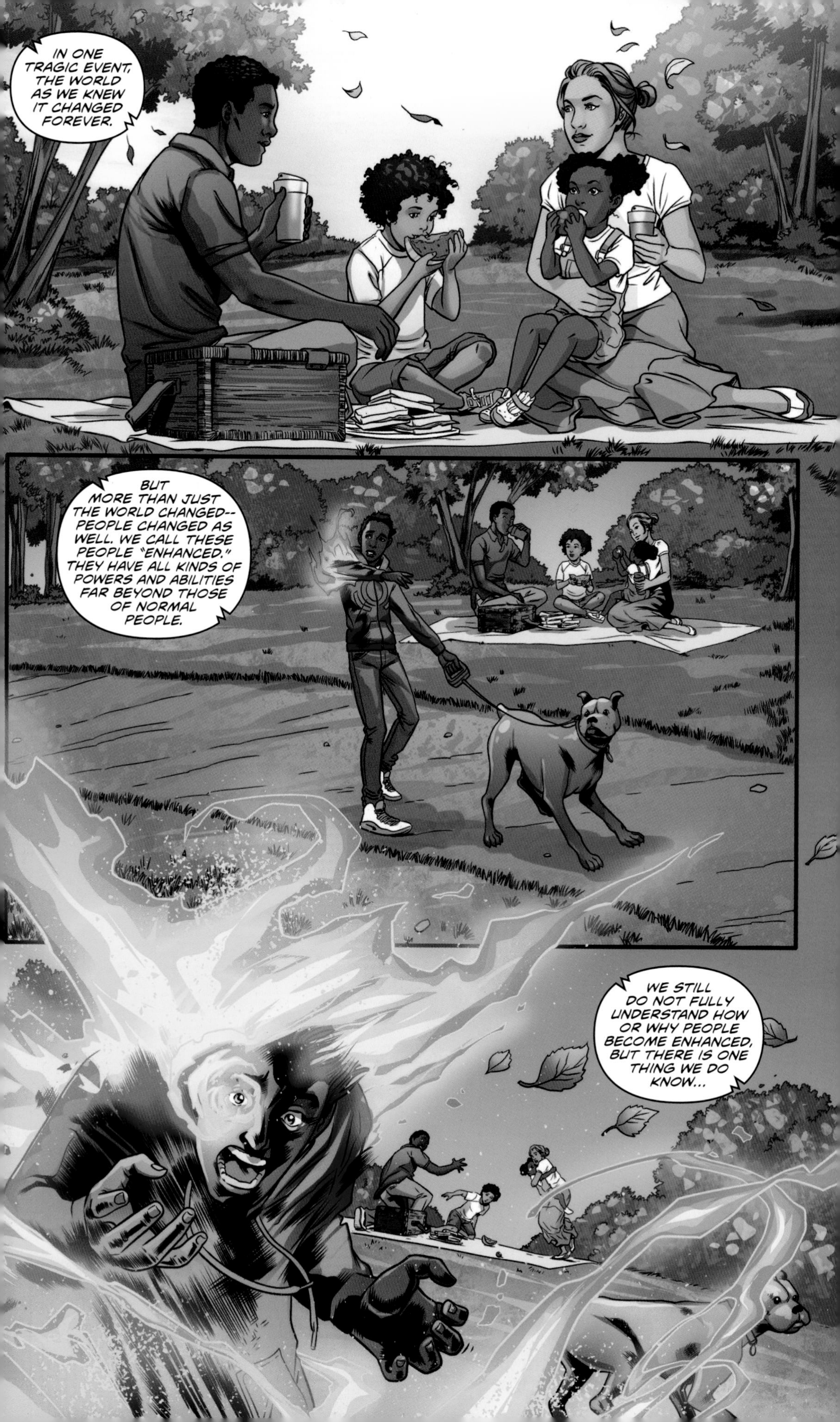
IN ONE TRAGIC EVENT, THE WORLD AS WE KNEW IT CHANGED FOREVER.
BUT MORE THAN JUST THE WORLD CHANGED-- PEOPLE CHANGED AS WELL. WE CALL THESE PEOPLE "ENHANCED." THEY HAVE ALL KINDS OF POWERS AND ABILITIES FAR BEYOND THOSE OF NORMAL PEOPLE.
WE STILL DO NOT FULLY UNDERSTAND HOW OR WHY PEOPLE BECOME ENHANCED, BUT THERE IS ONE THING WE DO KNOW...

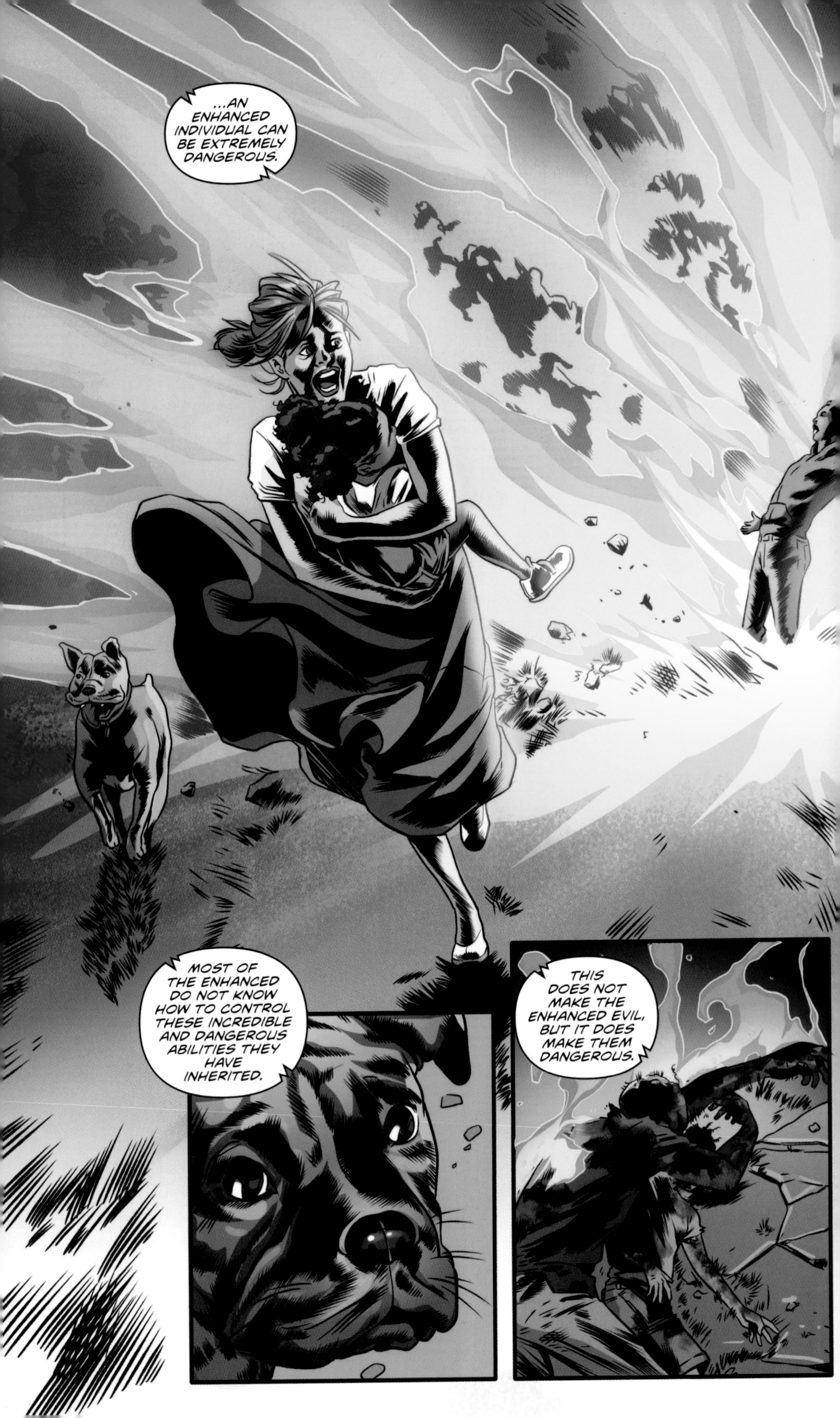
...AN ENHANCED INDIVIDUAL CAN BE EXTREMELY DANGEROUS.
MOST OF THE ENHANCED DO NOT KNOW HOW TO CONTROL THESE INCREDIBLE AND DANGEROUS ABILITIES THEY HAVE INHERITED.
THIS DOES NOT MAKE THE ENHANCED EVIL, BUT IT DOES MAKE THEM DANGEROUS.

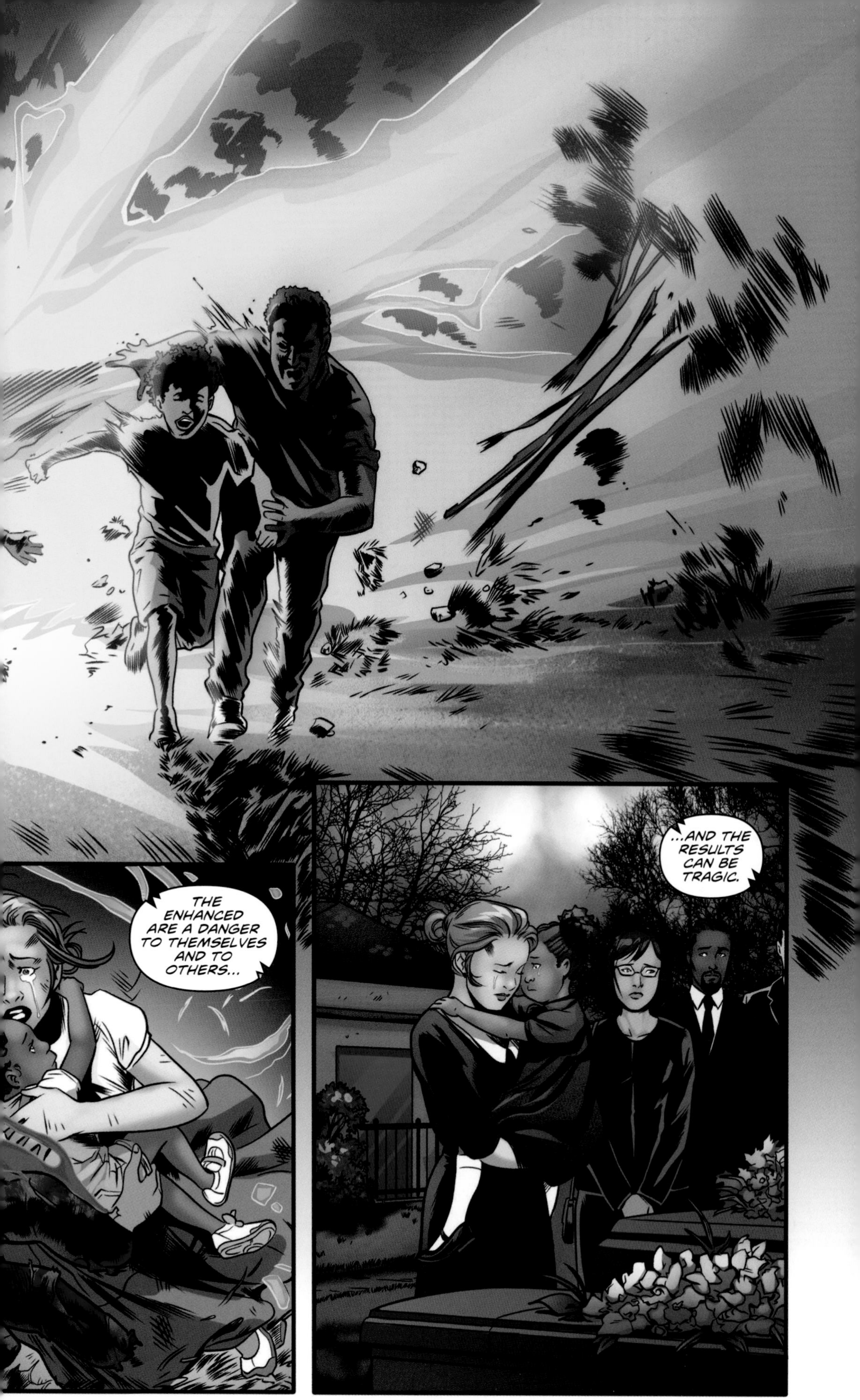
THE ENHANCED ARE A DANGER TO THEMSELVES AND TO OTHERS...
...AND THE RESULTS CAN BE TRAGIC.

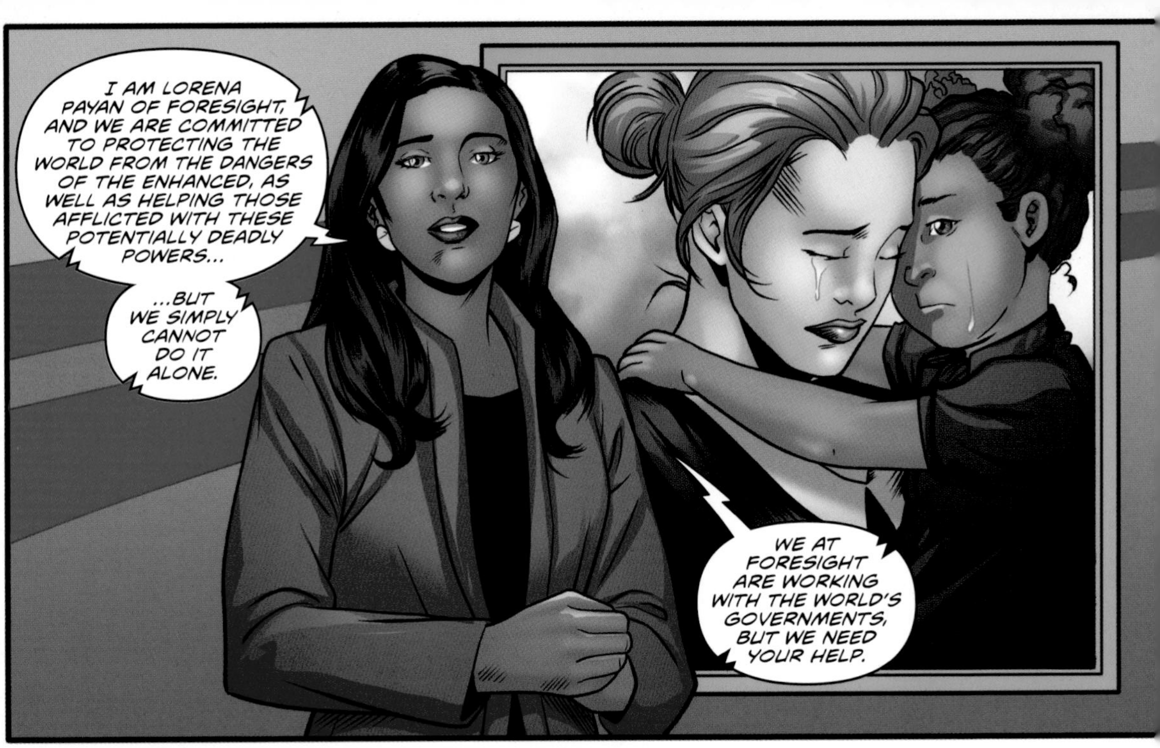
I AM LORENA PAYAN OF FORESIGHT, AND WE ARE COMMITTED TO PROTECTING THE WORLD FROM THE DANGERS OF THE ENHANCED, AS WELL AS HELPING THOSE AFFLICTED WITH THESE POTENTIALLY DEADLY POWERS...
...BUT WE SIMPLY CANNOT DO IT ALONE.
WE AT FORESIGHT ARE WORKING WITH THE WORLD'S GOVERNMENTS, BUT WE NEED YOUR HELP.
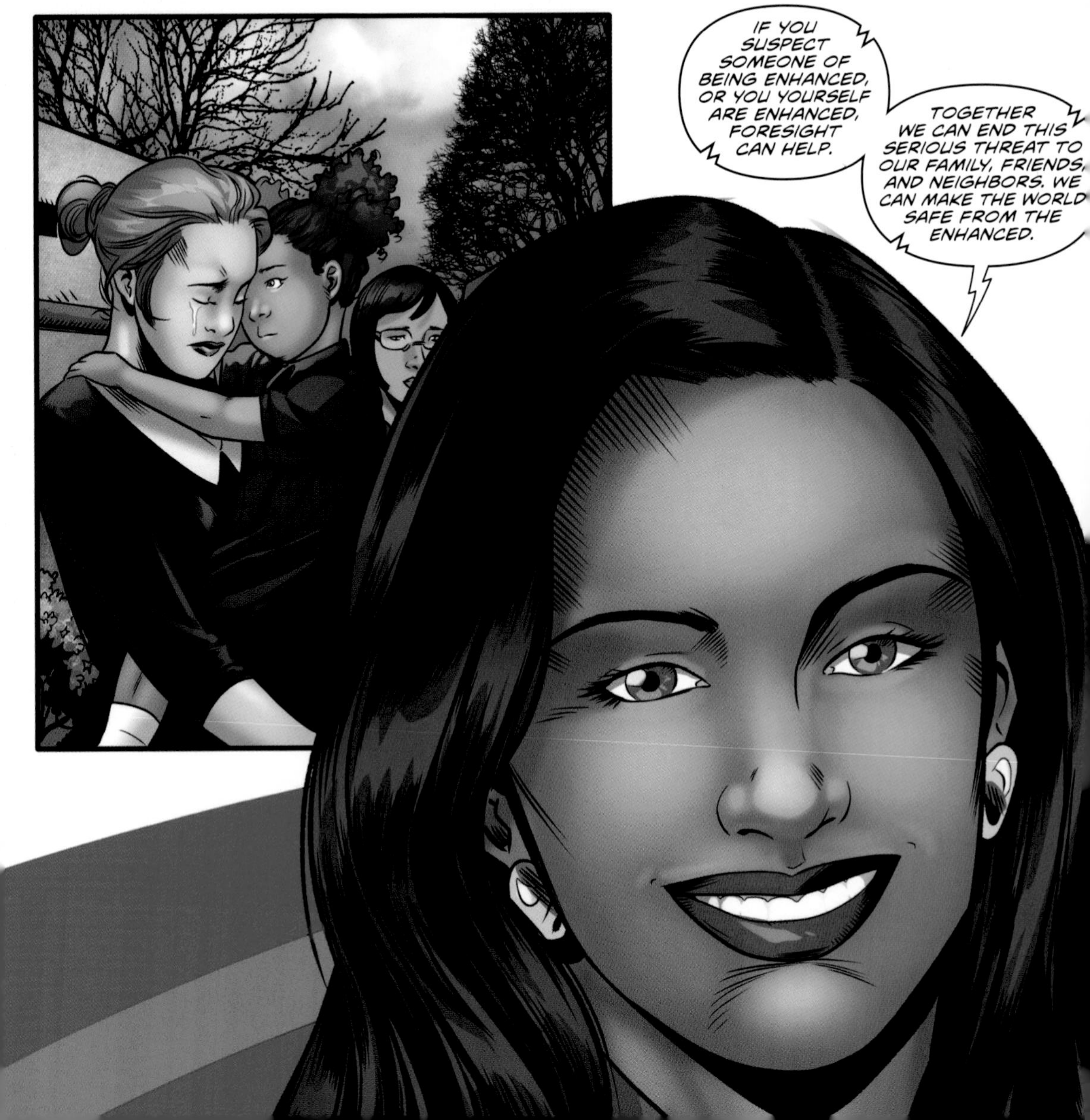
IF YOU SUSPECT SOMEONE OF BEING ENHANCED, OR YOU YOURSELF ARE ENHANCED, FORESIGHT CAN HELP.
TOGETHER WE CAN END THIS SERIOUS THREAT TO OUR FAMILY, FRIENDS, AND NEIGHBORS. WE CAN MAKE THE WORLD SAFE FROM THE ENHANCED.

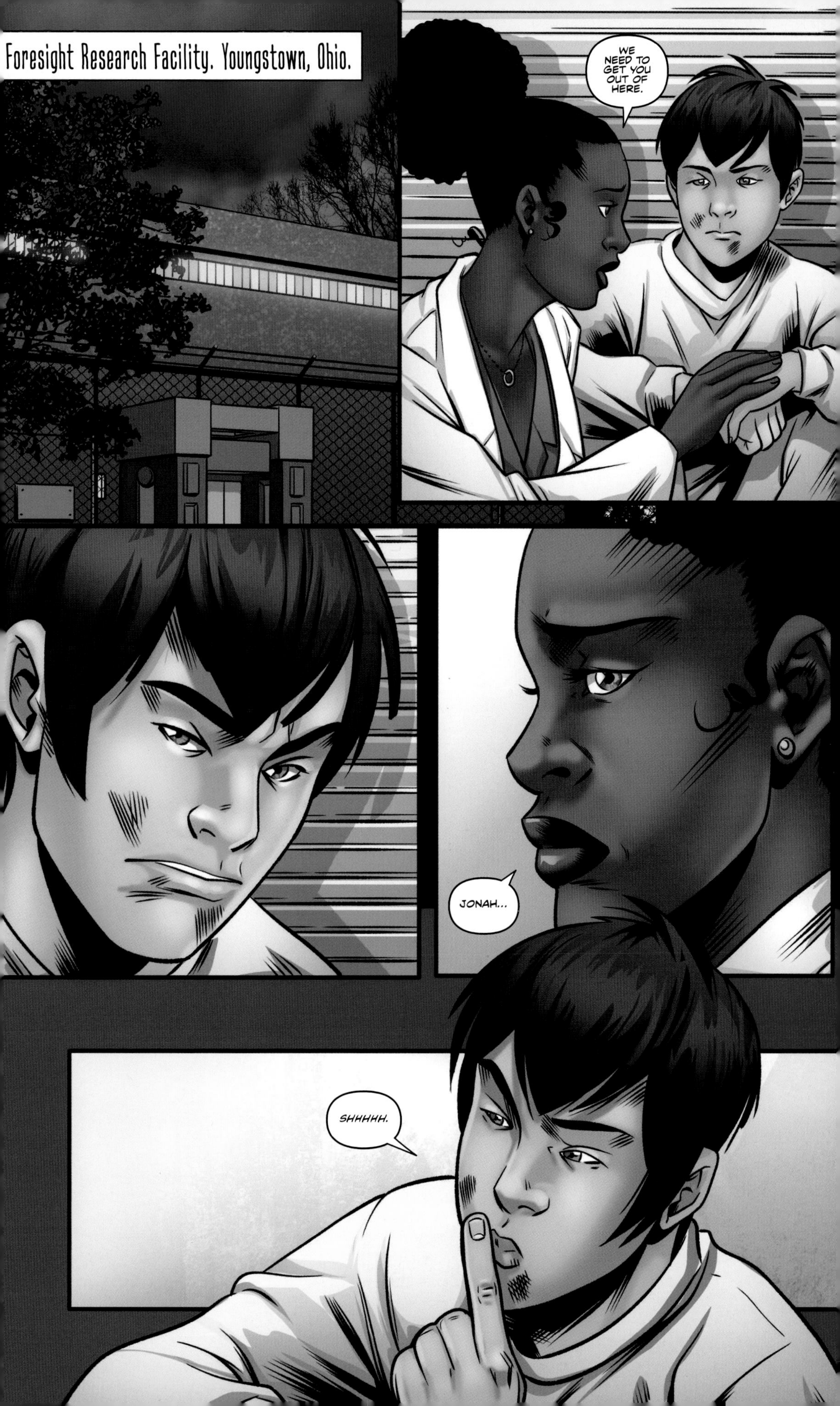
Foresight Research Facility. Youngstown, Ohio.
WE NEED TO GET YOU OUT OF HERE.
JONAH...
SHHHHH.

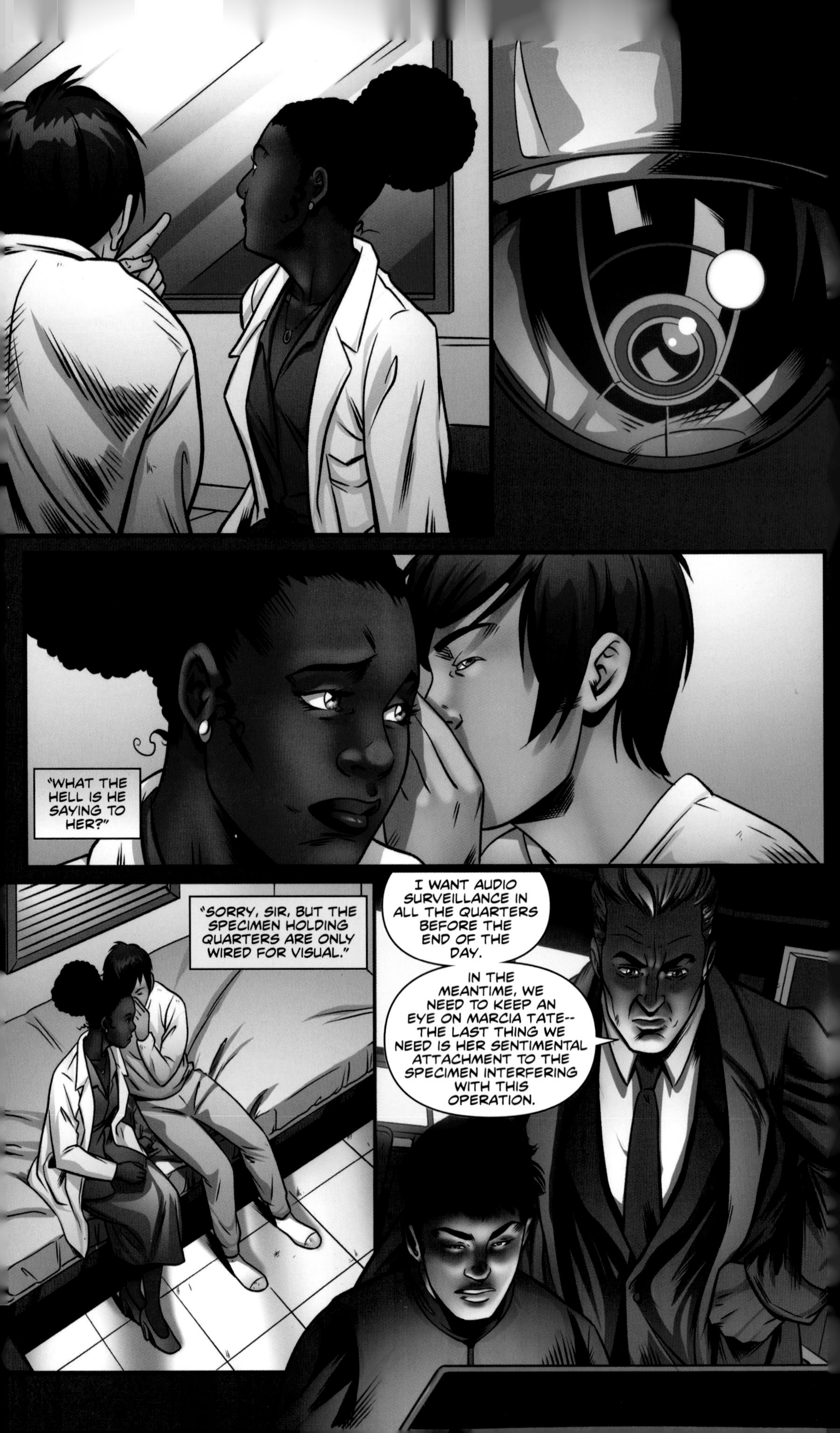
"WHAT THE HELL IS HE SAYING TO HER?"
"SORRY, SIR, BUT THE SPECIMEN HOLDING QUARTERS ARE ONLY WIRED FOR VISUAL."
I WANT AUDIO SURVEILLANCE IN ALL THE QUARTERS BEFORE THE END OF THE DAY.
IN THE MEANTIME, WE NEED TO KEEP AN EYE ON MARCIA TATE-- THE LAST THING WE NEED IS HER SENTIMENTAL ATTACHMENT TO THE SPECIMEN INTERFERING WITH THIS OPERATION.

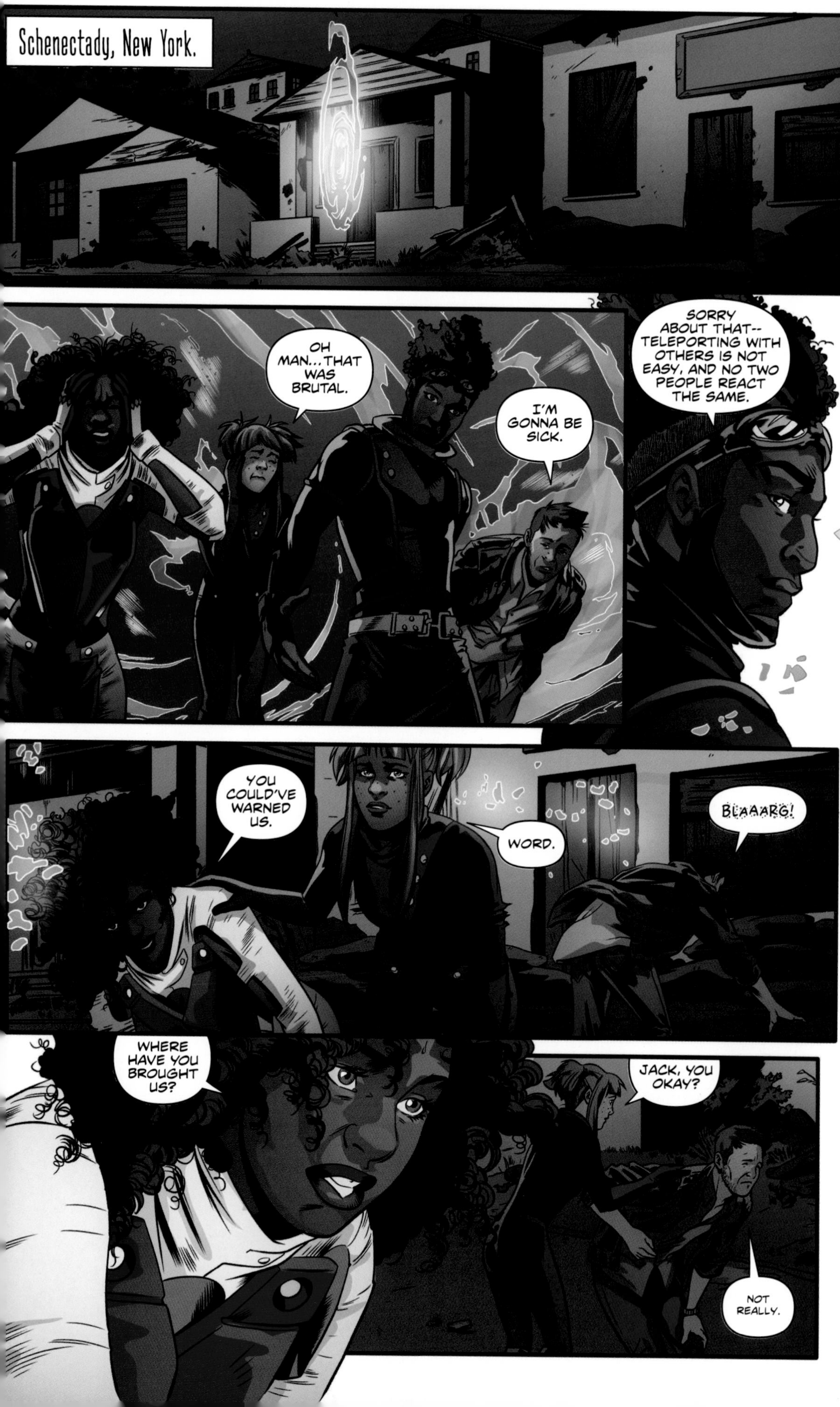
Schenectady, New York.
OH MAN...THAT WAS BRUTAL.
I'M GONNA BE SICK.
SORRY ABOUT THAT-- TELEPORTING WITH OTHERS IS NOT EASY, AND NO TWO PEOPLE REACT THE SAME.
YOU COULD'VE WARNED US.
WORD.
BLAAARG!
WHERE HAVE YOU BROUGHT US?
JACK, YOU OKAY?
NOT REALLY.

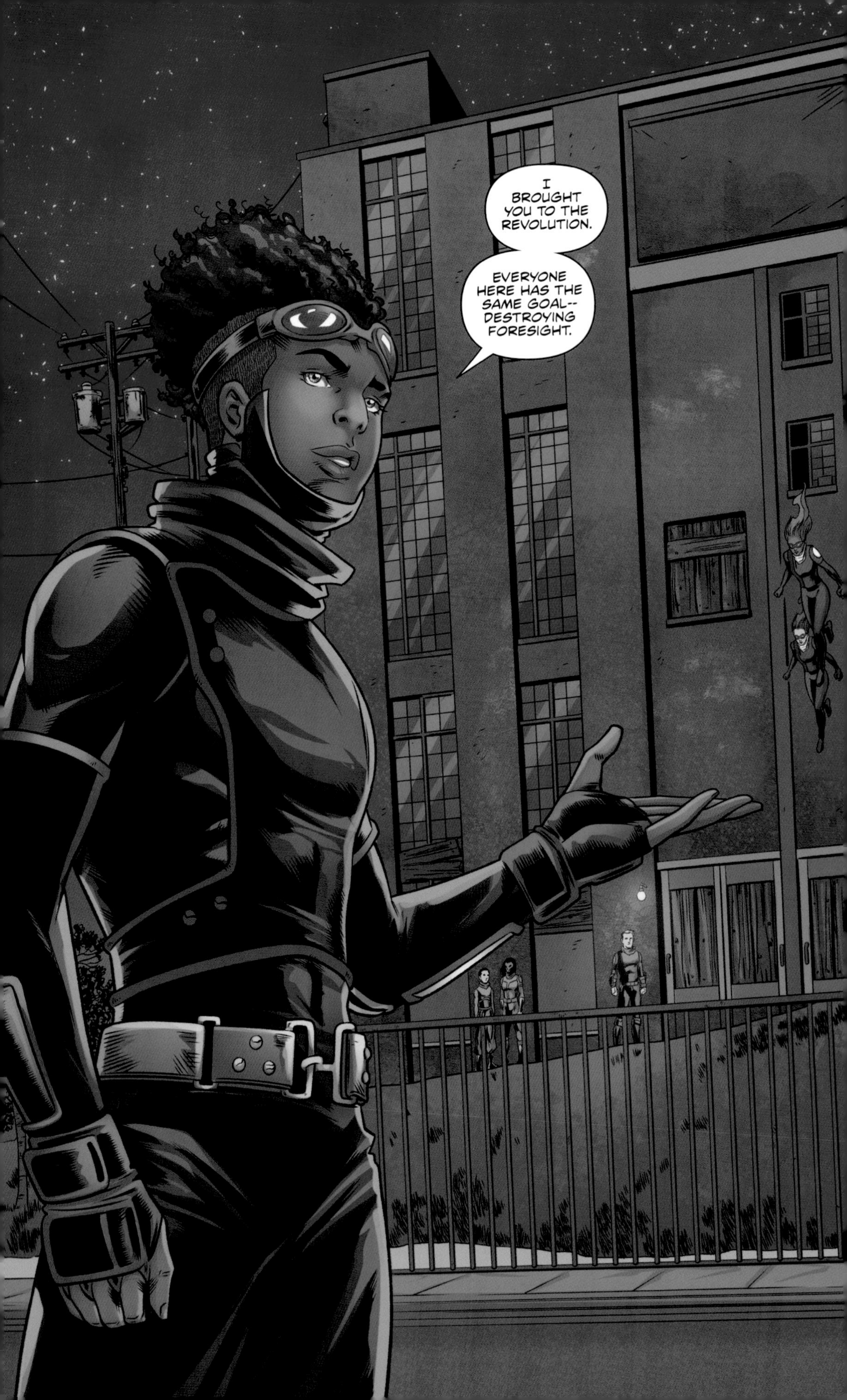
I BROUGHT YOU TO THE REVOLUTION.
EVERYONE HERE HAS THE SAME GOAL-- DESTROYING FORESIGHT.

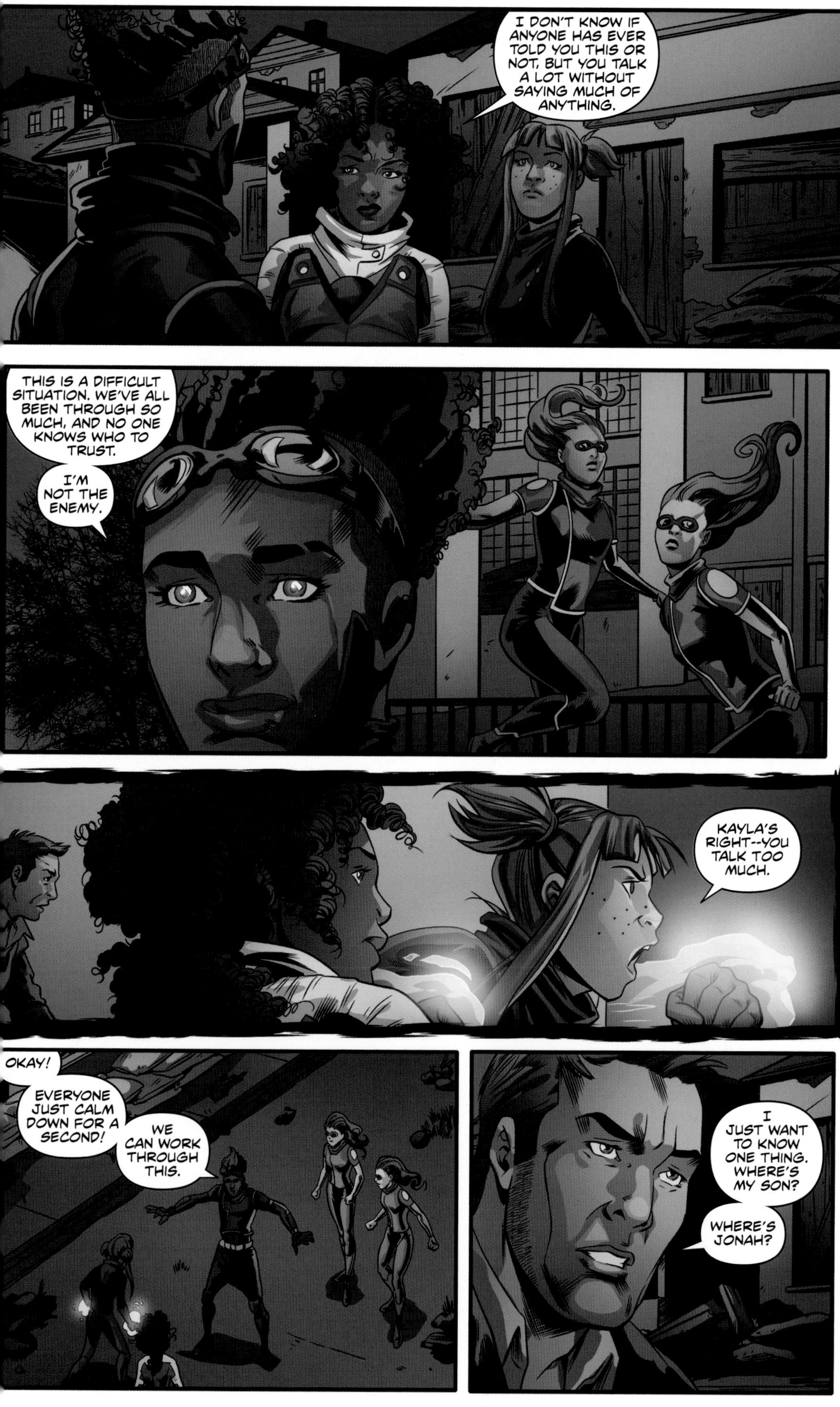
I DON'T KNOW IF ANYONE HAS EVER TOLD YOU THIS OR NOT, BUT YOU TALK A LOT WITHOUT SAYING MUCH OF ANYTHING.
THIS IS A DIFFICULT SITUATION. WE'VE ALL BEEN THROUGH SO MUCH, AND NO ONE KNOWS WHO TO TRUST.
I'M NOT THE ENEMY.
KAYLA'S RIGHT--YOU TALK TOO MUCH.
OKAY!
EVERYONE JUST CALM DOWN FOR A SECOND!
WE CAN WORK THROUGH THIS.
I JUST WANT TO KNOW ONE THING. WHERE'S MY SON?
WHERE'S JONAH?

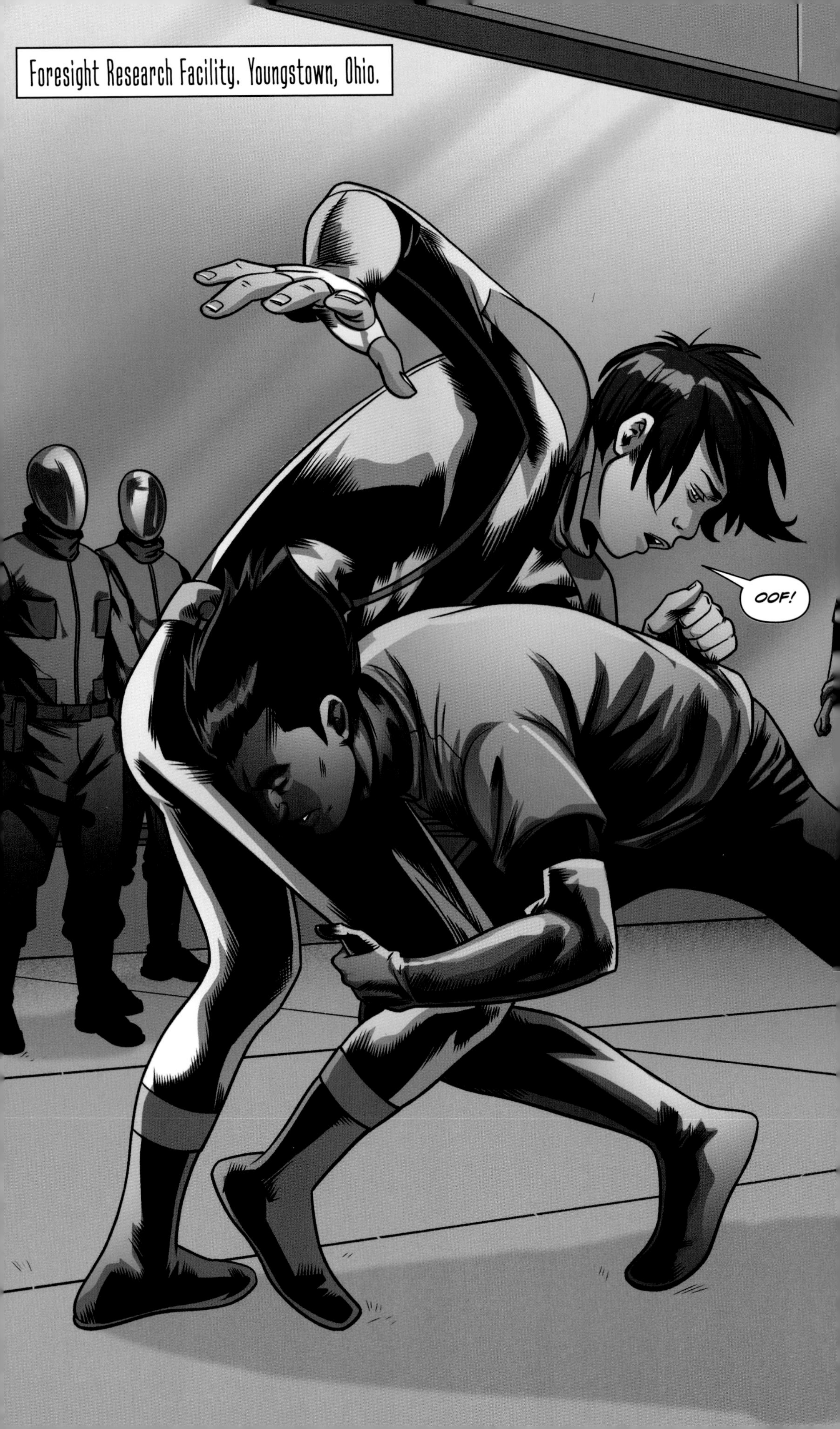
Foresight Research Facility. Youngstown, Ohio.
OOF!

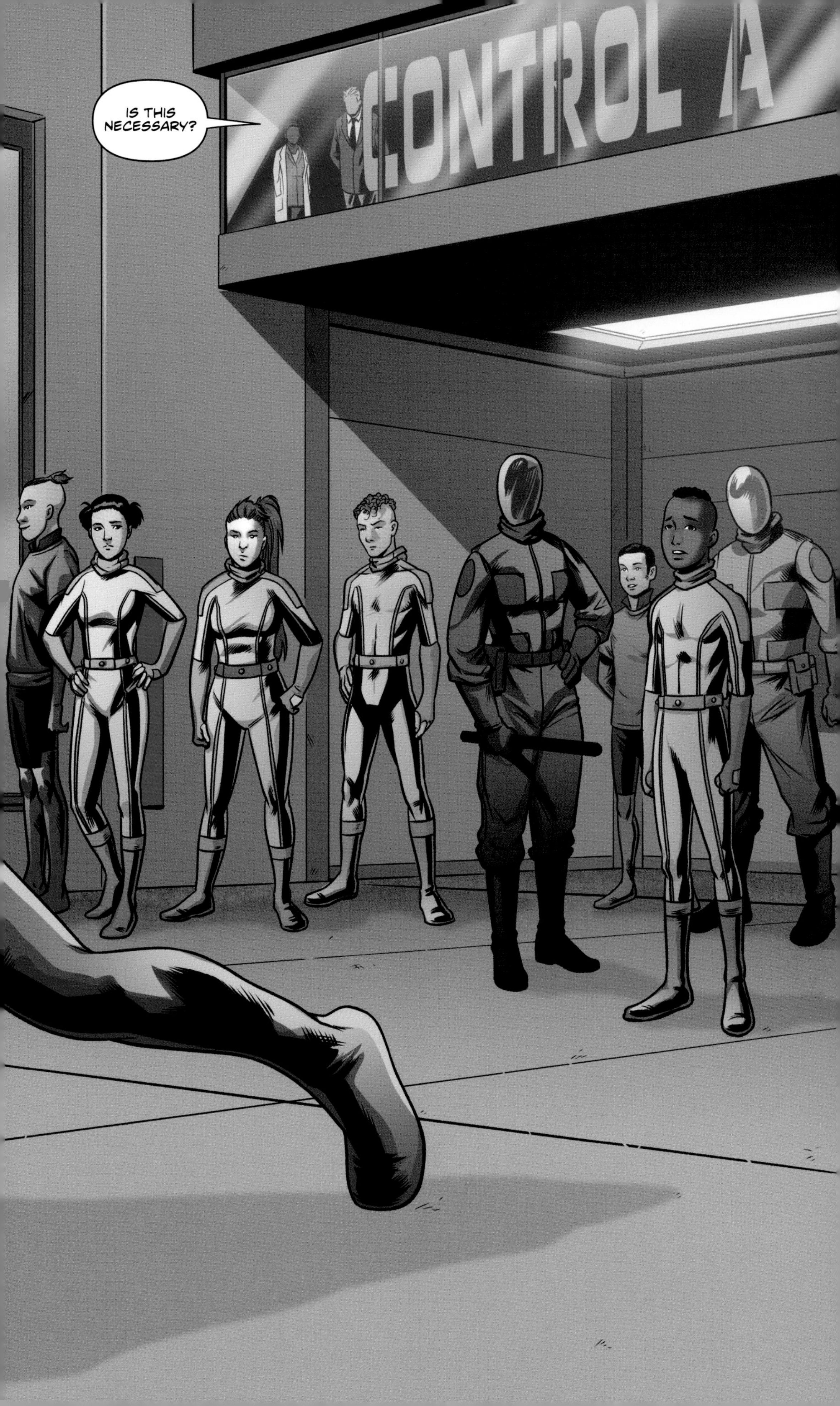
IS THIS NECESSARY?
CONTROL A

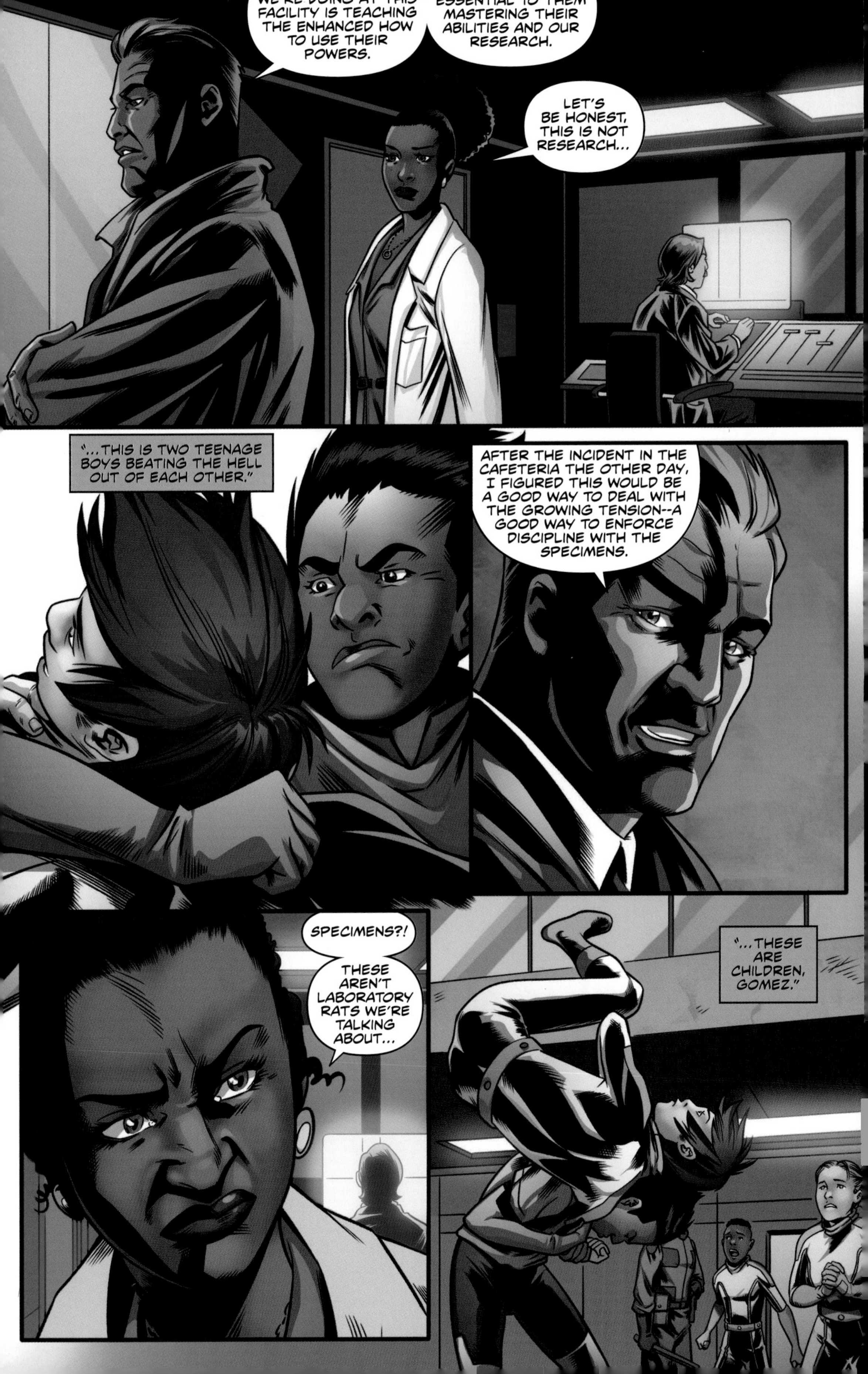
PART OF THE RESEARCH WE'RE DOING AT THIS FACILITY IS TEACHING THE ENHANCED HOW TO USE THEIR POWERS.
COMBAT TRAINING IS AN ESSENTIAL TO THEM MASTERING THEIR ABILITIES AND OUR RESEARCH.
LET'S BE HONEST, THIS IS NOT RESEARCH...
"...THIS IS TWO TEENAGE BOYS BEATING THE HELL OUT OF EACH OTHER."
AFTER THE INCIDENT IN THE CAFETERIA THE OTHER DAY, I FIGURED THIS WOULD BE A GOOD WAY TO DEAL WITH THE GROWING TENSION--A GOOD WAY TO ENFORCE DISCIPLINE WITH THE SPECIMENS.
SPECIMENS?!
THESE AREN'T LABORATORY RATS WE'RE TALKING ABOUT...
"...THESE ARE CHILDREN, GOMEZ."

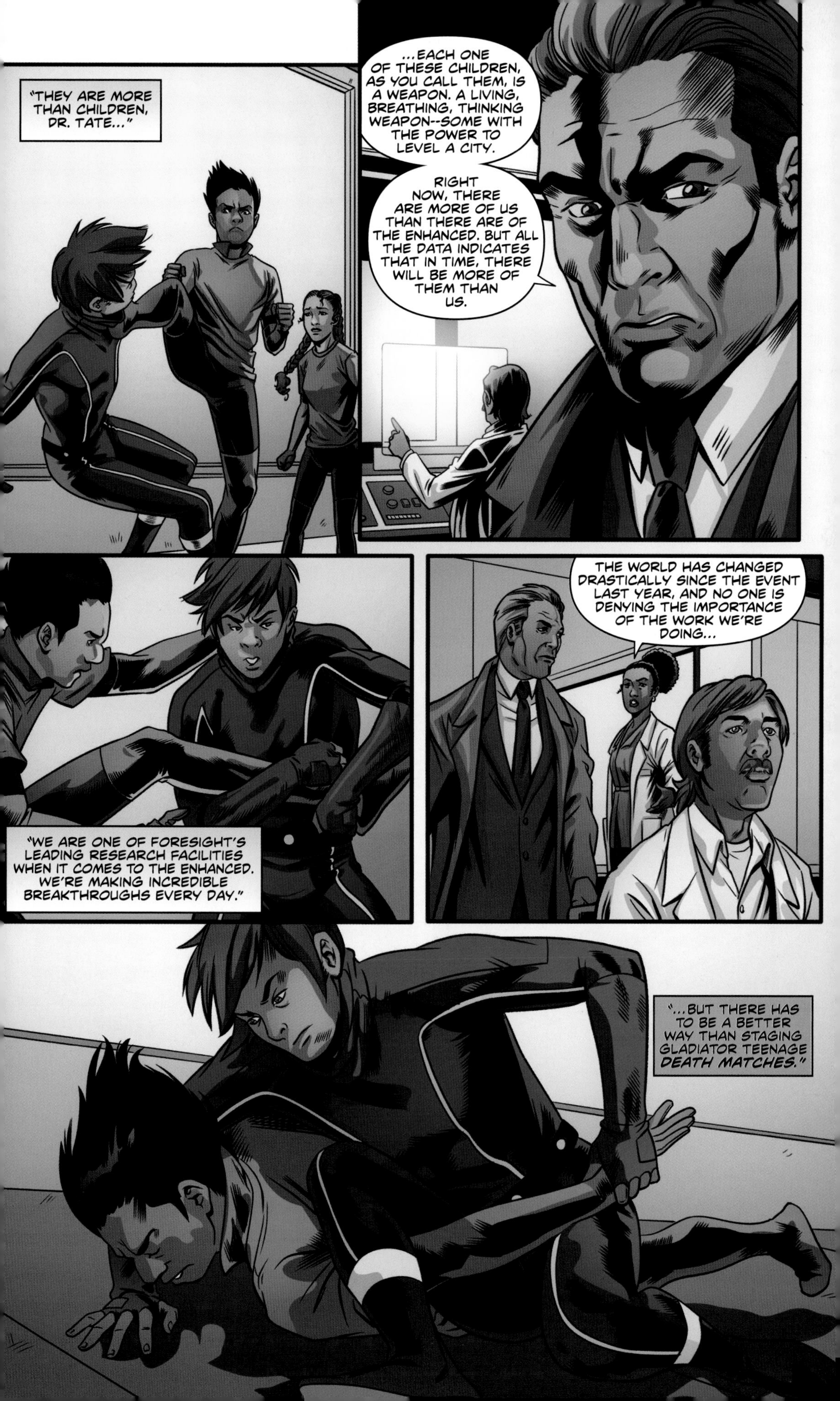
"THEY ARE MORE THAN CHILDREN, DR. TATE..."
...EACH ONE OF THESE CHILDREN, AS YOU CALL THEM, IS A WEAPON. A LIVING, BREATHING, THINKING WEAPON--SOME WITH THE POWER TO LEVEL A CITY.
RIGHT NOW, THERE ARE MORE OF US THAN THERE ARE OF THE ENHANCED. BUT ALL THE DATA INDICATES THAT IN TIME, THERE WILL BE MORE OF THEM THAN US.
"WE ARE ONE OF FORESIGHT'S LEADING RESEARCH FACILITIES WHEN IT COMES TO THE ENHANCED. WE'RE MAKING INCREDIBLE BREAKTHROUGHS EVERY DAY."
THE WORLD HAS CHANGED DRASTICALLY SINCE THE EVENT LAST YEAR, AND NO ONE IS DENYING THE IMPORTANCE OF THE WORK WE'RE DOING...
"...BUT THERE HAS TO BE A BETTER WAY THAN STAGING GLADIATOR TEENAGE DEATH MATCHES."

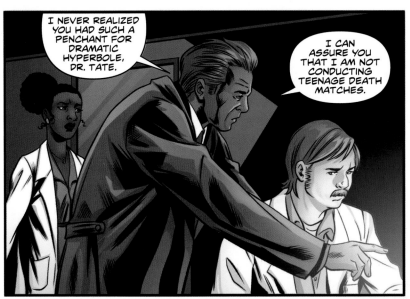

I NEVER REALIZED YOU HAD SUCH A PENCHANT FOR DRAMATIC HYPERBOLE, DR. TATE.

I CAN ASSURE YOU THAT I AM NOT CONDUCTING TEENAGE DEATH MATCHES.

VERNE, LOWER THE PHYSICAL STRENGTH LEVELS ON THE WATKINS SPECIMEN BY SEVENTY-FIVE PERCENT, BUT HOLD STEADY WITH HIS PAIN THRESHOLD.

"...STRENGTH LEVELS ARE DECREASED. HE WON'T BE ABLE TO HOLD HIS OWN IN THE FIGHT."

I THOUGHT YOU SAID THIS WASN'T A DEATH MATCH.

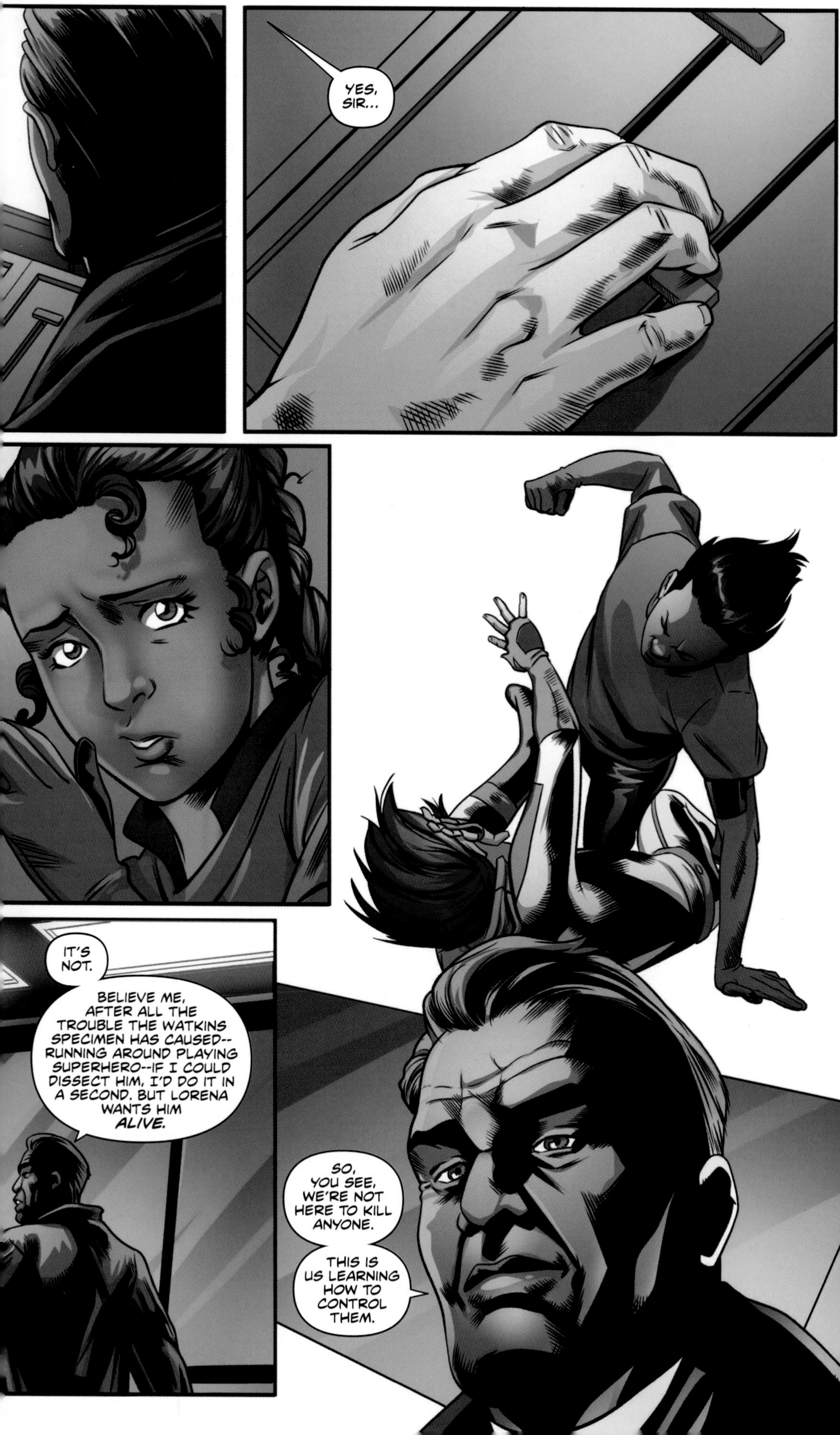
YES, SIR...
IT'S NOT.
BELIEVE ME, AFTER ALL THE TROUBLE THE WATKINS SPECIMEN HAS CAUSED-- RUNNING AROUND PLAYING SUPERHERO--IF I COULD DISSECT HIM, I'D DO IT IN A SECOND. BUT LORENA WANTS HIM *ALIVE.*
SO, YOU SEE, WE'RE NOT HERE TO KILL ANYONE.
THIS IS US LEARNING HOW TO CONTROL THEM.

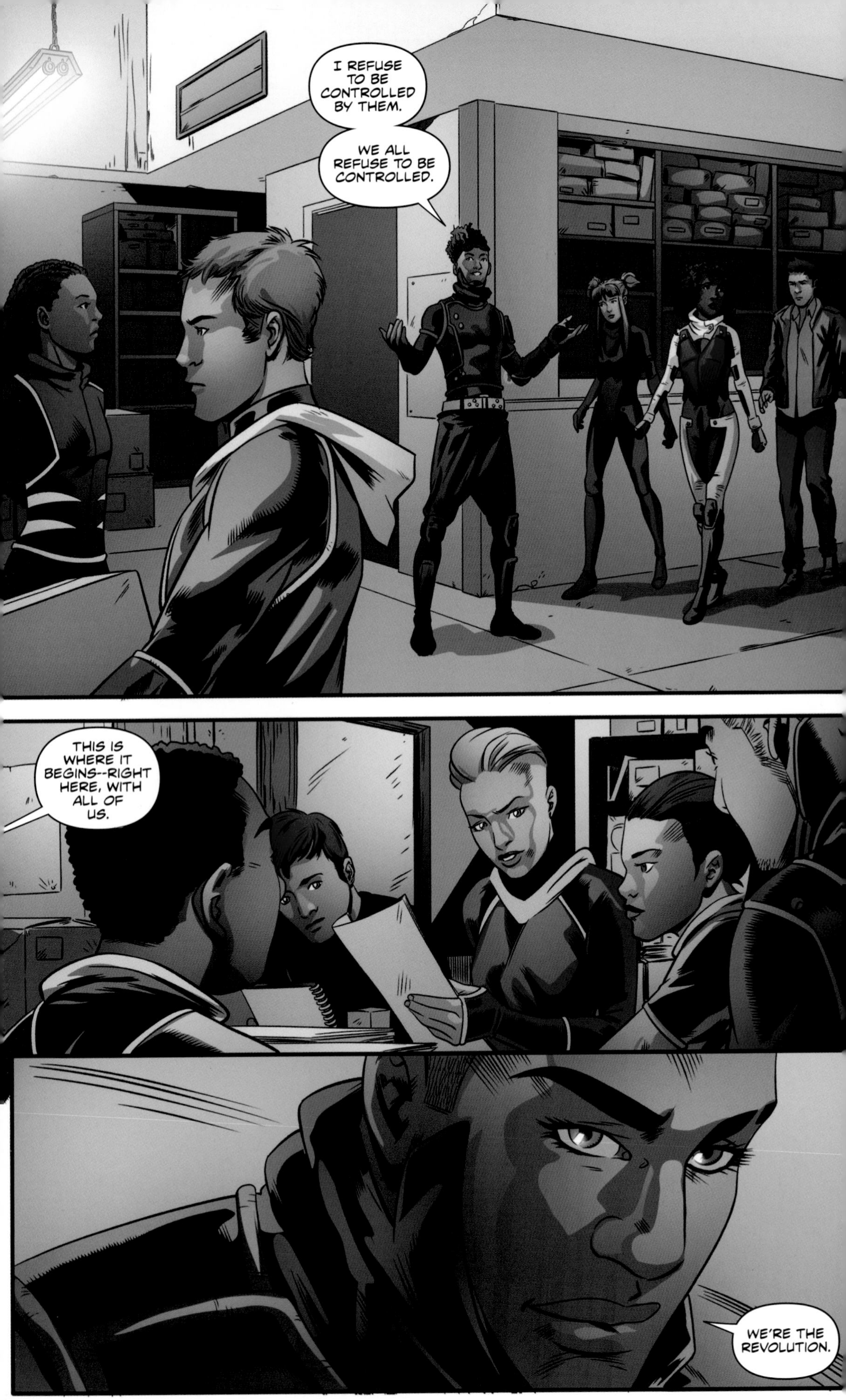
I REFUSE TO BE CONTROLLED BY THEM.
WE ALL REFUSE TO BE CONTROLLED.
THIS IS WHERE IT BEGINS--RIGHT HERE, WITH ALL OF US.
WE'RE THE REVOLUTION.

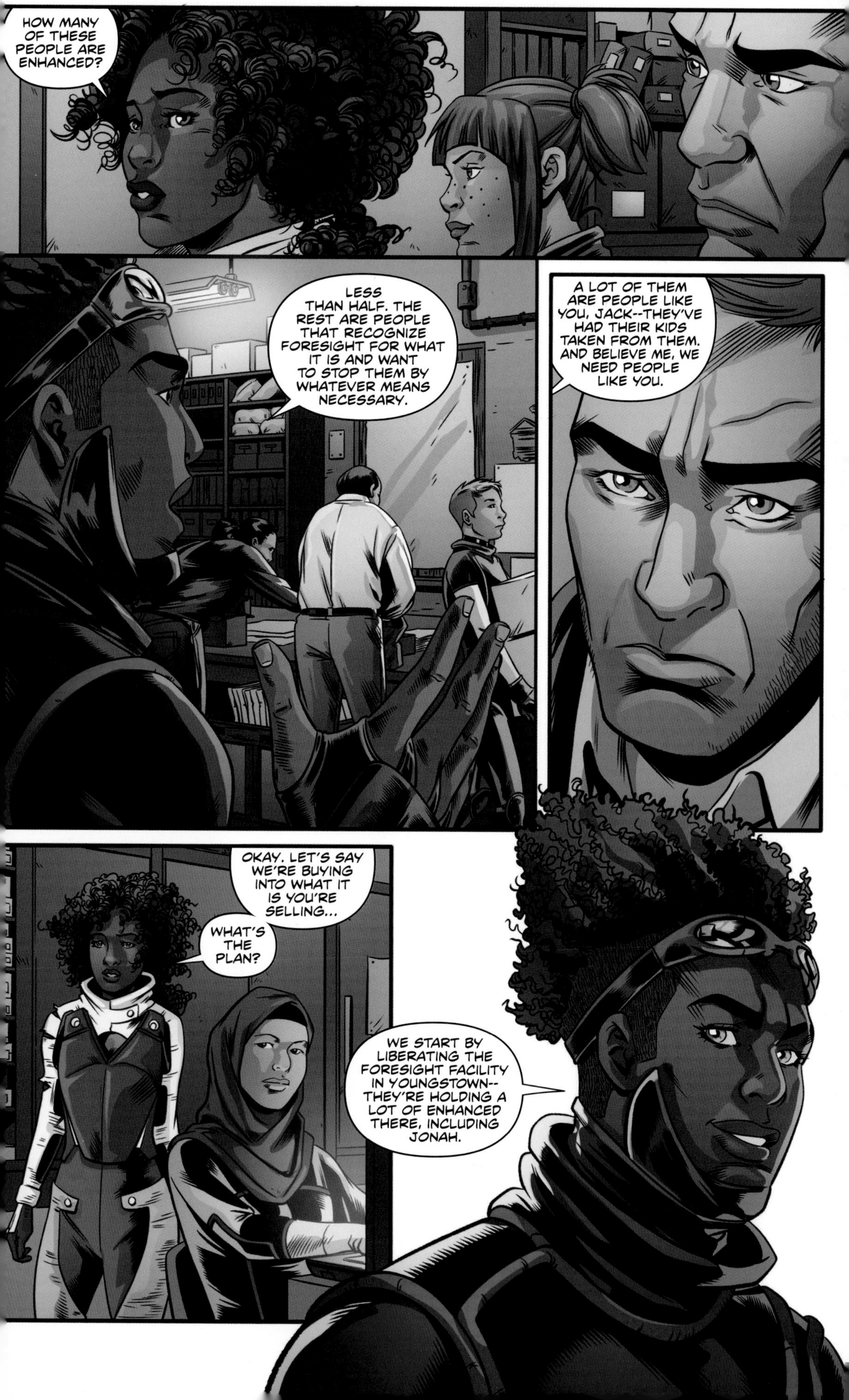

HOW MANY OF THESE PEOPLE ARE ENHANCED?
LESS THAN HALF. THE REST ARE PEOPLE THAT RECOGNIZE FORESIGHT FOR WHAT IT IS AND WANT TO STOP THEM BY WHATEVER MEANS NECESSARY.
A LOT OF THEM ARE PEOPLE LIKE YOU, JACK--THEY'VE HAD THEIR KIDS TAKEN FROM THEM. AND BELIEVE ME, WE NEED PEOPLE LIKE YOU.
OKAY. LET'S SAY WE'RE BUYING INTO WHAT IT IS YOU'RE SELLING...
WHAT'S THE PLAN?
WE START BY LIBERATING THE FORESIGHT FACILITY IN YOUNGSTOWN--THEY'RE HOLDING A LOT OF ENHANCED THERE, INCLUDING JONAH.

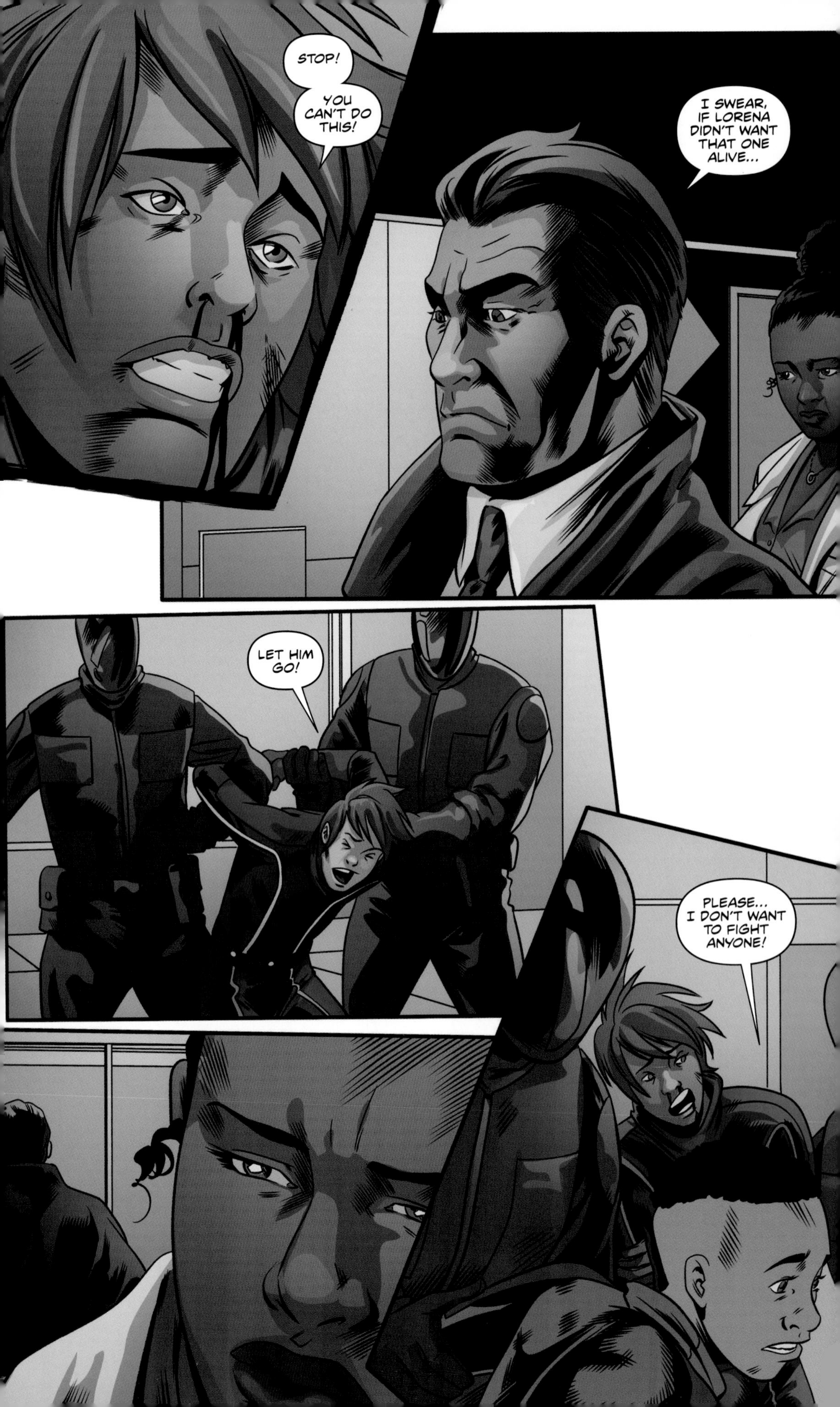
STOP!
YOU CAN'T DO THIS!
I SWEAR, IF LORENA DIDN'T WANT THAT ONE ALIVE...
LET HIM GO!
PLEASE... I DON'T WANT TO FIGHT ANYONE!

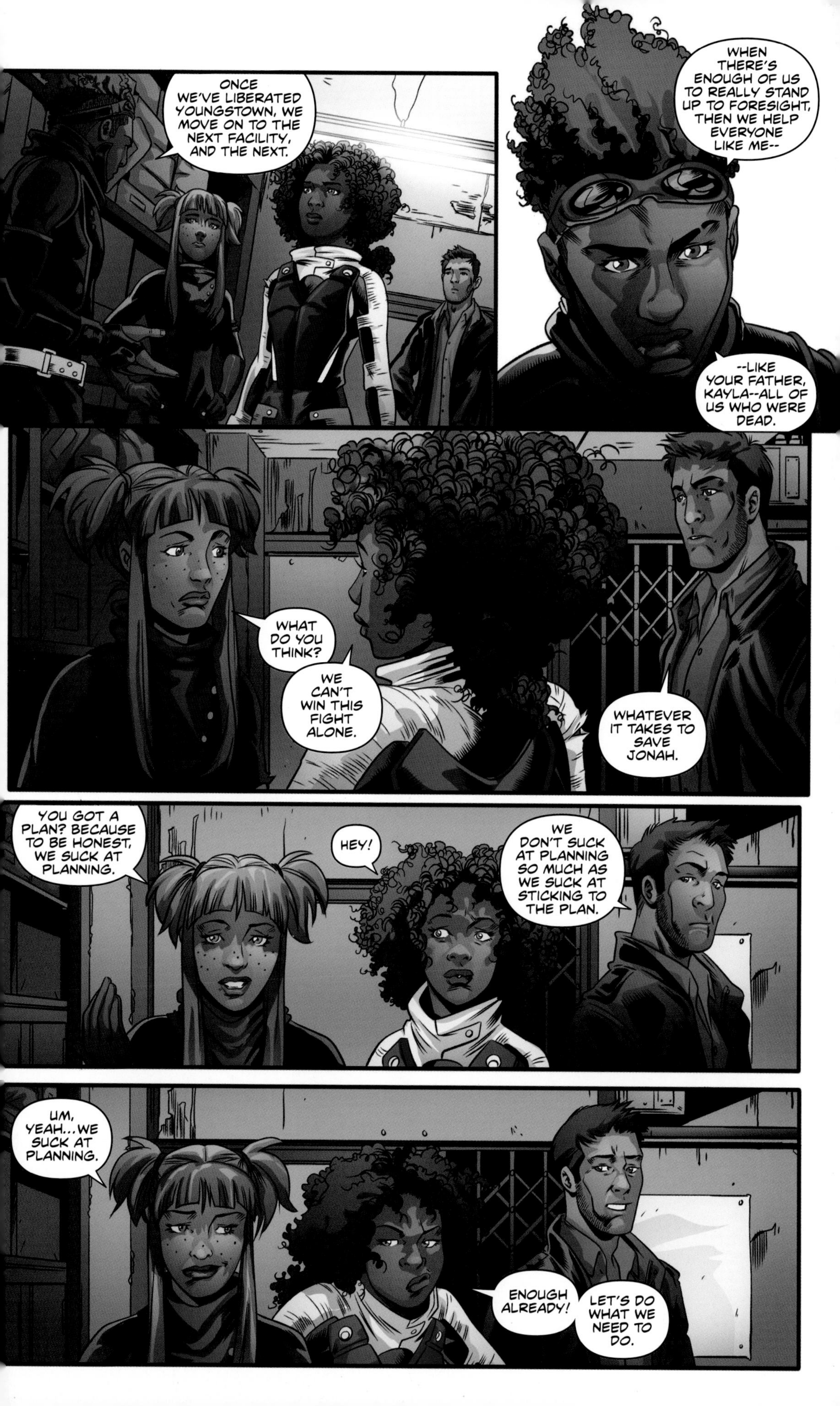

ONCE WE'VE LIBERATED YOUNGSTOWN, WE MOVE ON TO THE NEXT FACILITY, AND THE NEXT.
WHEN THERE'S ENOUGH OF US TO REALLY STAND UP TO FORESIGHT, THEN WE HELP EVERYONE LIKE ME--
--LIKE YOUR FATHER, KAYLA--ALL OF US WHO WERE DEAD.
WHAT DO YOU THINK?
WE CAN'T WIN THIS FIGHT ALONE.
WHATEVER IT TAKES TO SAVE JONAH.
YOU GOT A PLAN? BECAUSE TO BE HONEST, WE SUCK AT PLANNING.
HEY!
WE DON'T SUCK AT PLANNING SO MUCH AS WE SUCK AT STICKING TO THE PLAN.
UM, YEAH...WE SUCK AT PLANNING.
ENOUGH ALREADY!
LET'S DO WHAT WE NEED TO DO.

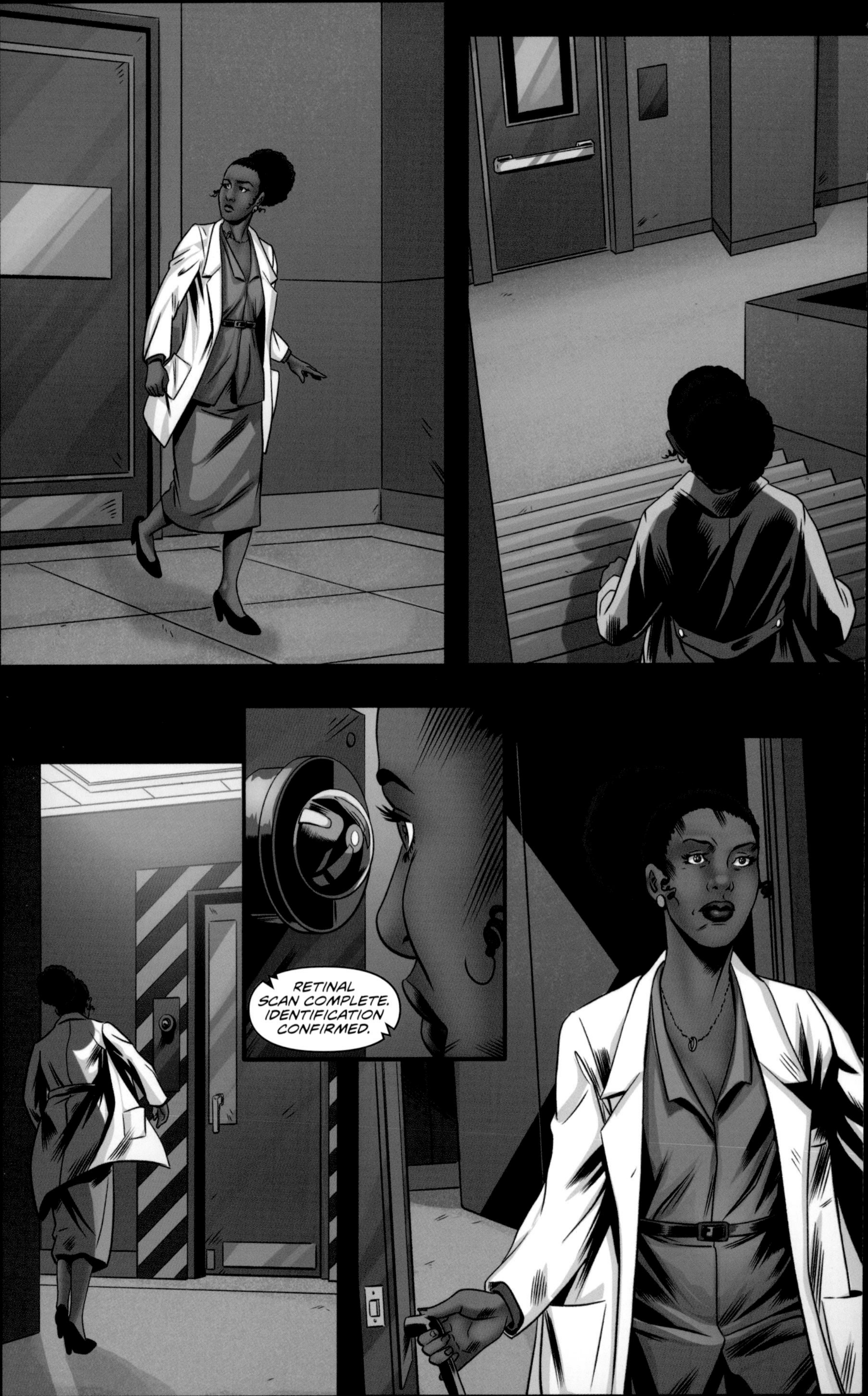
RETINAL SCAN COMPLETE. IDENTIFICATION CONFIRMED.

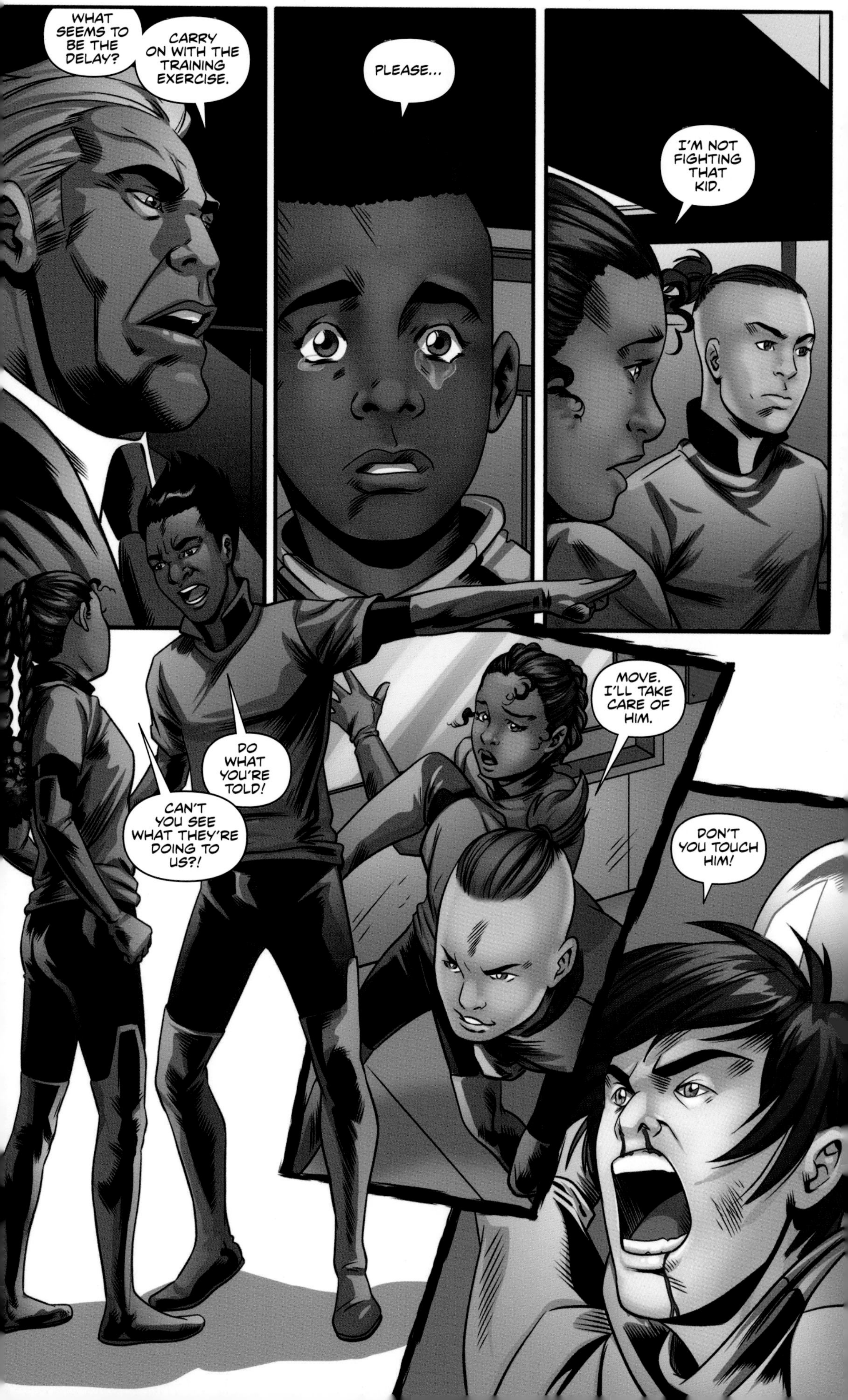
WHAT SEEMS TO BE THE DELAY?
CARRY ON WITH THE TRAINING EXERCISE.
PLEASE...
I'M NOT FIGHTING THAT KID.
DO WHAT YOU'RE TOLD!
CAN'T YOU SEE WHAT THEY'RE DOING TO US?!
MOVE. I'LL TAKE CARE OF HIM.
DON'T YOU TOUCH HIM!

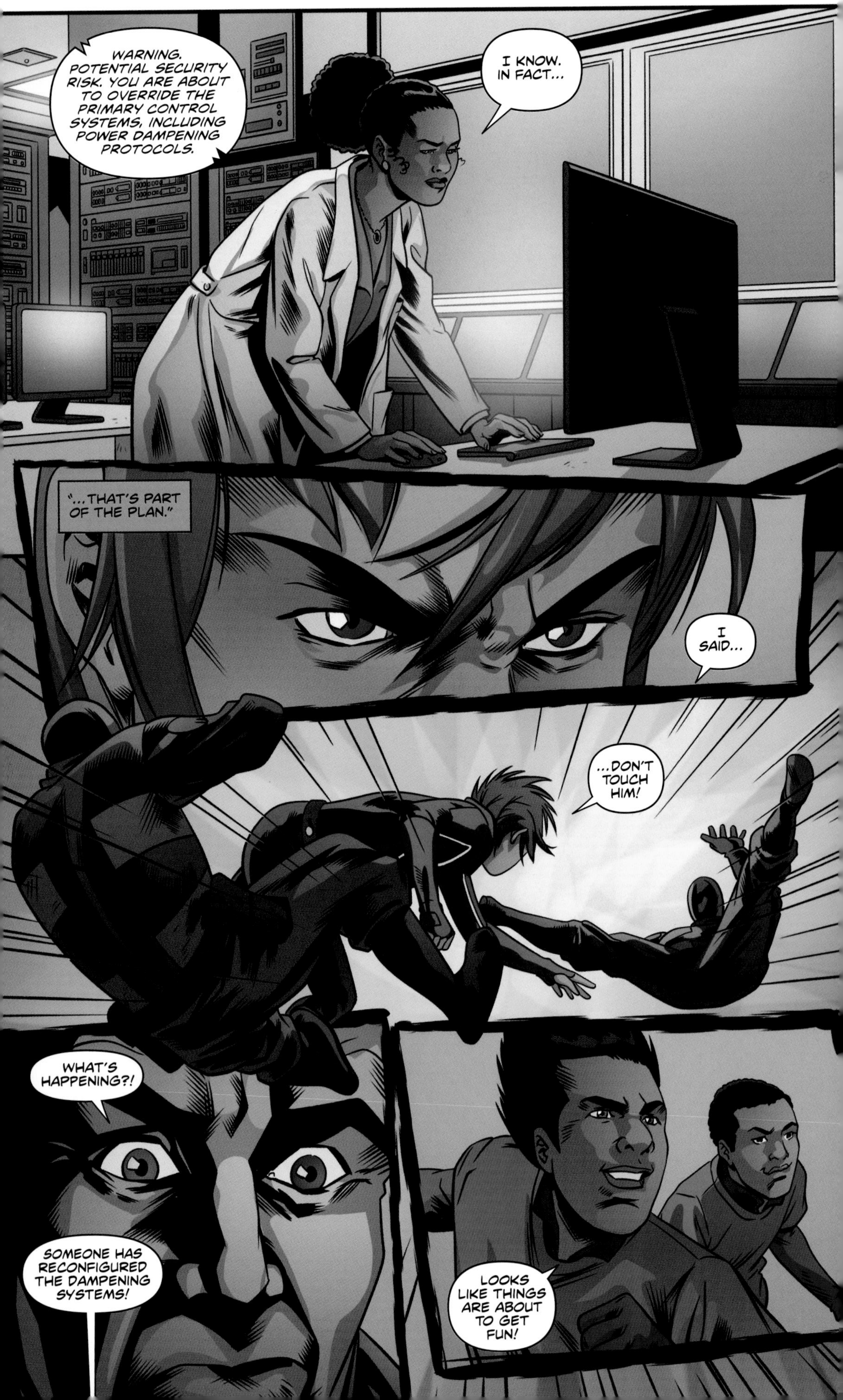
WARNING. POTENTIAL SECURITY RISK. YOU ARE ABOUT TO OVERRIDE THE PRIMARY CONTROL SYSTEMS, INCLUDING POWER DAMPENING PROTOCOLS.
I KNOW. IN FACT...
"...THAT'S PART OF THE PLAN."
I SAID...
...DON'T TOUCH HIM!
WHAT'S HAPPENING?!
SOMEONE HAS RECONFIGURED THE DAMPENING SYSTEMS!
LOOKS LIKE THINGS ARE ABOUT TO GET FUN!

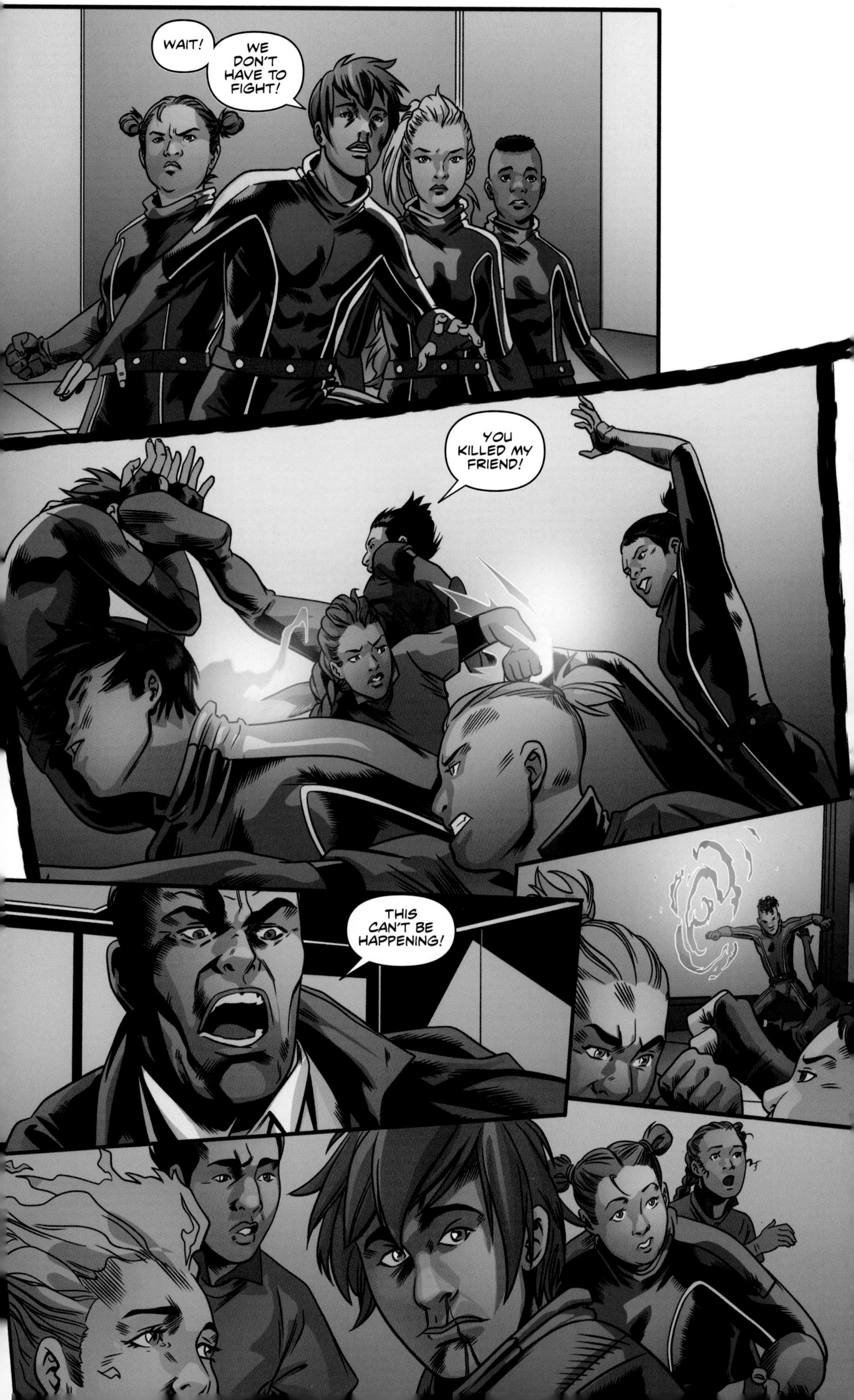
WAIT!
WE DON'T HAVE TO FIGHT!
YOU KILLED MY FRIEND!
THIS CAN'T BE HAPPENING!

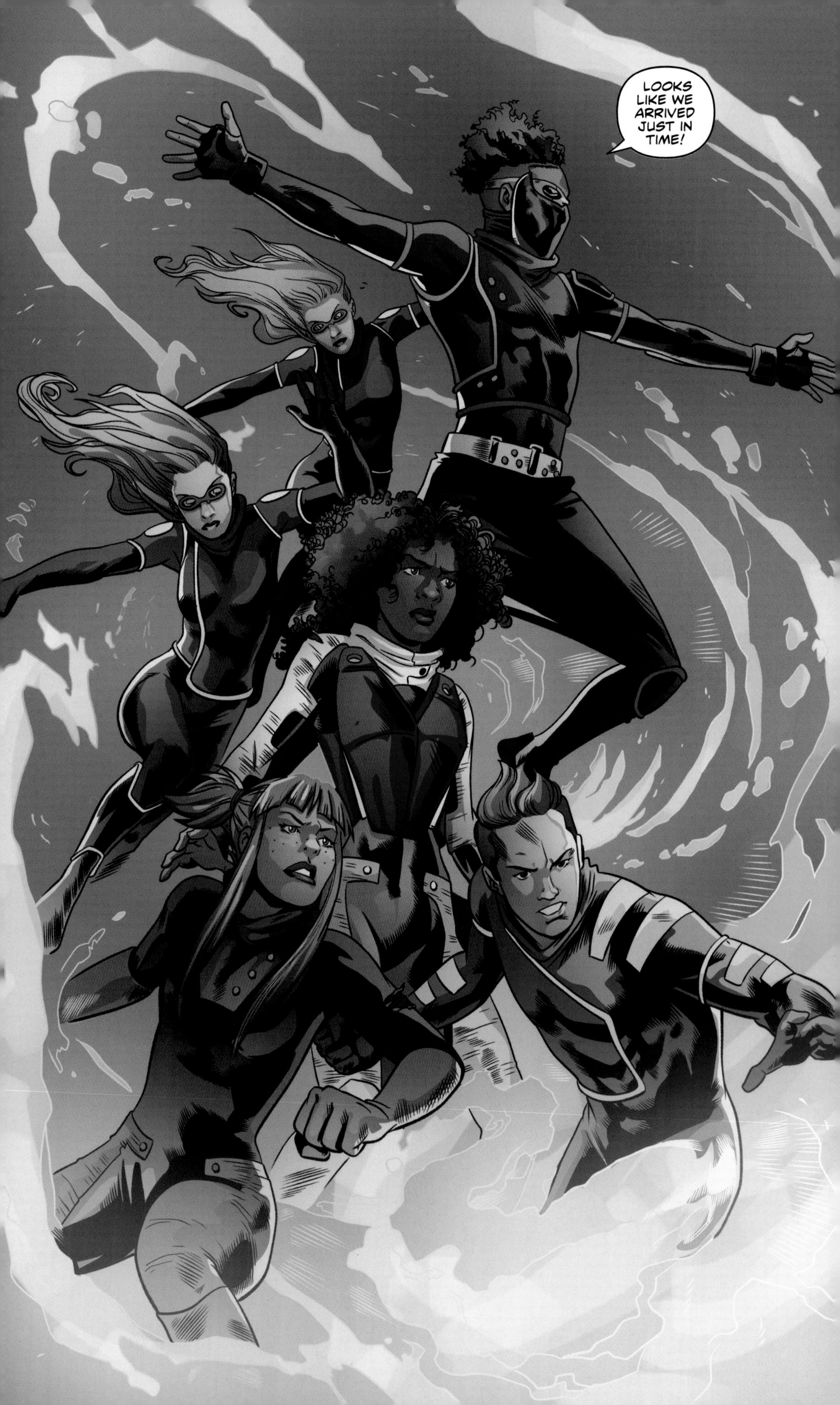
LOOKS LIKE WE ARRIVED JUST IN TIME!

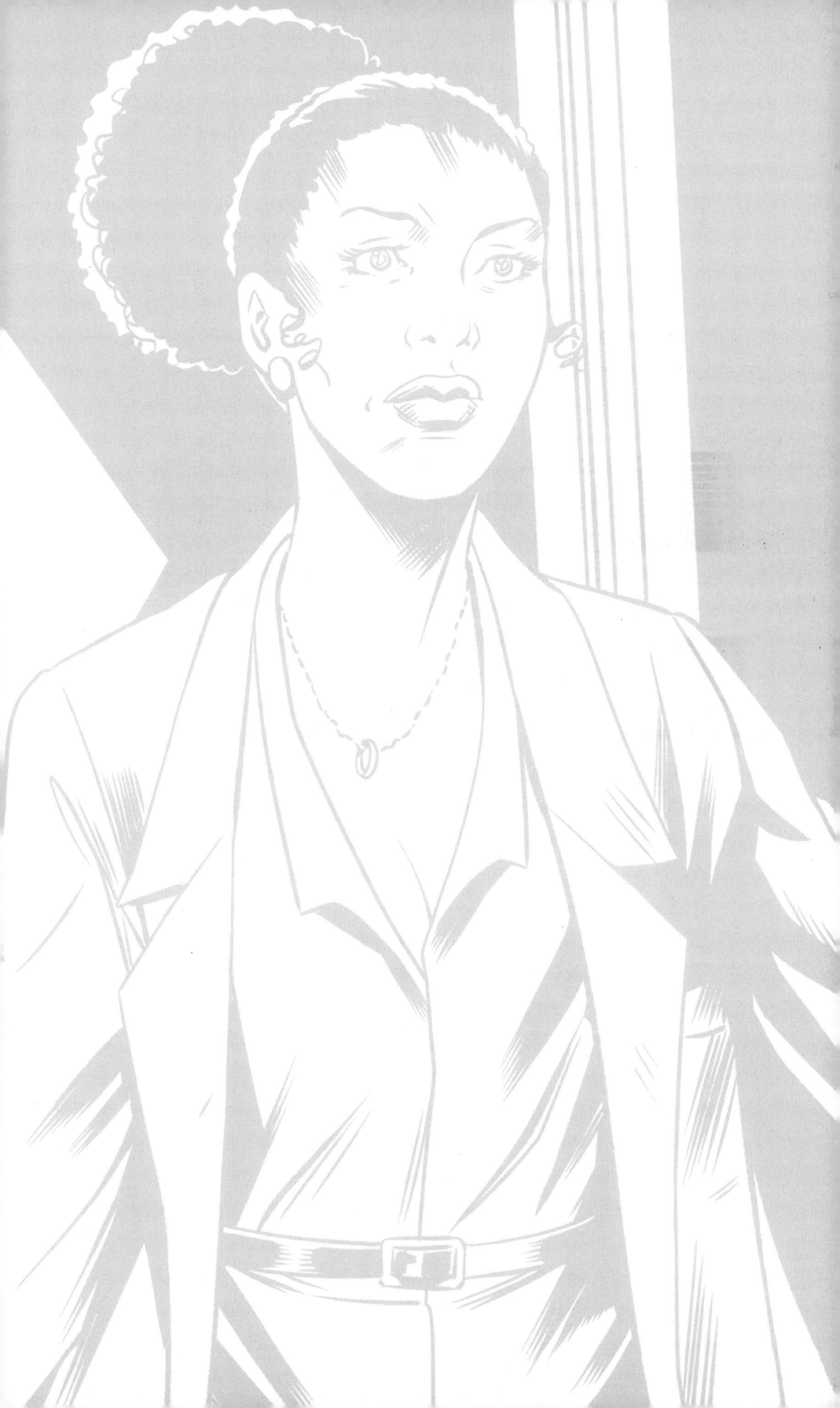

CHAPTER FIVE

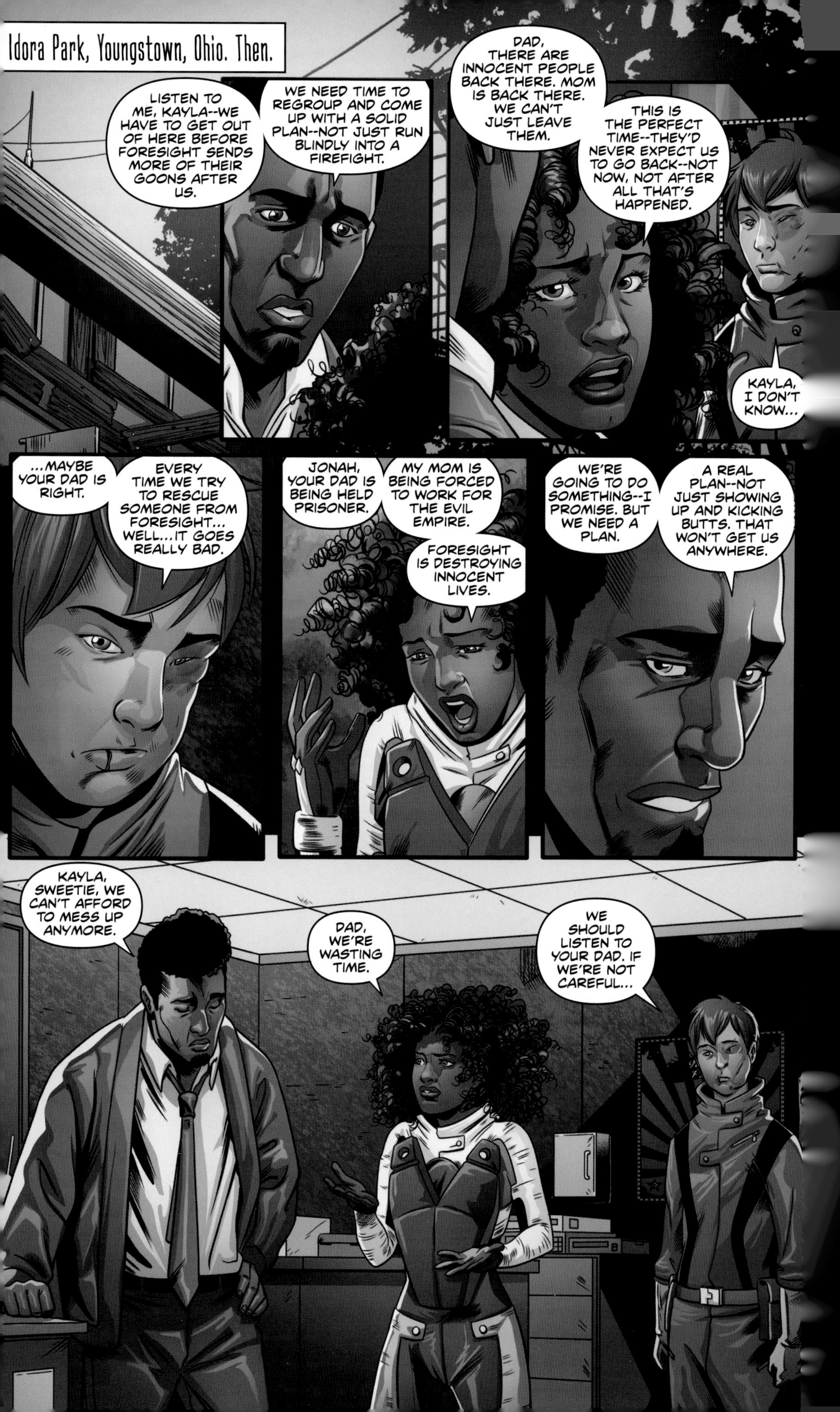
Idora Park, Youngstown, Ohio. Then.
LISTEN TO ME, KAYLA--WE HAVE TO GET OUT OF HERE BEFORE FORESIGHT SENDS MORE OF THEIR GOONS AFTER US.
WE NEED TIME TO REGROUP AND COME UP WITH A SOLID PLAN--NOT JUST RUN BLINDLY INTO A FIREFIGHT.
DAD, THERE ARE INNOCENT PEOPLE BACK THERE. MOM IS BACK THERE. WE CAN'T JUST LEAVE THEM.
THIS IS THE PERFECT TIME--THEY'D NEVER EXPECT US TO GO BACK--NOT NOW, NOT AFTER ALL THAT'S HAPPENED.
KAYLA, I DON'T KNOW...
...MAYBE YOUR DAD IS RIGHT.
EVERY TIME WE TRY TO RESCUE SOMEONE FROM FORESIGHT... WELL...IT GOES REALLY BAD.
JONAH, YOUR DAD IS BEING HELD PRISONER.
MY MOM IS BEING FORCED TO WORK FOR THE EVIL EMPIRE.
FORESIGHT IS DESTROYING INNOCENT LIVES.
WE'RE GOING TO DO SOMETHING--I PROMISE. BUT WE NEED A PLAN.
A REAL PLAN--NOT JUST SHOWING UP AND KICKING BUTTS. THAT WON'T GET US ANYWHERE.
KAYLA, SWEETIE, WE CAN'T AFFORD TO MESS UP ANYMORE.
DAD, WE'RE WASTING TIME.
WE SHOULD LISTEN TO YOUR DAD. IF WE'RE NOT CAREFUL...

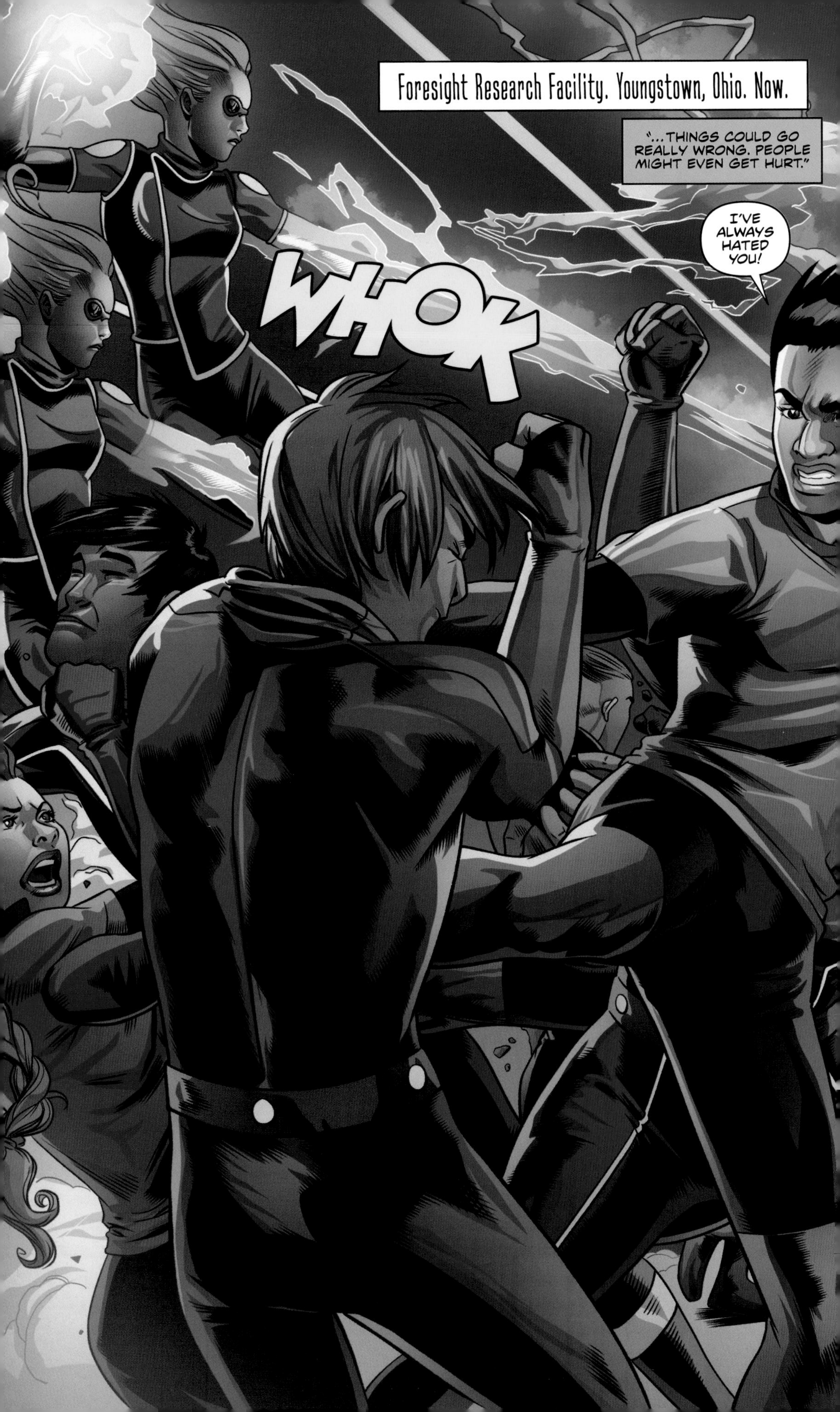
Foresight Research Facility. Youngstown, Ohio. Now.
"...THINGS COULD GO REALLY WRONG. PEOPLE MIGHT EVEN GET HURT."
I'VE ALWAYS HATED YOU!
WHOK

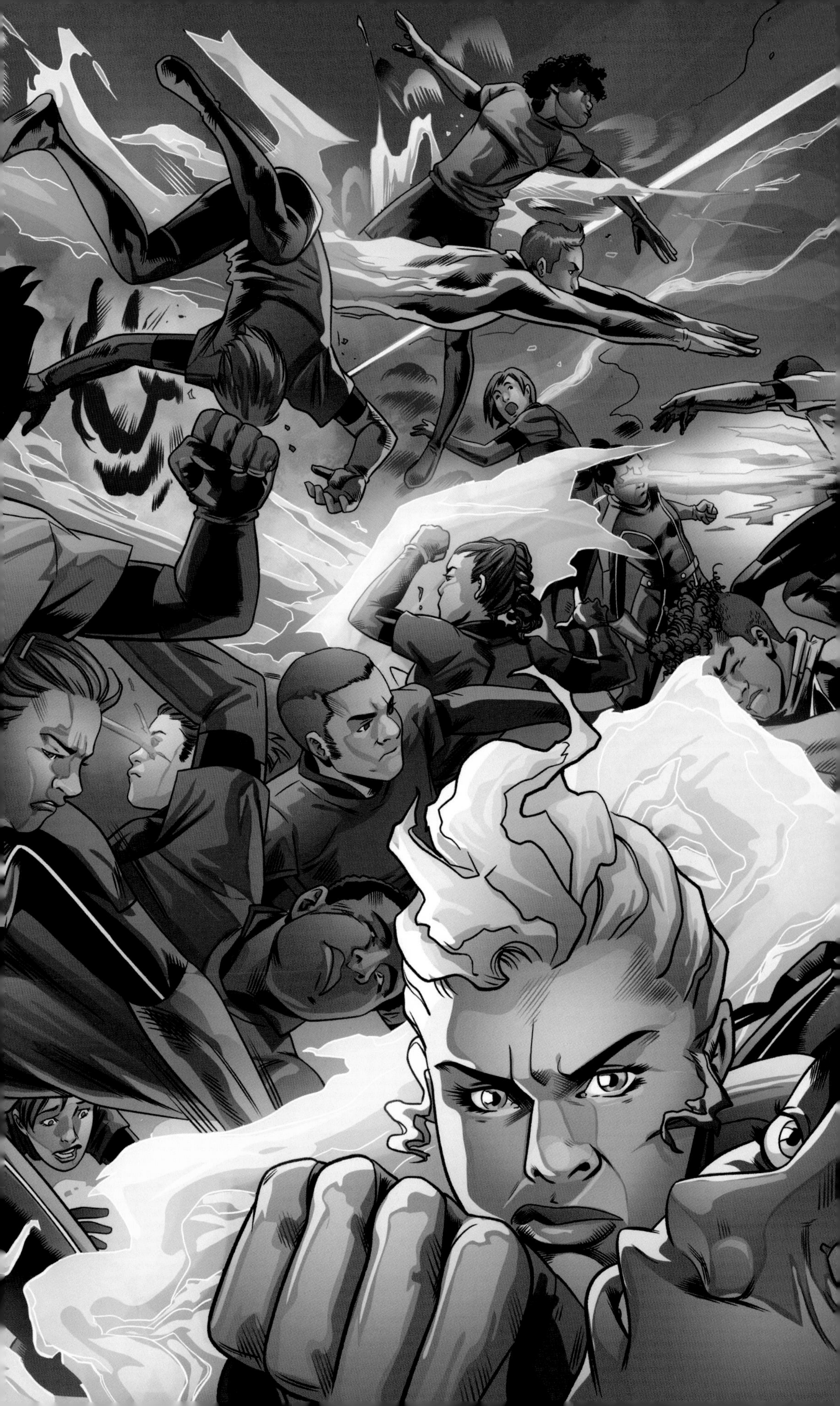

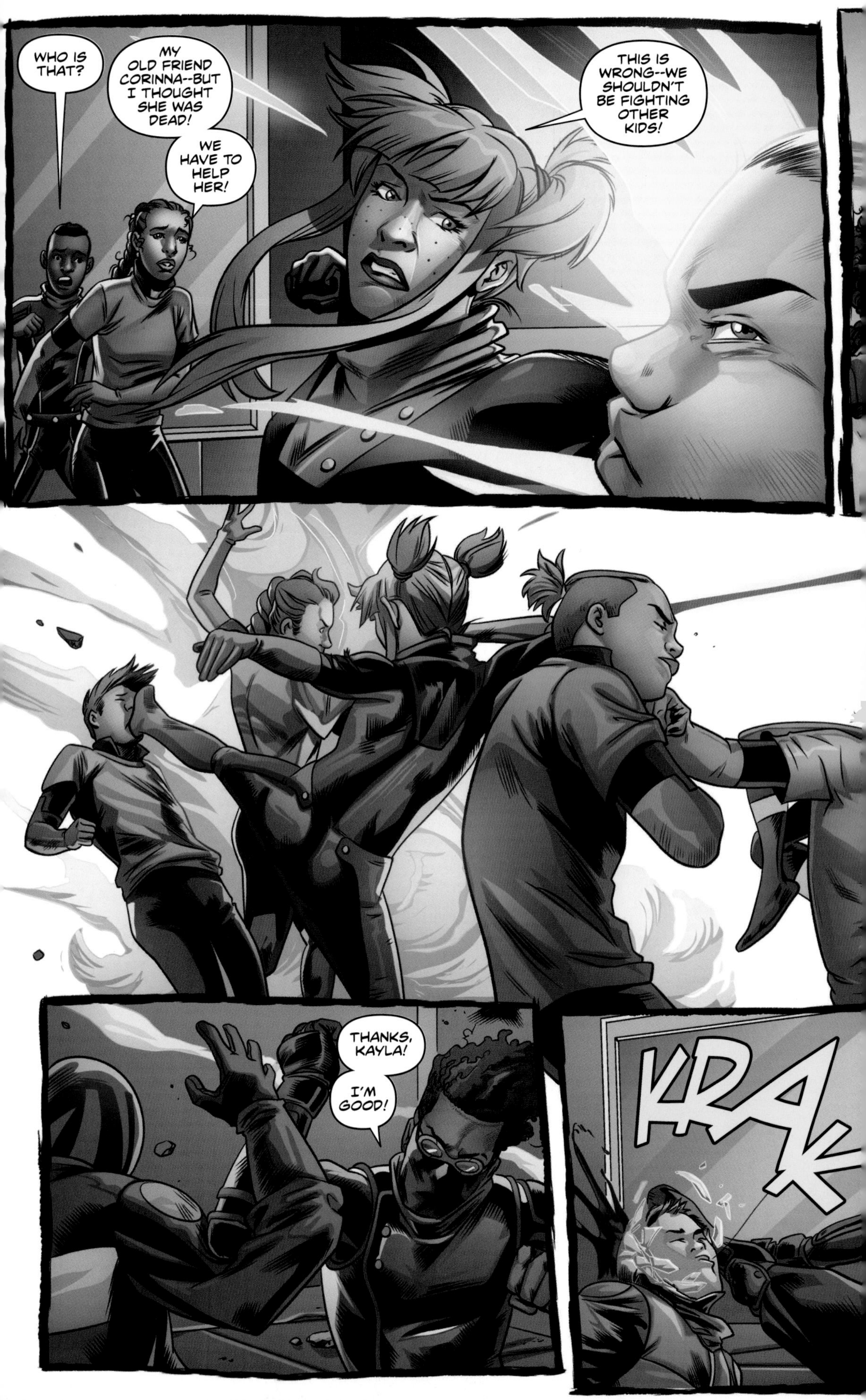
WHO IS THAT?
MY OLD FRIEND CORINNA--BUT I THOUGHT SHE WAS DEAD!
WE HAVE TO HELP HER!
THIS IS WRONG--WE SHOULDN'T BE FIGHTING OTHER KIDS!
THANKS, KAYLA!
I'M GOOD!
KRAK

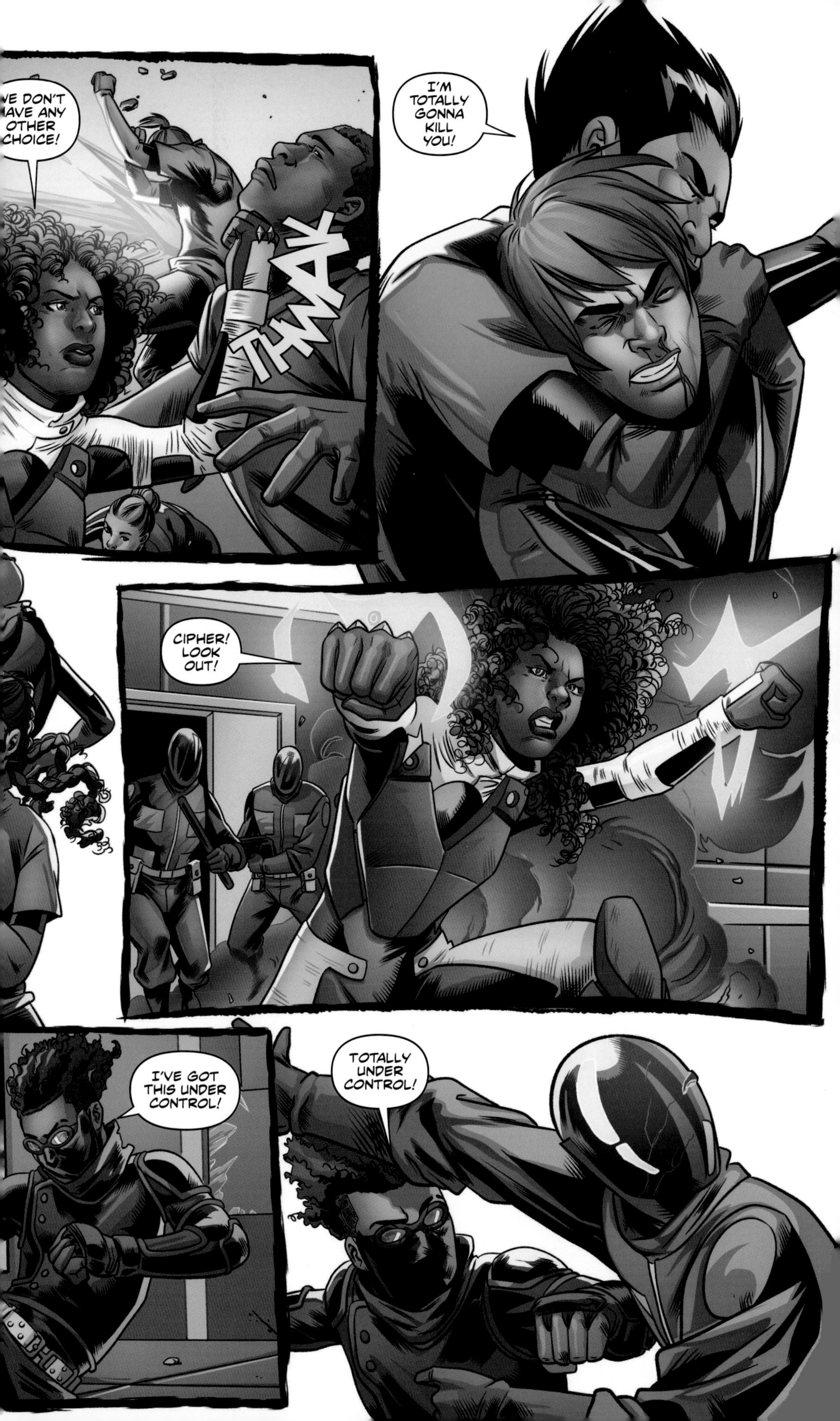
WE DON'T HAVE ANY OTHER CHOICE!
THWAK
I'M TOTALLY GONNA KILL YOU!
CIPHER! LOOK OUT!
I'VE GOT THIS UNDER CONTROL!
TOTALLY UNDER CONTROL!

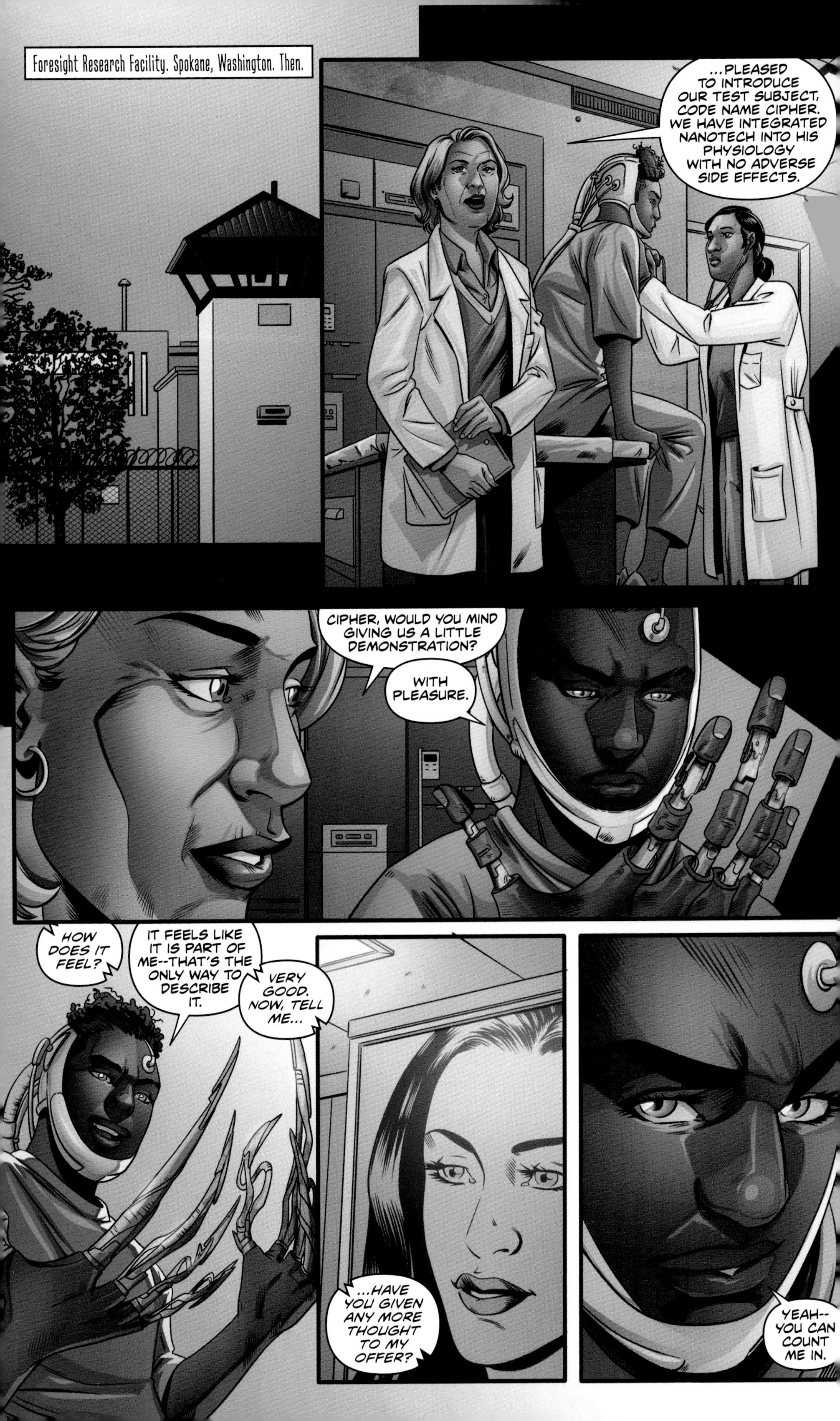
Foresight Research Facility. Spokane, Washington. Then.
...PLEASED TO INTRODUCE OUR TEST SUBJECT, CODE NAME CIPHER. WE HAVE INTEGRATED NANOTECH INTO HIS PHYSIOLOGY WITH NO ADVERSE SIDE EFFECTS.
CIPHER, WOULD YOU MIND GIVING US A LITTLE DEMONSTRATION?
WITH PLEASURE.
HOW DOES IT FEEL?
IT FEELS LIKE IT IS PART OF ME--THAT'S THE ONLY WAY TO DESCRIBE IT.
VERY GOOD. NOW, TELL ME...
...HAVE YOU GIVEN ANY MORE THOUGHT TO MY OFFER?
YEAH--YOU CAN COUNT ME IN.

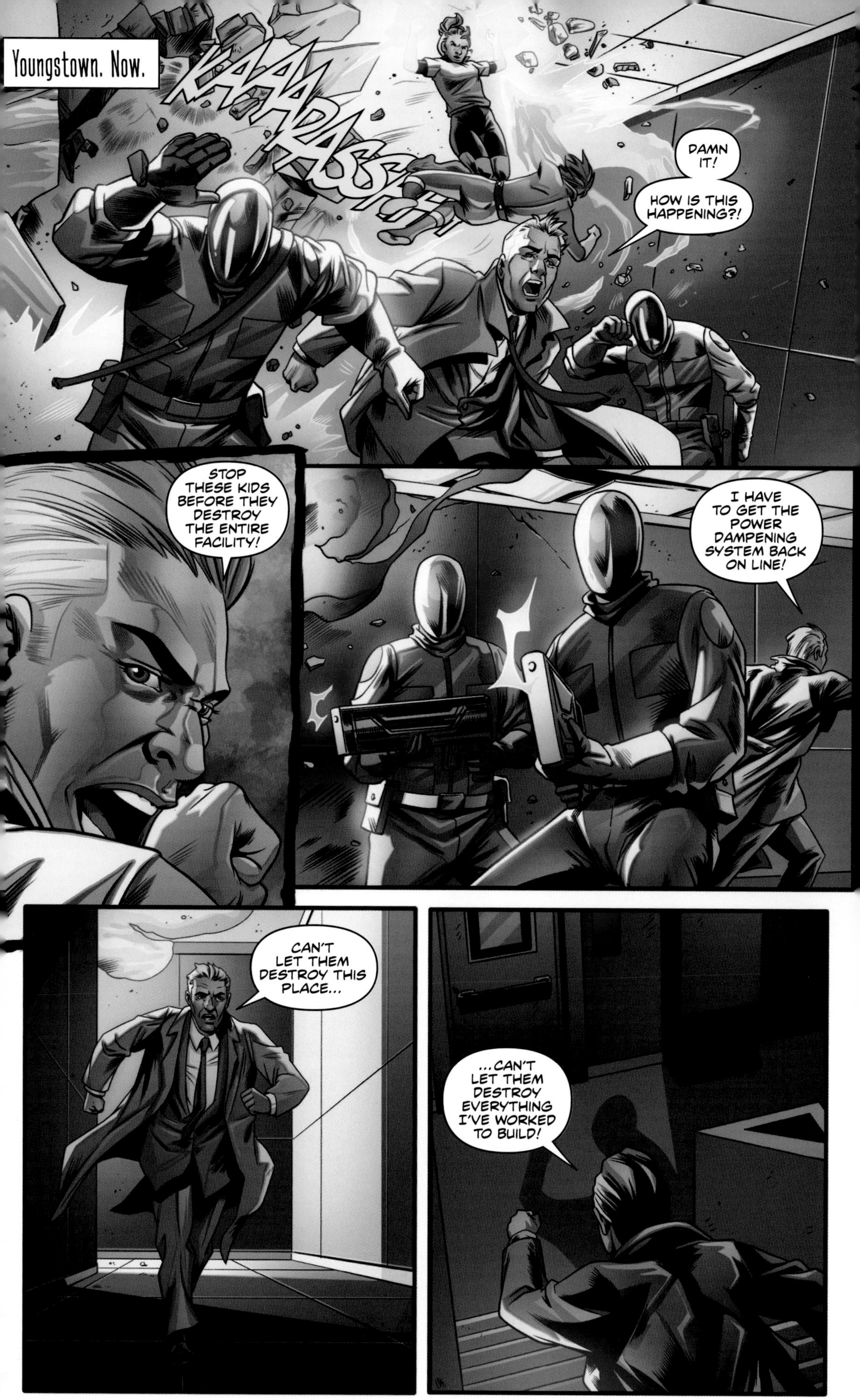
Youngstown. Now.
KAAARASSSHH
DAMN IT!
HOW IS THIS HAPPENING?!
STOP THESE KIDS BEFORE THEY DESTROY THE ENTIRE FACILITY!
I HAVE TO GET THE POWER DAMPENING SYSTEM BACK ON LINE!
CAN'T LET THEM DESTROY THIS PLACE...
...CAN'T LET THEM DESTROY EVERYTHING I'VE WORKED TO BUILD!

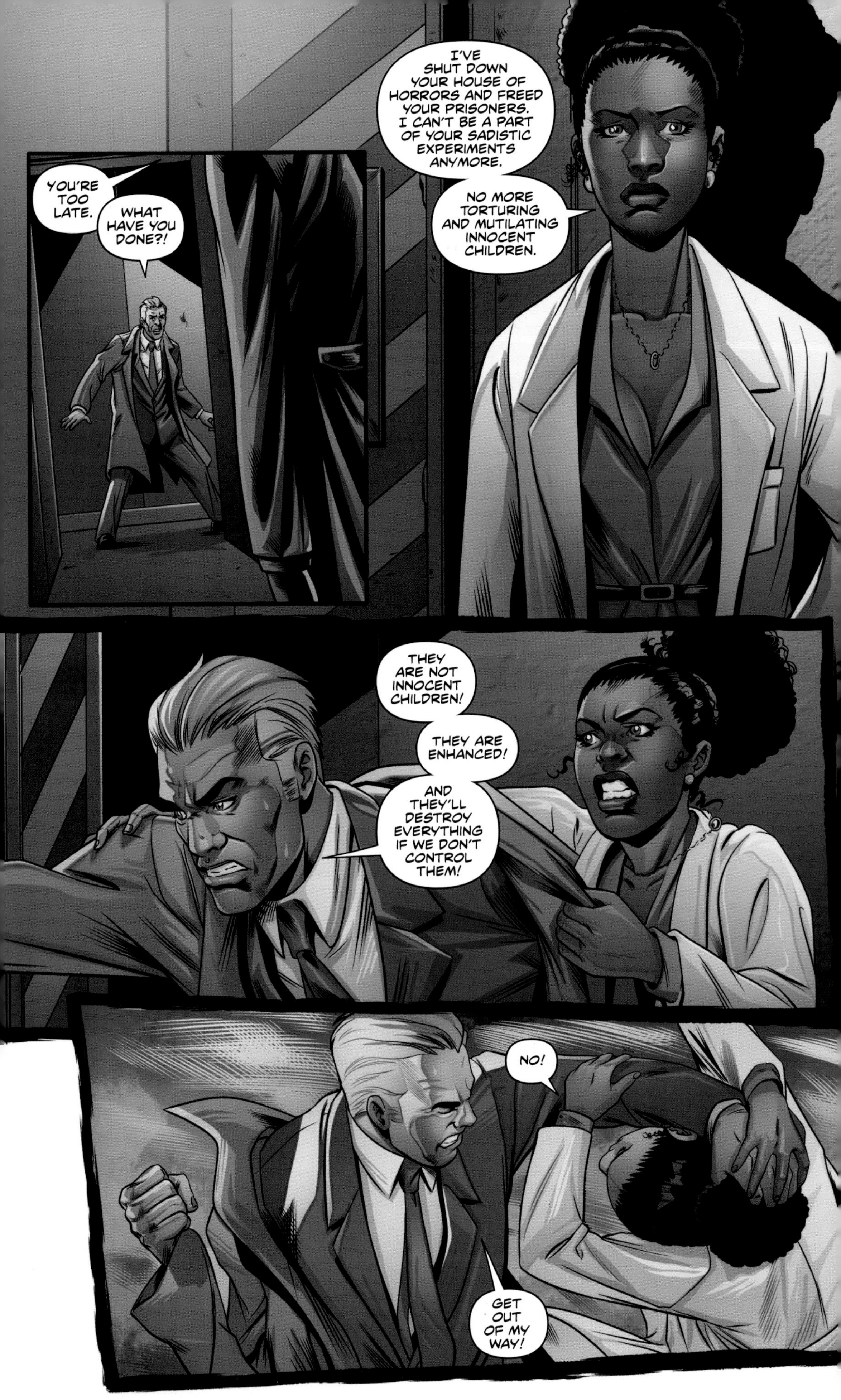
I'VE SHUT DOWN YOUR HOUSE OF HORRORS AND FREED YOUR PRISONERS. I CAN'T BE A PART OF YOUR SADISTIC EXPERIMENTS ANYMORE.
YOU'RE TOO LATE.
WHAT HAVE YOU DONE?!
NO MORE TORTURING AND MUTILATING INNOCENT CHILDREN.
THEY ARE NOT INNOCENT CHILDREN!
THEY ARE ENHANCED!
AND THEY'LL DESTROY EVERYTHING IF WE DON'T CONTROL THEM!
NO!
GET OUT OF MY WAY!

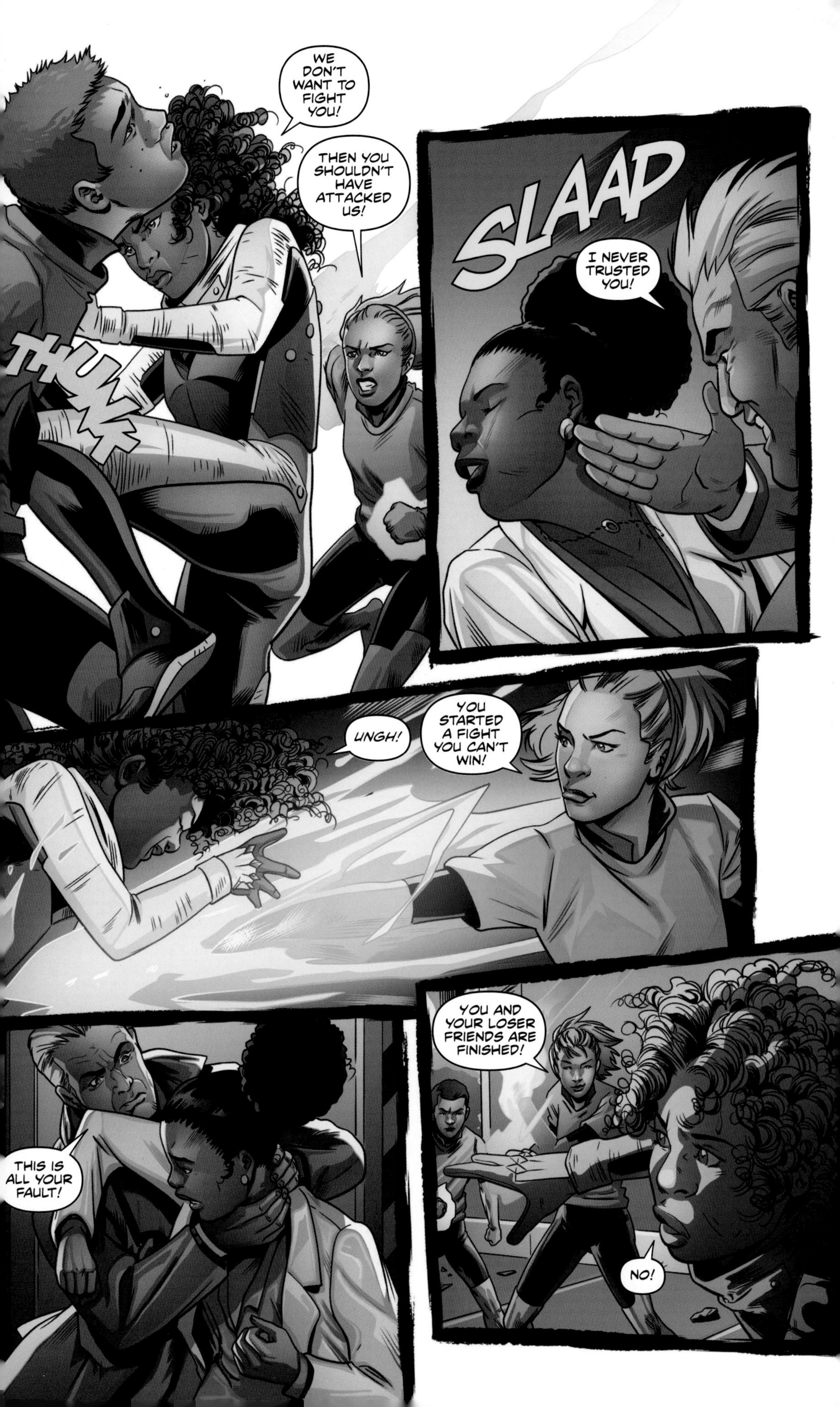

WE DON'T WANT TO FIGHT YOU!
THEN YOU SHOULDN'T HAVE ATTACKED US!
THUNK
SLAAP
I NEVER TRUSTED YOU!
UNGH!
YOU STARTED A FIGHT YOU CAN'T WIN!
THIS IS ALL YOUR FAULT!
YOU AND YOUR LOSER FRIENDS ARE FINISHED!
NO!

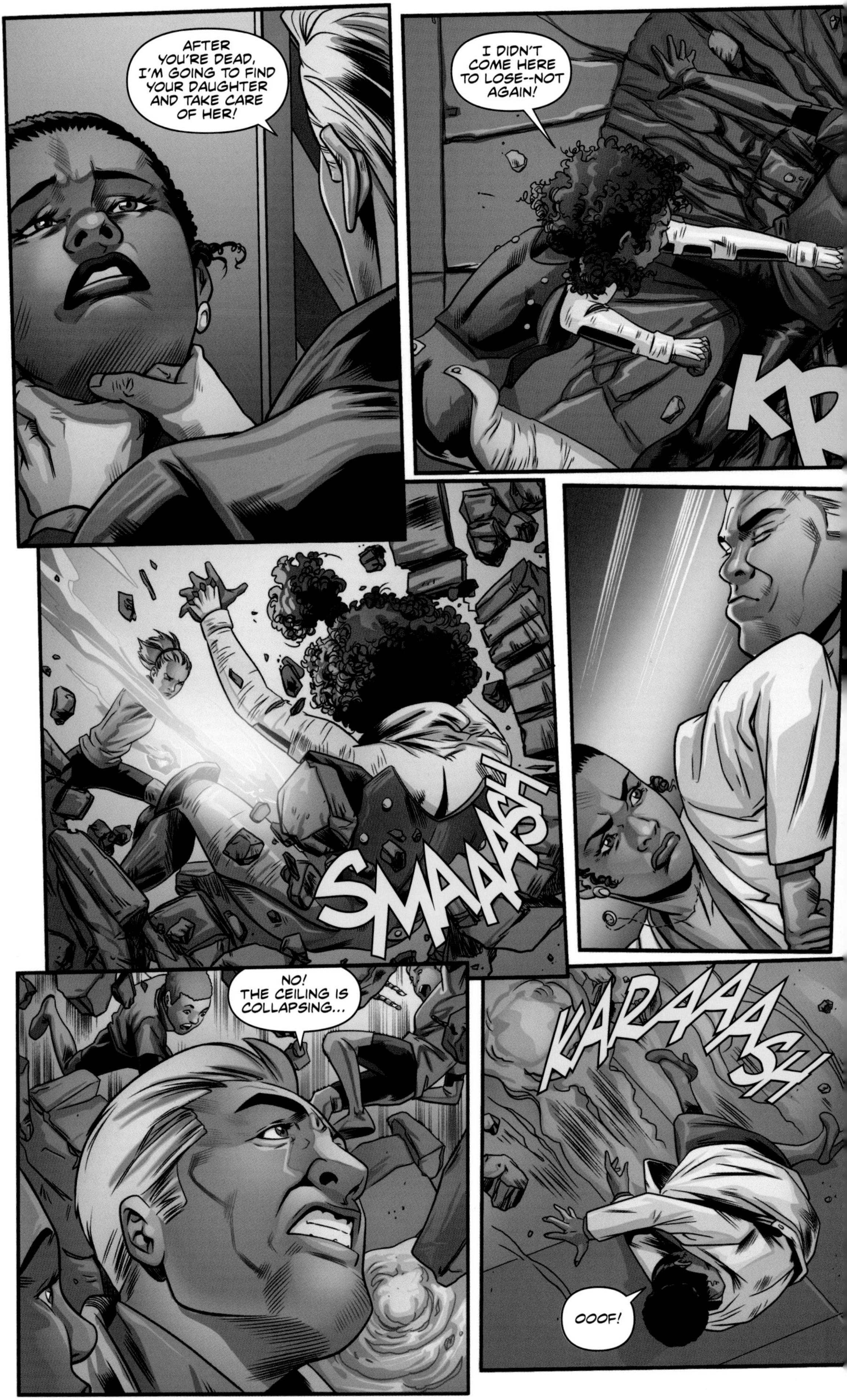
AFTER YOU'RE DEAD, I'M GOING TO FIND YOUR DAUGHTER AND TAKE CARE OF HER!
I DIDN'T COME HERE TO LOSE--NOT AGAIN!
KR
SMAAASH
NO! THE CEILING IS COLLAPSING...
KARAAAASH
OOOF!

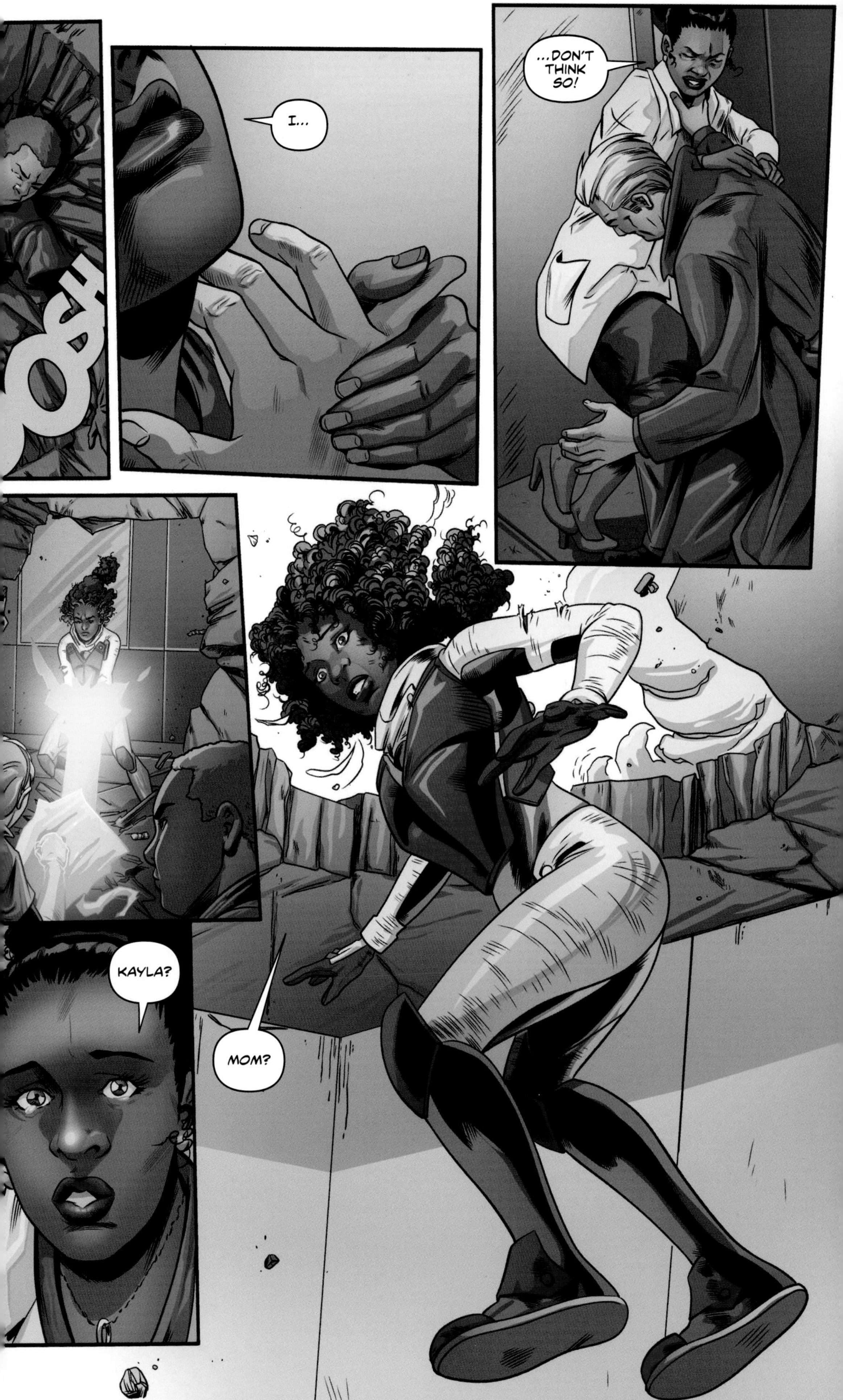
I...
...DON'T THINK SO!
KAYLA?
MOM?

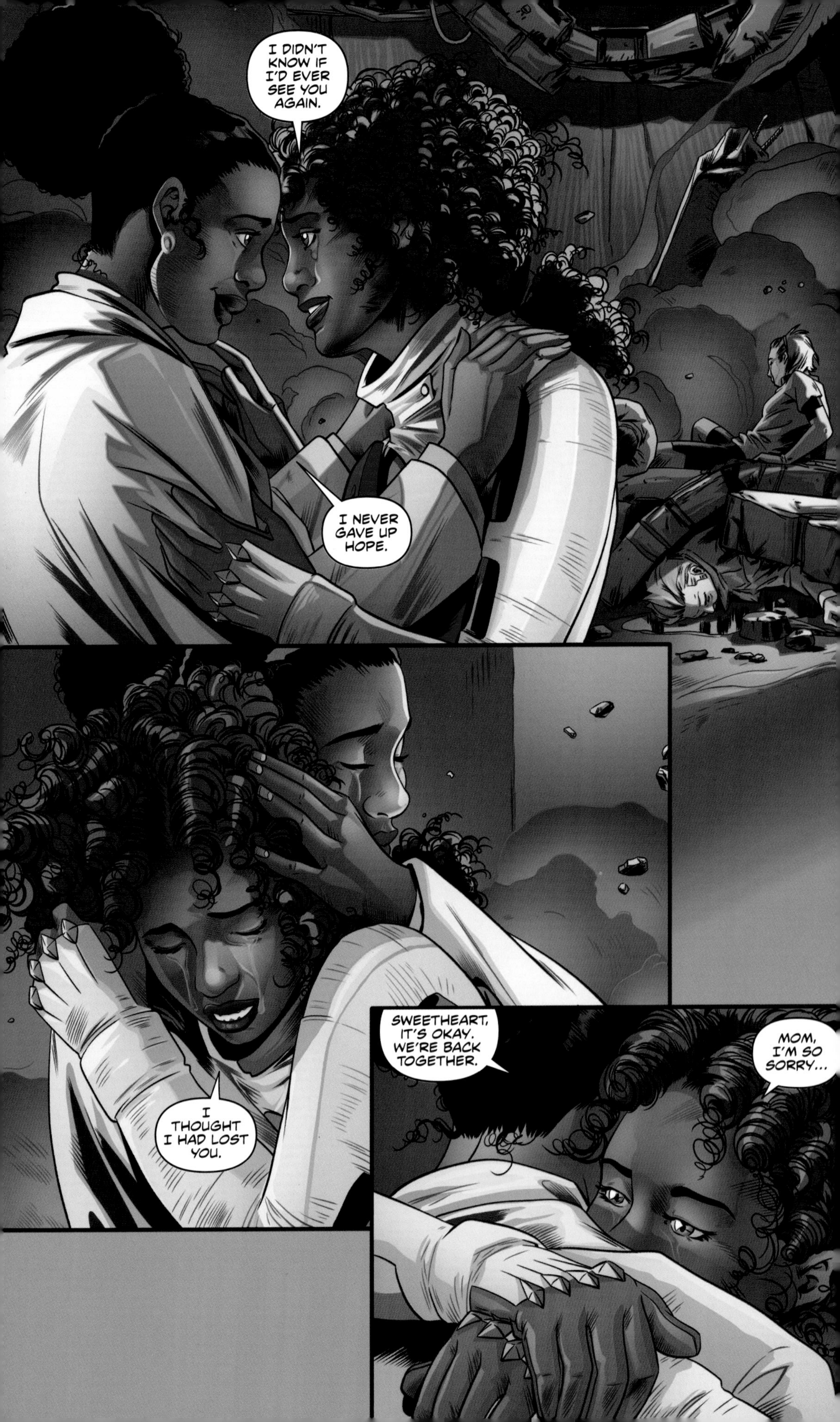
I DIDN'T KNOW IF I'D EVER SEE YOU AGAIN.
I NEVER GAVE UP HOPE.
I THOUGHT I HAD LOST YOU.
SWEETHEART, IT'S OKAY. WE'RE BACK TOGETHER.
MOM, I'M SO SORRY...

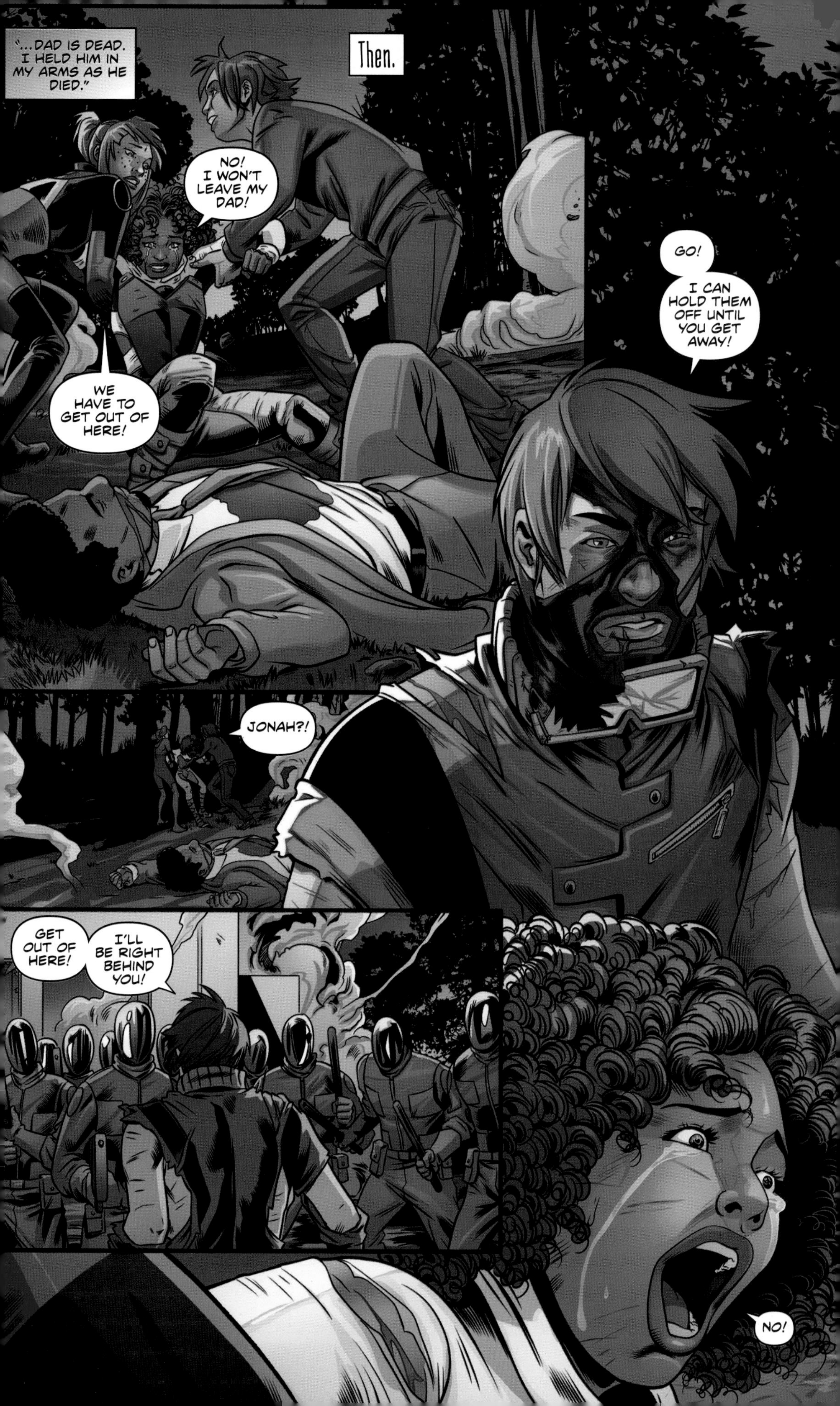
"...DAD IS DEAD. I HELD HIM IN MY ARMS AS HE DIED."
Then.
NO! I WON'T LEAVE MY DAD!
WE HAVE TO GET OUT OF HERE!
GO!
I CAN HOLD THEM OFF UNTIL YOU GET AWAY!
JONAH?!
GET OUT OF HERE!
I'LL BE RIGHT BEHIND YOU!
NO!

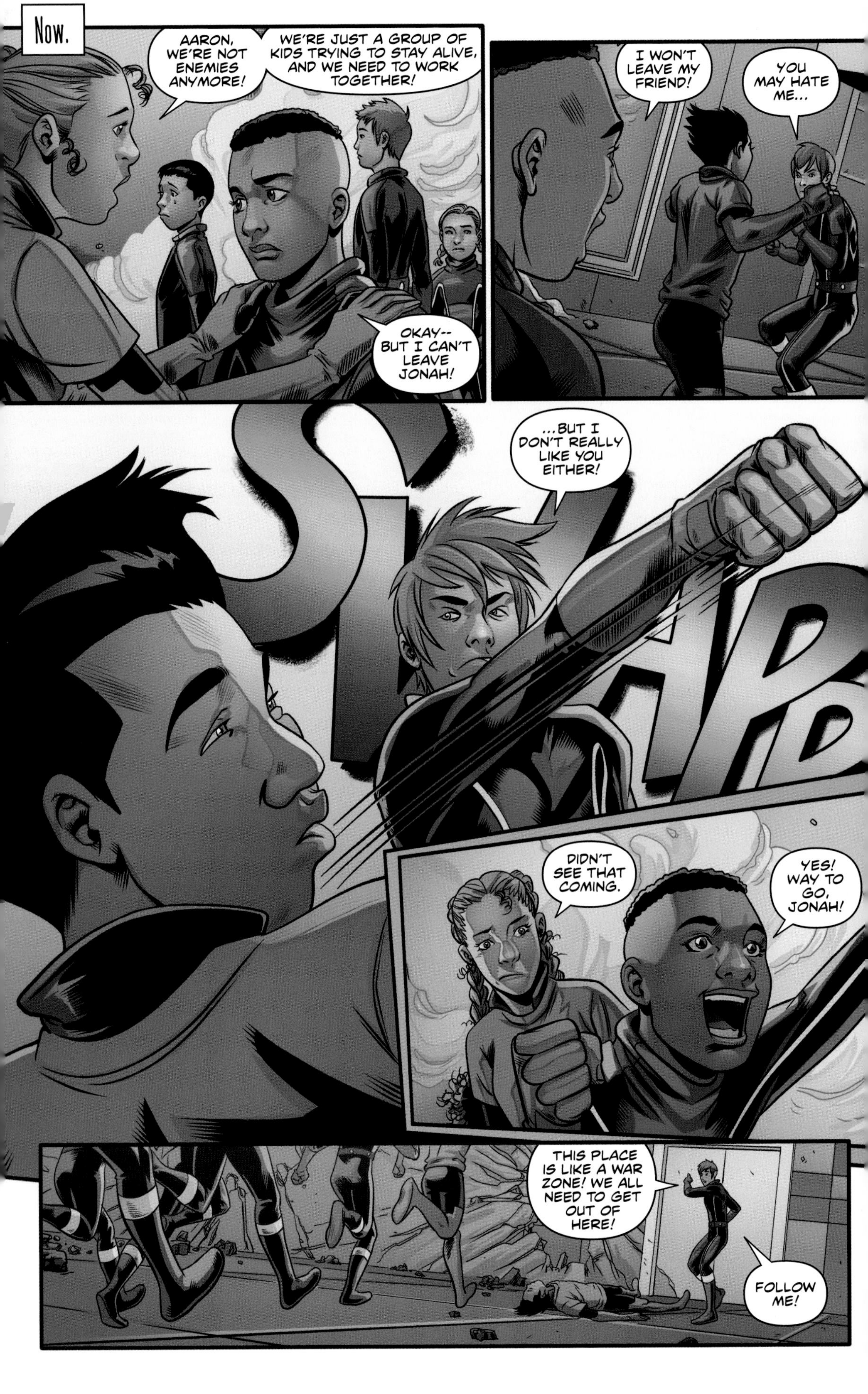

Now.
AARON, WE'RE NOT ENEMIES ANYMORE!
WE'RE JUST A GROUP OF KIDS TRYING TO STAY ALIVE, AND WE NEED TO WORK TOGETHER!
OKAY-- BUT I CAN'T LEAVE JONAH!
I WON'T LEAVE MY FRIEND!
YOU MAY HATE ME...
...BUT I DON'T REALLY LIKE YOU EITHER!
DIDN'T SEE THAT COMING.
YES! WAY TO GO, JONAH!
THIS PLACE IS LIKE A WAR ZONE! WE ALL NEED TO GET OUT OF HERE!
FOLLOW ME!

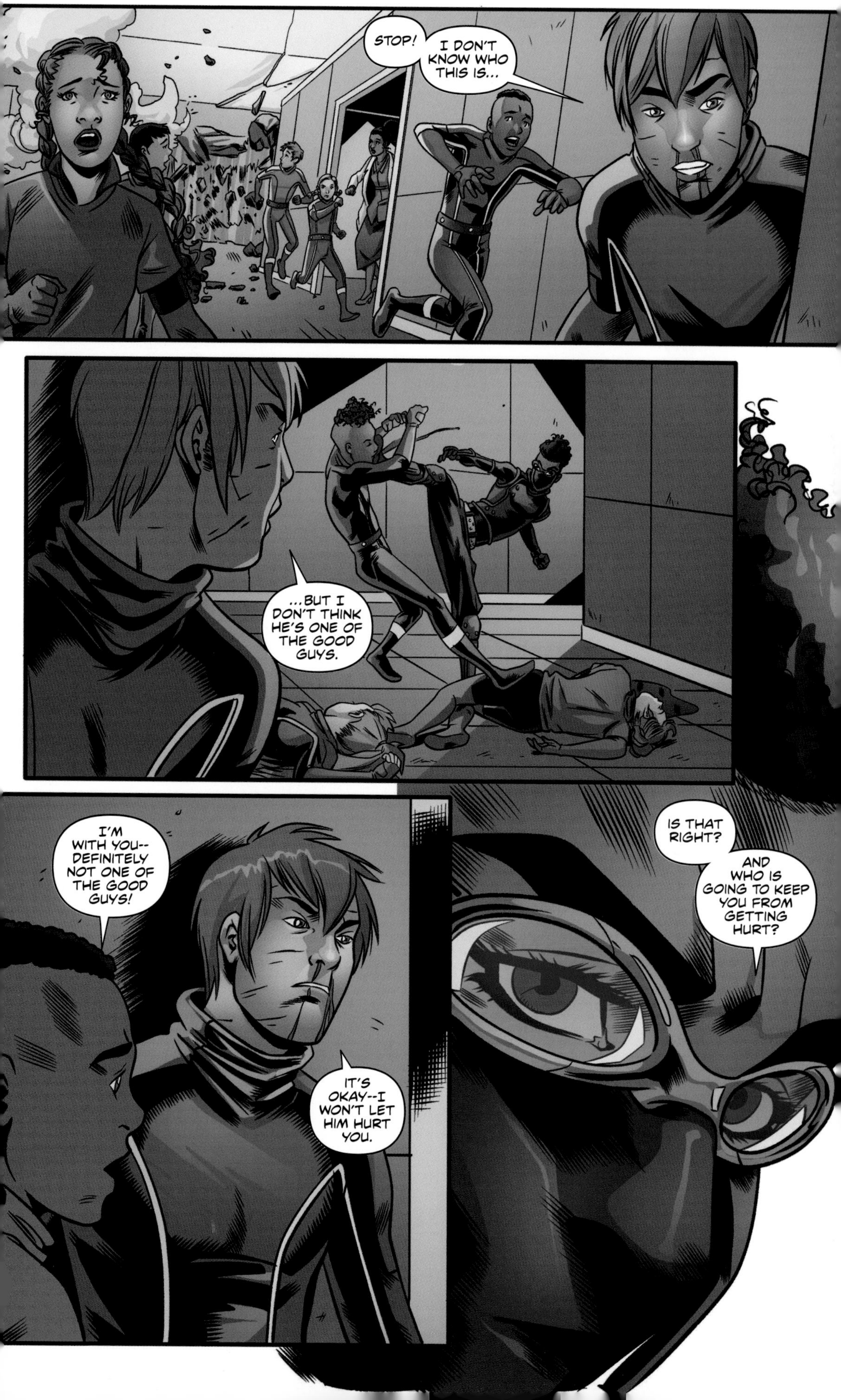
STOP!
I DON'T KNOW WHO THIS IS...
...BUT I DON'T THINK HE'S ONE OF THE GOOD GUYS.
I'M WITH YOU--DEFINITELY NOT ONE OF THE GOOD GUYS!
IT'S OKAY--I WON'T LET HIM HURT YOU.
IS THAT RIGHT?
AND WHO IS GOING TO KEEP YOU FROM GETTING HURT?

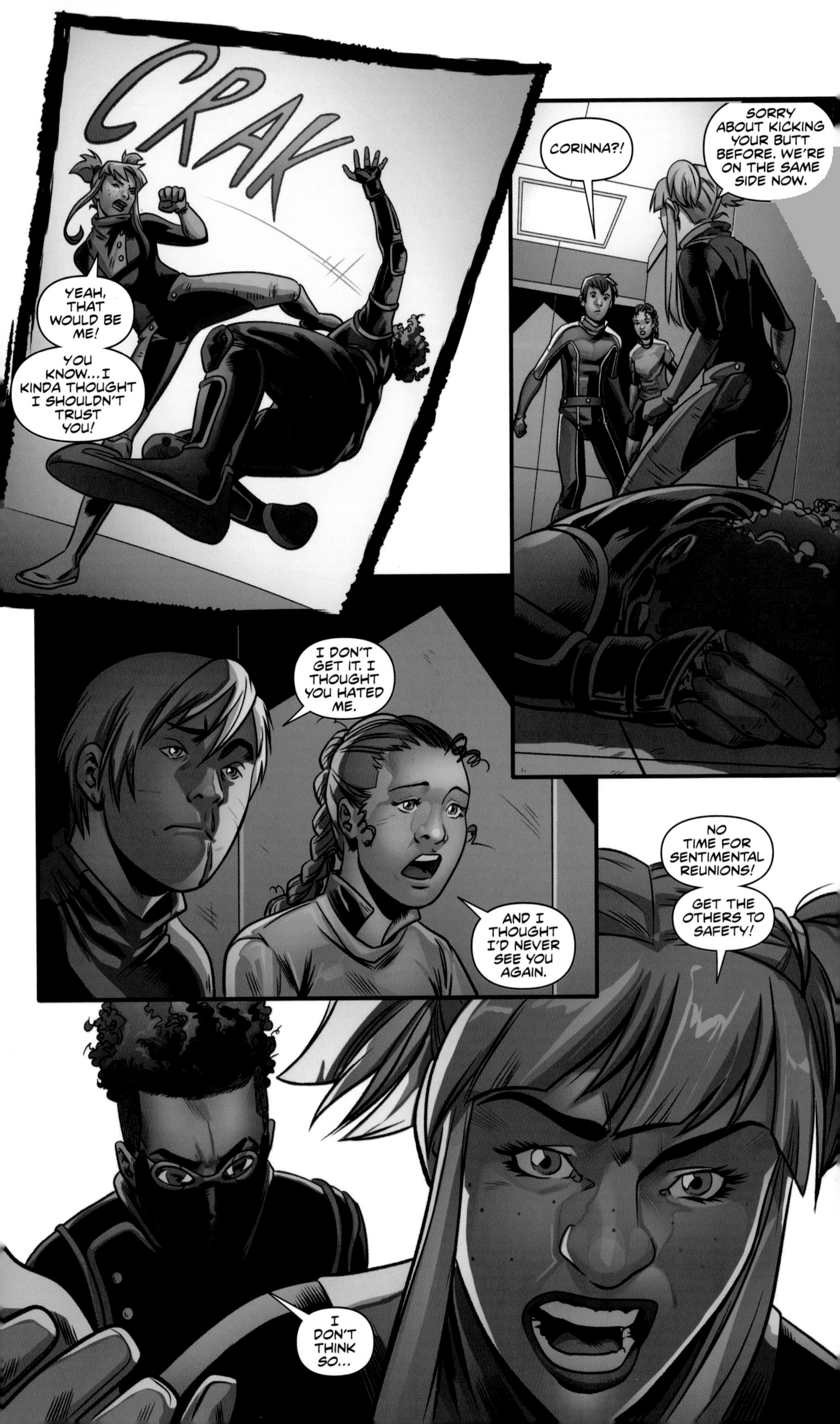
CRAK
YEAH, THAT WOULD BE ME!
YOU KNOW... I KINDA THOUGHT I SHOULDN'T TRUST YOU!
CORINNA?!
SORRY ABOUT KICKING YOUR BUTT BEFORE. WE'RE ON THE SAME SIDE NOW.
I DON'T GET IT. I THOUGHT YOU HATED ME.
AND I THOUGHT I'D NEVER SEE YOU AGAIN.
NO TIME FOR SENTIMENTAL REUNIONS!
GET THE OTHERS TO SAFETY!
I DON'T THINK SO...

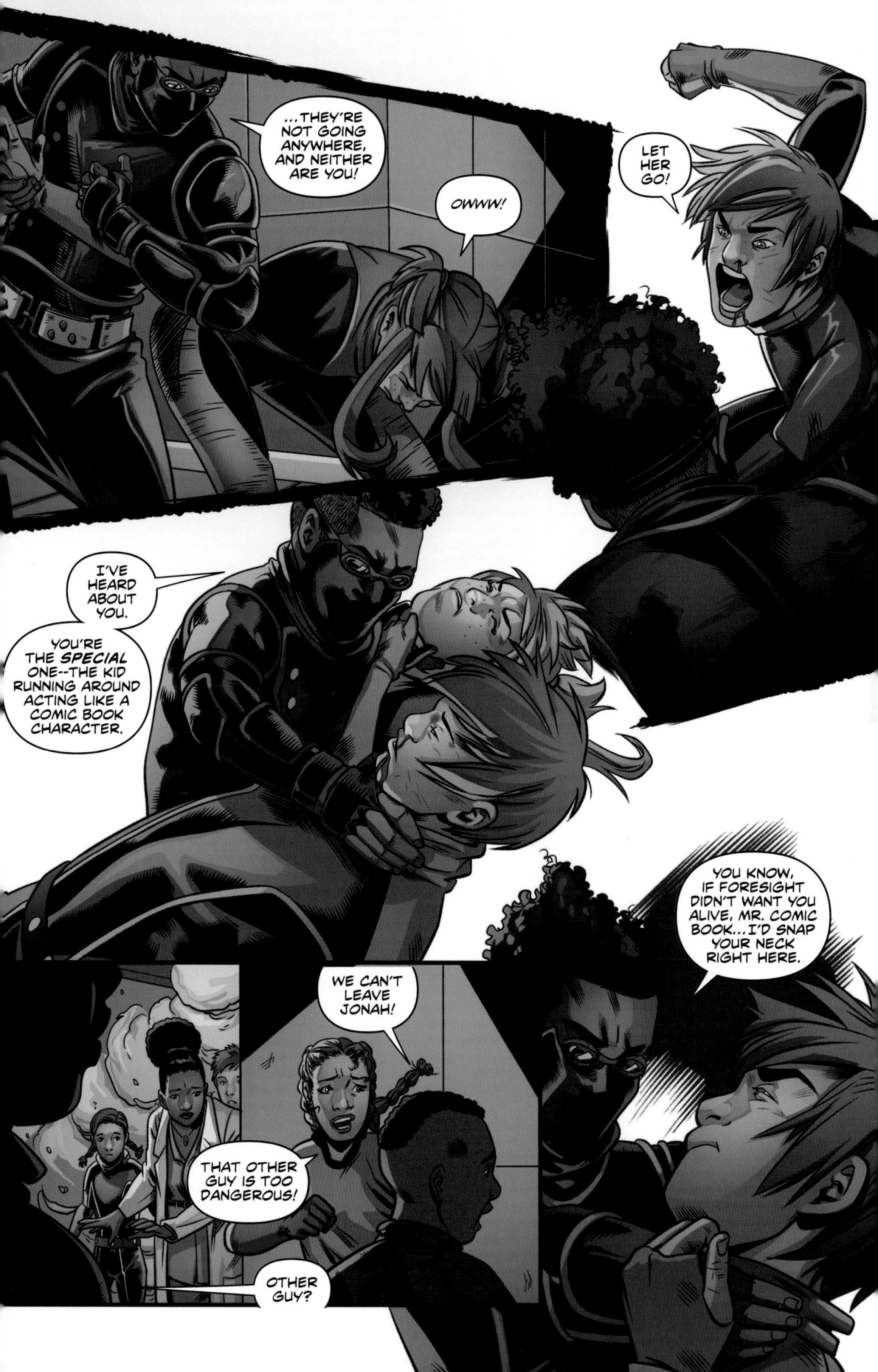
...THEY'RE NOT GOING ANYWHERE, AND NEITHER ARE YOU!
OWWW!
LET HER GO!
I'VE HEARD ABOUT YOU.
YOU'RE THE SPECIAL ONE--THE KID RUNNING AROUND ACTING LIKE A COMIC BOOK CHARACTER.
YOU KNOW, IF FORESIGHT DIDN'T WANT YOU ALIVE, MR. COMIC BOOK...I'D SNAP YOUR NECK RIGHT HERE.
WE CAN'T LEAVE JONAH!
THAT OTHER GUY IS TOO DANGEROUS!
OTHER GUY?

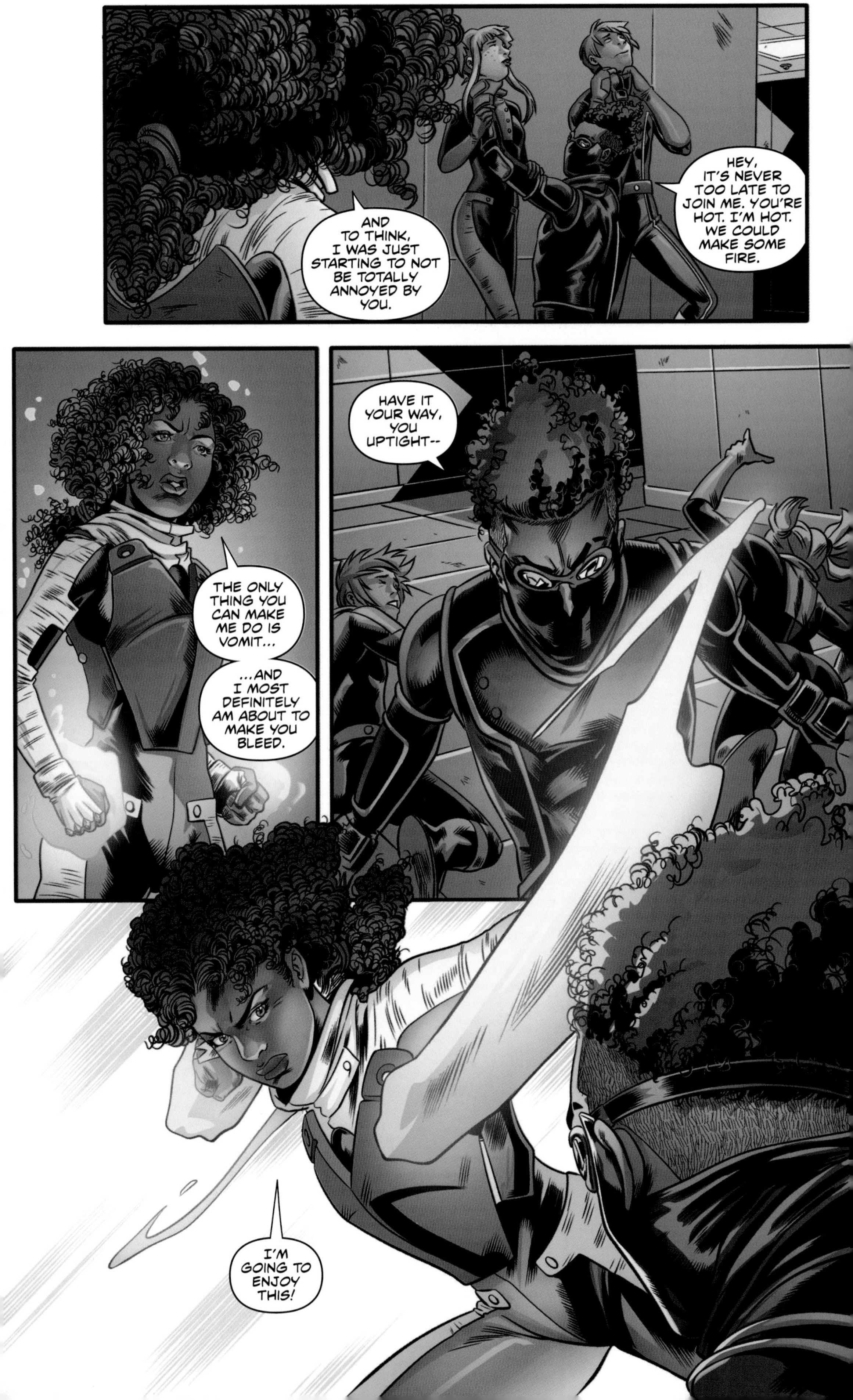
AND TO THINK, I WAS JUST STARTING TO NOT BE TOTALLY ANNOYED BY YOU.
HEY, IT'S NEVER TOO LATE TO JOIN ME. YOU'RE HOT. I'M HOT. WE COULD MAKE SOME FIRE.
THE ONLY THING YOU CAN MAKE ME DO IS VOMIT...
...AND I MOST DEFINITELY AM ABOUT TO MAKE YOU BLEED.
HAVE IT YOUR WAY, YOU UPTIGHT--
I'M GOING TO ENJOY THIS!

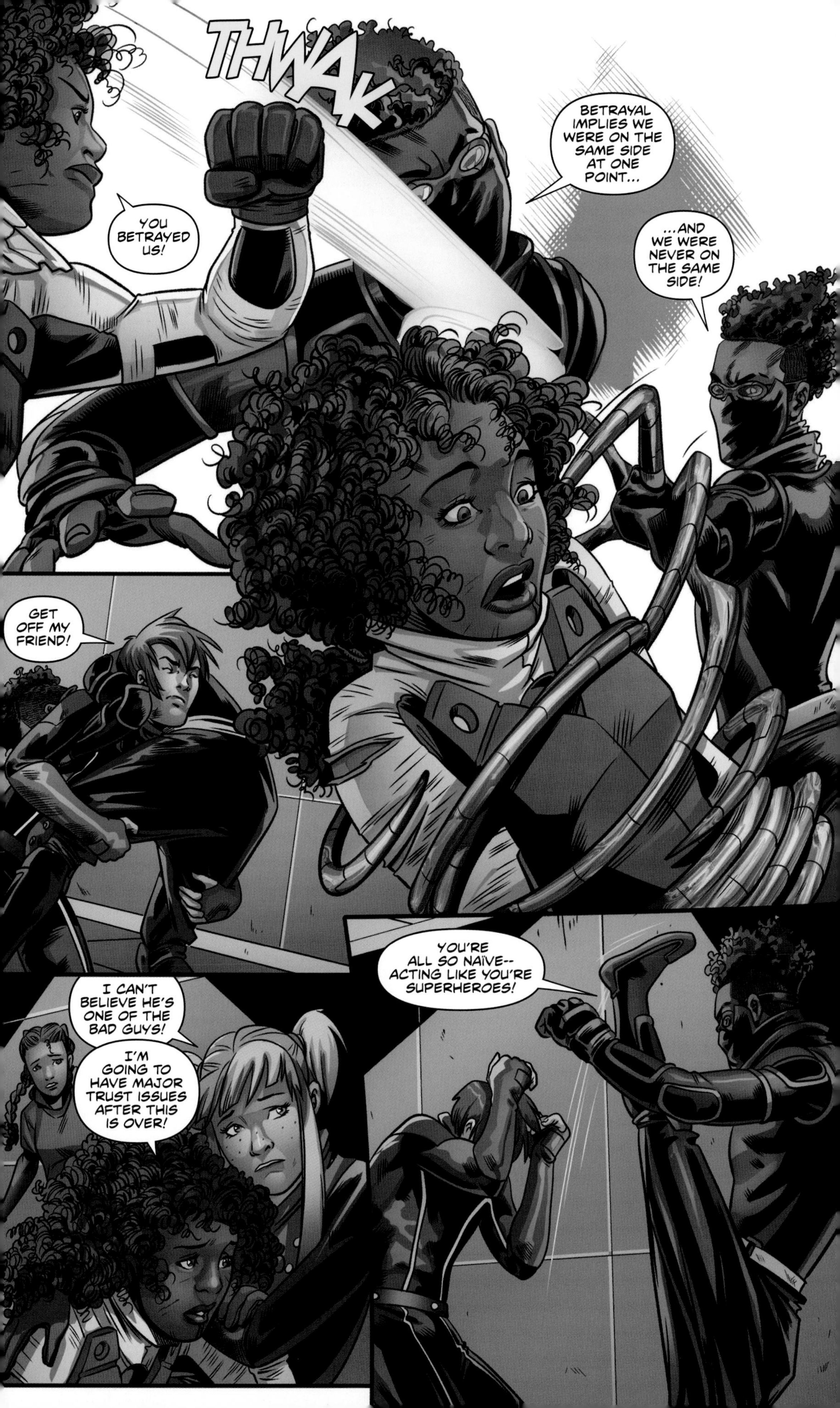
THWAK
YOU BETRAYED US!
BETRAYAL IMPLIES WE WERE ON THE SAME SIDE AT ONE POINT...
...AND WE WERE NEVER ON THE SAME SIDE!
GET OFF MY FRIEND!
YOU'RE ALL SO NAÏVE-- ACTING LIKE YOU'RE SUPERHEROES!
I CAN'T BELIEVE HE'S ONE OF THE BAD GUYS!
I'M GOING TO HAVE MAJOR TRUST ISSUES AFTER THIS IS OVER!

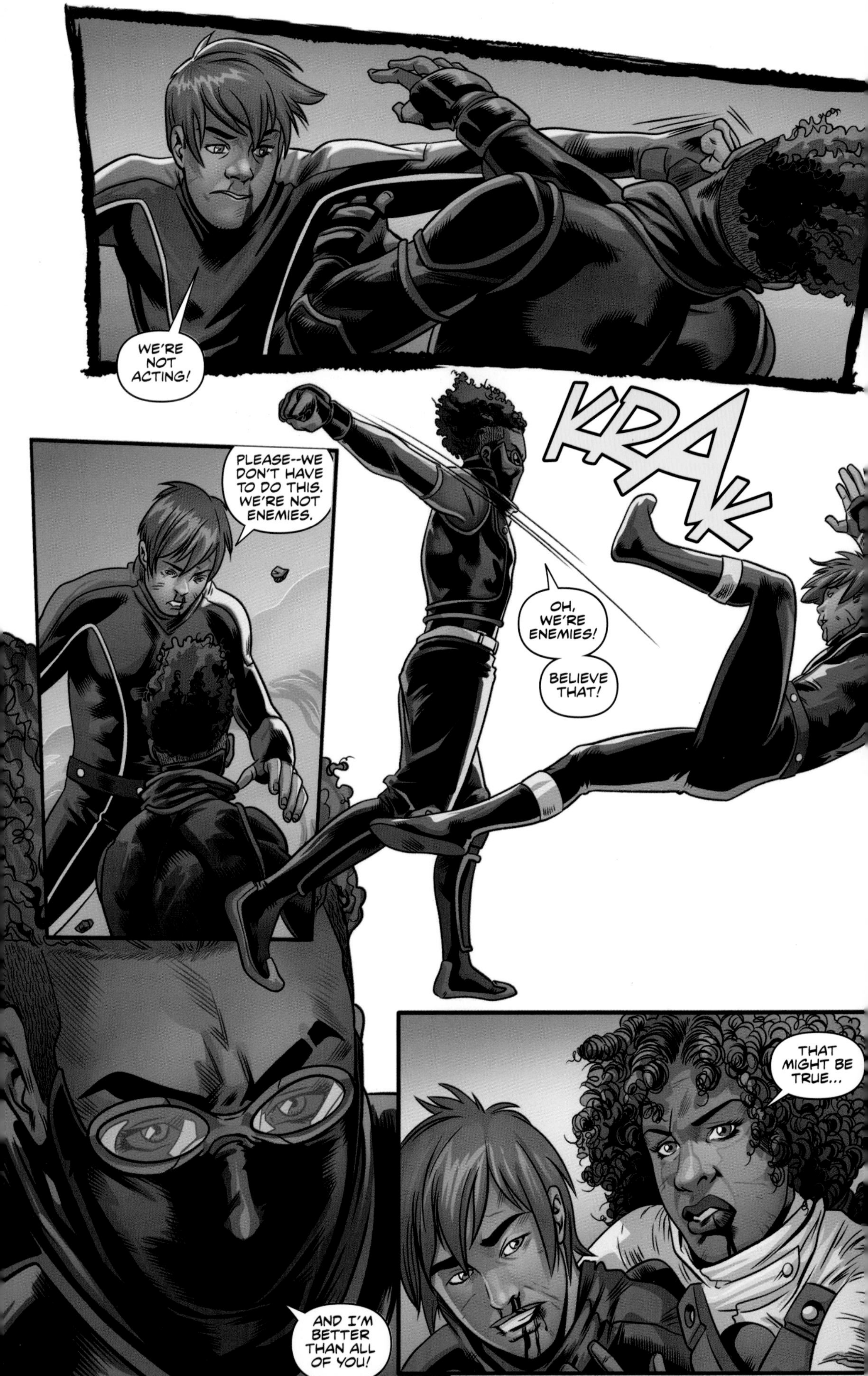
WE'RE NOT ACTING!
KRAK
PLEASE--WE DON'T HAVE TO DO THIS. WE'RE NOT ENEMIES.
OH, WE'RE ENEMIES!
BELIEVE THAT!
THAT MIGHT BE TRUE...
AND I'M BETTER THAN ALL OF YOU!

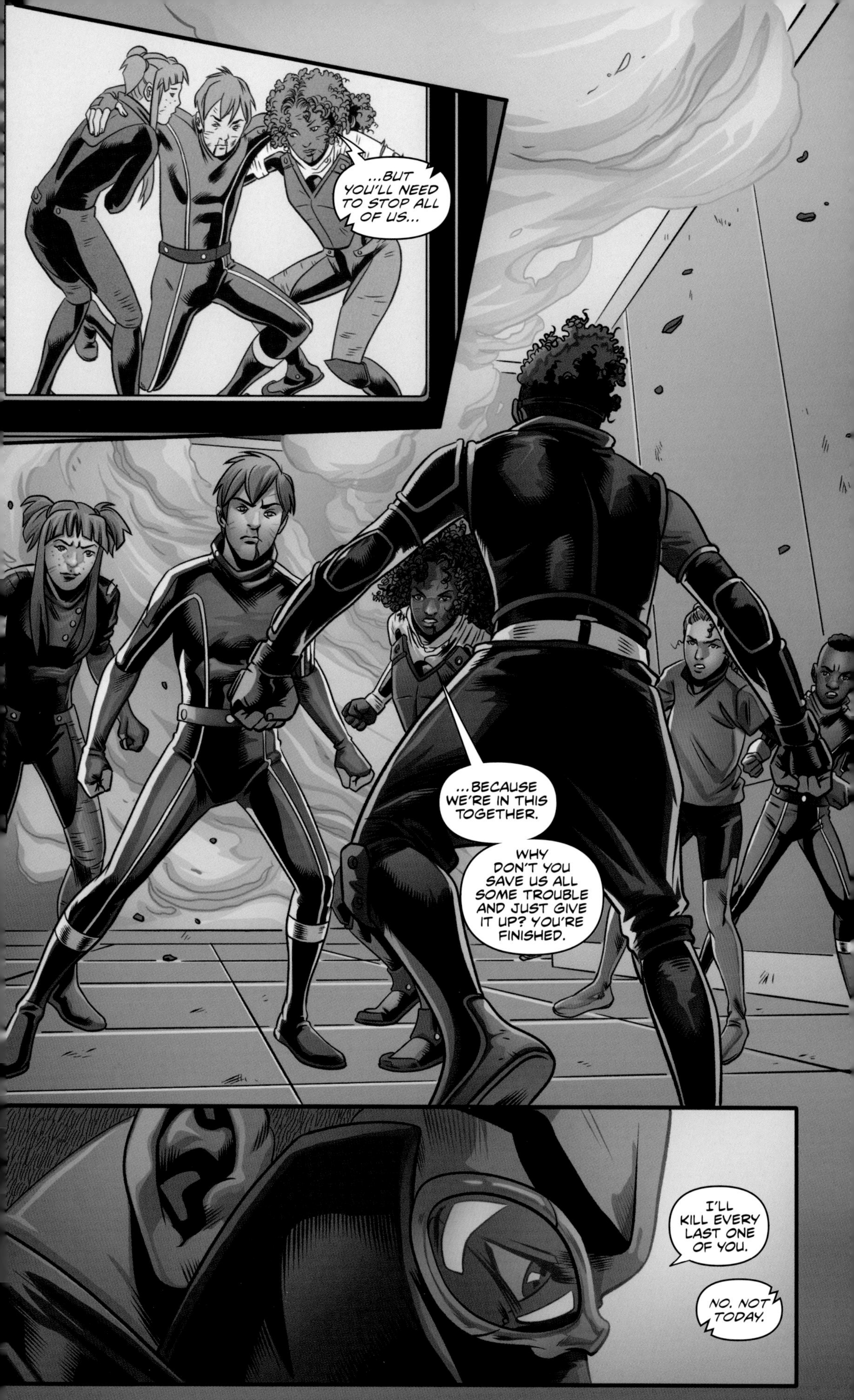
...BUT YOU'LL NEED TO STOP ALL OF US...
...BECAUSE WE'RE IN THIS TOGETHER.
WHY DON'T YOU SAVE US ALL SOME TROUBLE AND JUST GIVE IT UP? YOU'RE FINISHED.
I'LL KILL EVERY LAST ONE OF YOU.
NO. NOT TODAY.

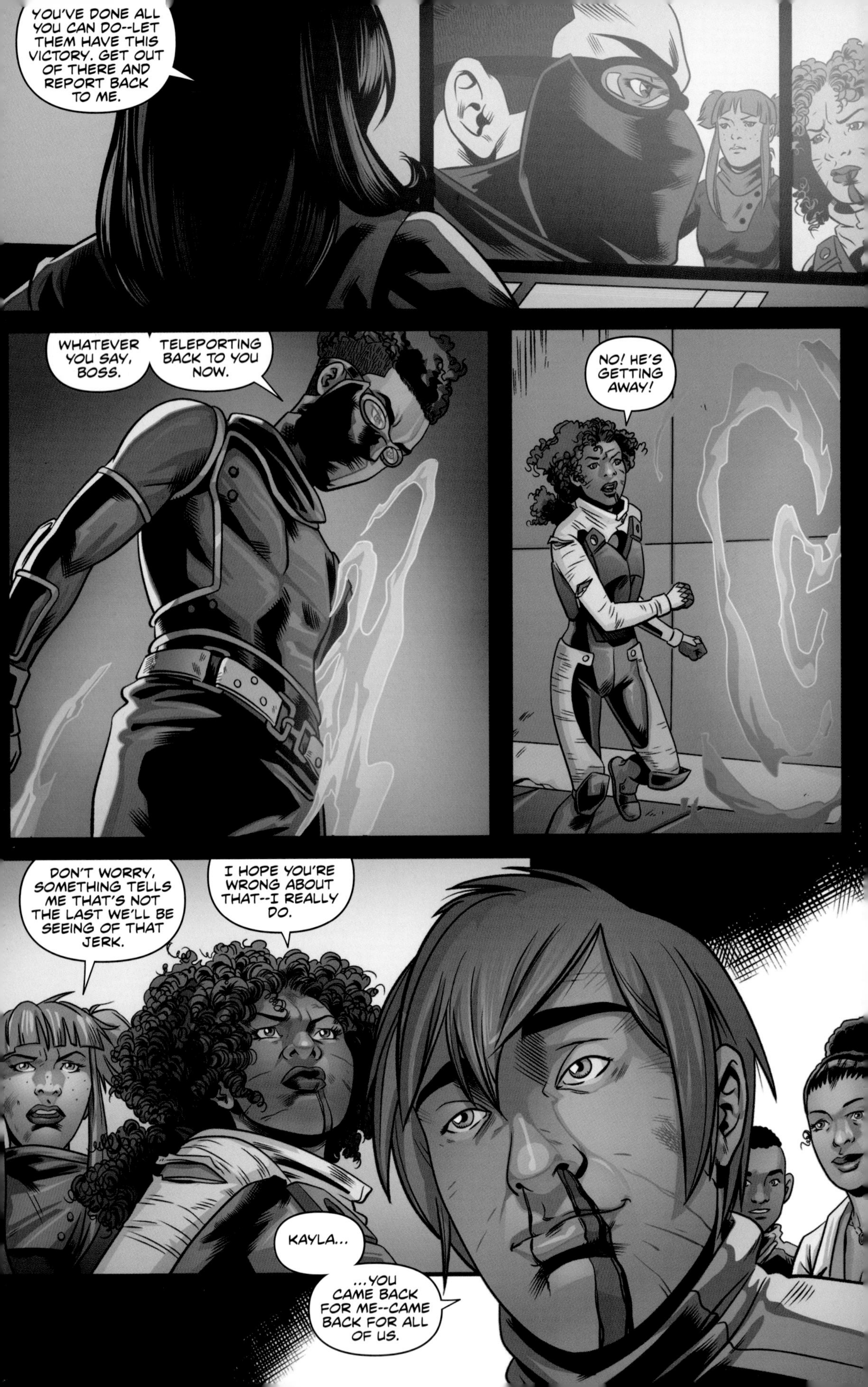
YOU'VE DONE ALL YOU CAN DO--LET THEM HAVE THIS VICTORY. GET OUT OF THERE AND REPORT BACK TO ME.
WHATEVER YOU SAY, BOSS.
TELEPORTING BACK TO YOU NOW.
NO! HE'S GETTING AWAY!
DON'T WORRY, SOMETHING TELLS ME THAT'S NOT THE LAST WE'LL BE SEEING OF THAT JERK.
I HOPE YOU'RE WRONG ABOUT THAT--I REALLY DO.
KAYLA...
...YOU CAME BACK FOR ME--CAME BACK FOR ALL OF US.

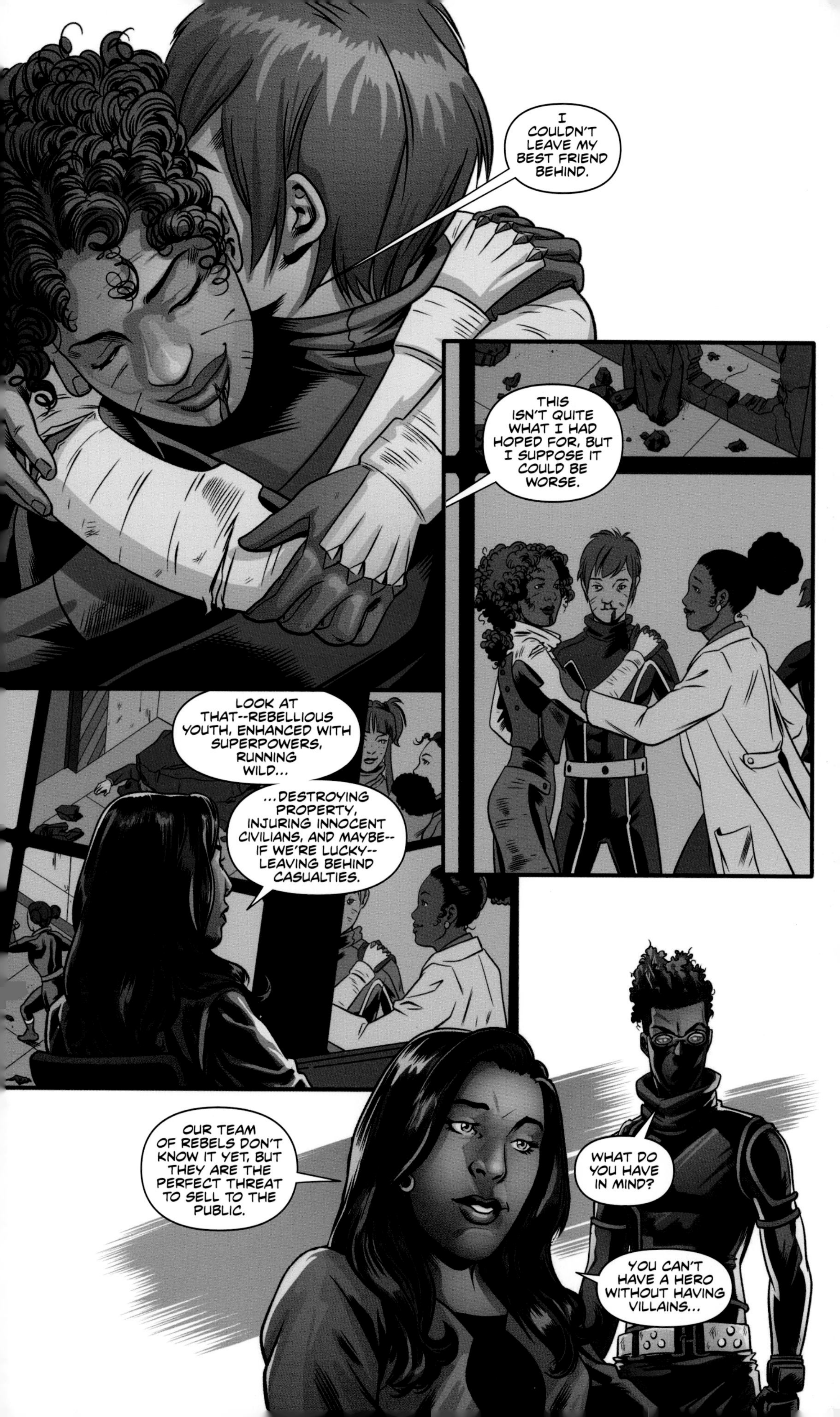
I COULDN'T LEAVE MY BEST FRIEND BEHIND.
THIS ISN'T QUITE WHAT I HAD HOPED FOR, BUT I SUPPOSE IT COULD BE WORSE.
LOOK AT THAT--REBELLIOUS YOUTH, ENHANCED WITH SUPERPOWERS, RUNNING WILD...
...DESTROYING PROPERTY, INJURING INNOCENT CIVILIANS, AND MAYBE--IF WE'RE LUCKY--LEAVING BEHIND CASUALTIES.
OUR TEAM OF REBELS DON'T KNOW IT YET, BUT THEY ARE THE PERFECT THREAT TO SELL TO THE PUBLIC.
WHAT DO YOU HAVE IN MIND?
YOU CAN'T HAVE A HERO WITHOUT HAVING VILLAINS...

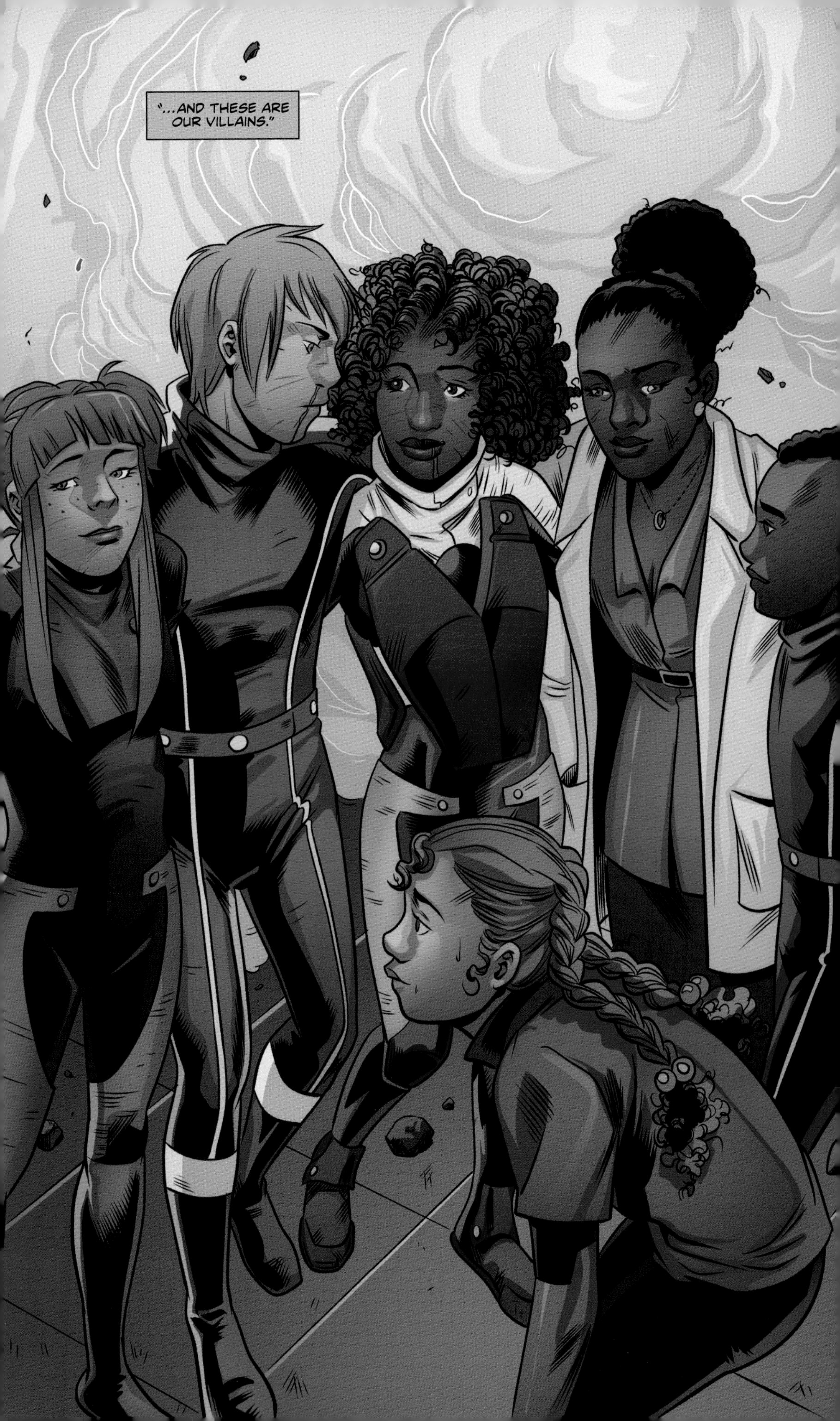
"...AND THESE ARE OUR VILLAINS."

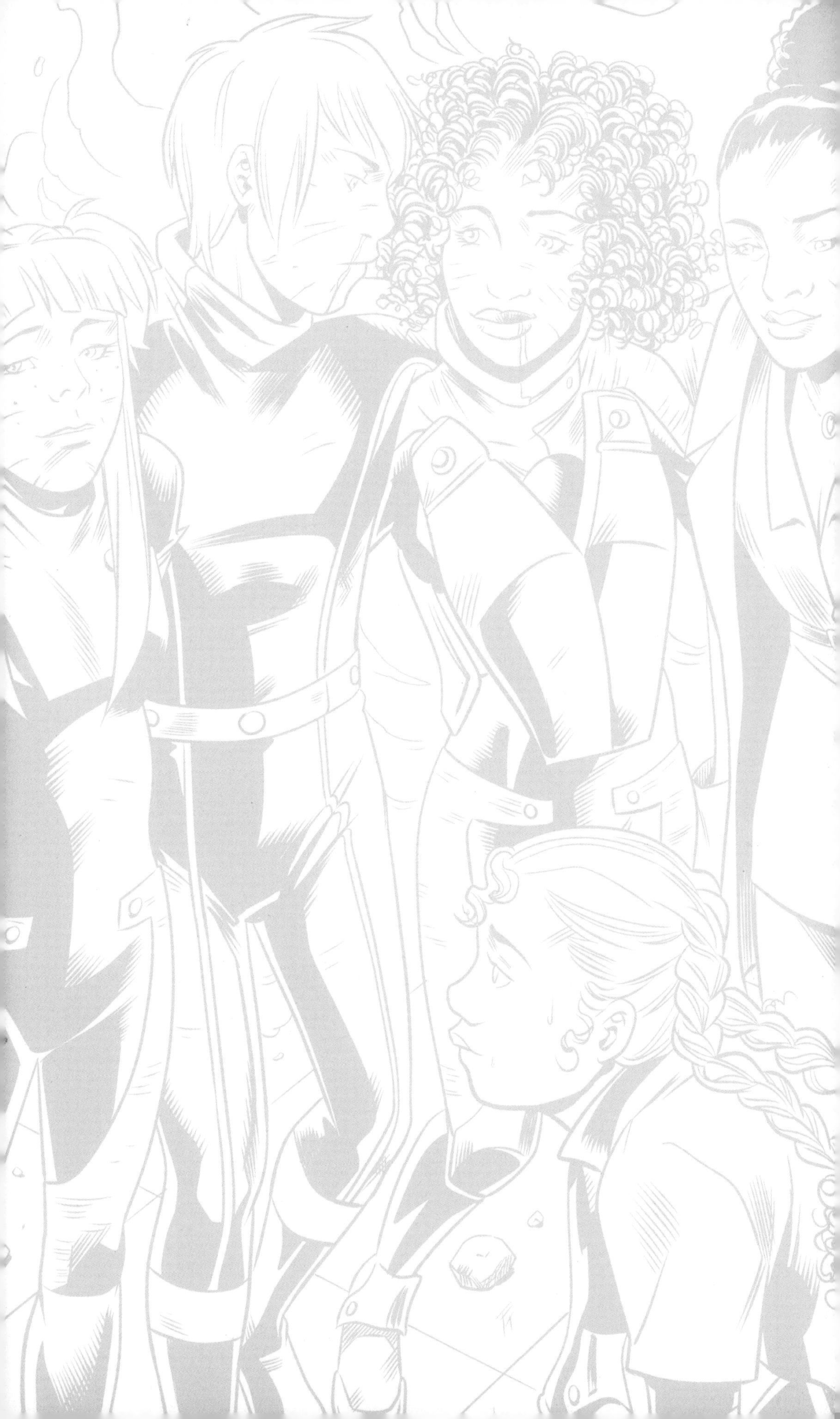

COVER GALLERY

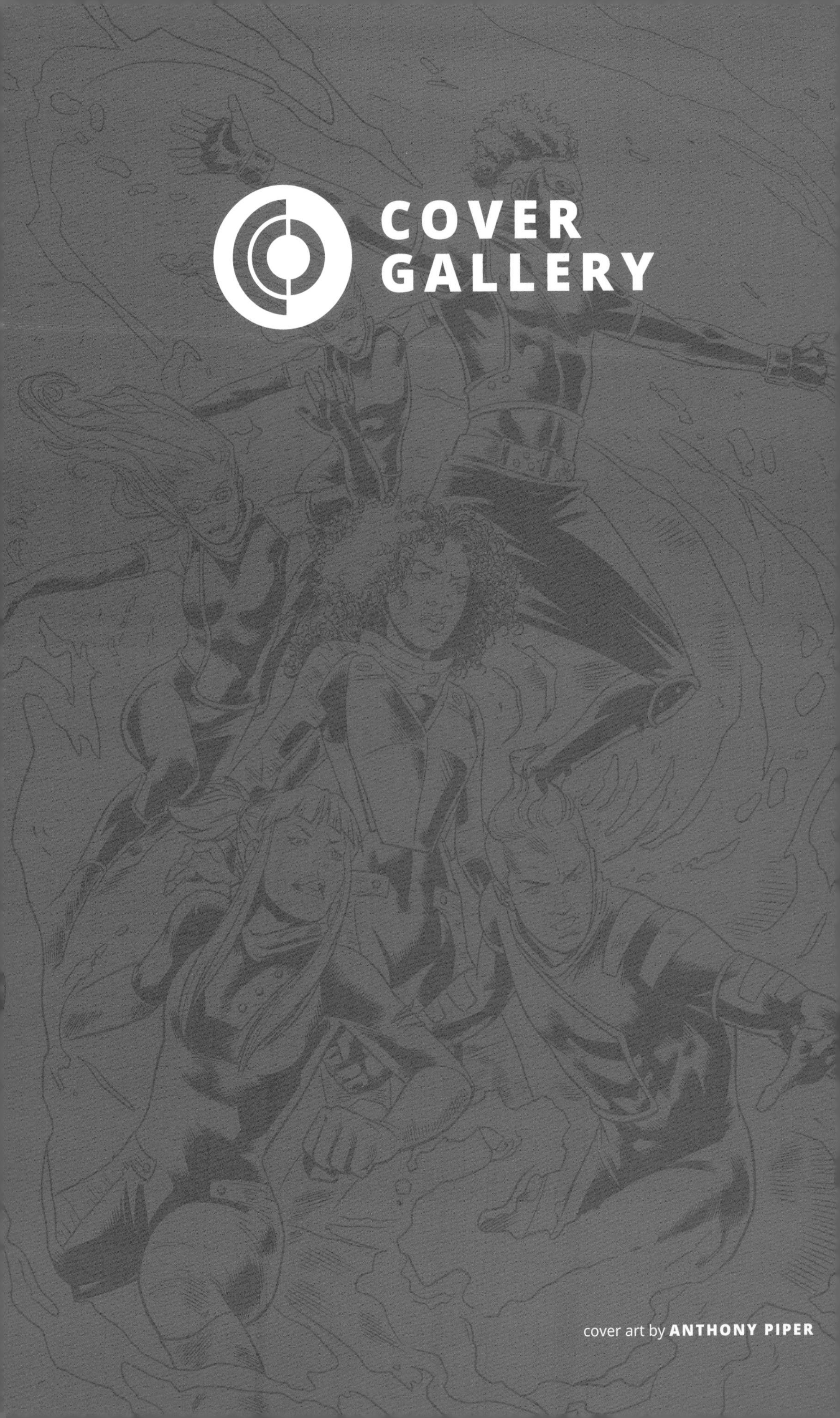

cover art by **ANTHONY PIPER**

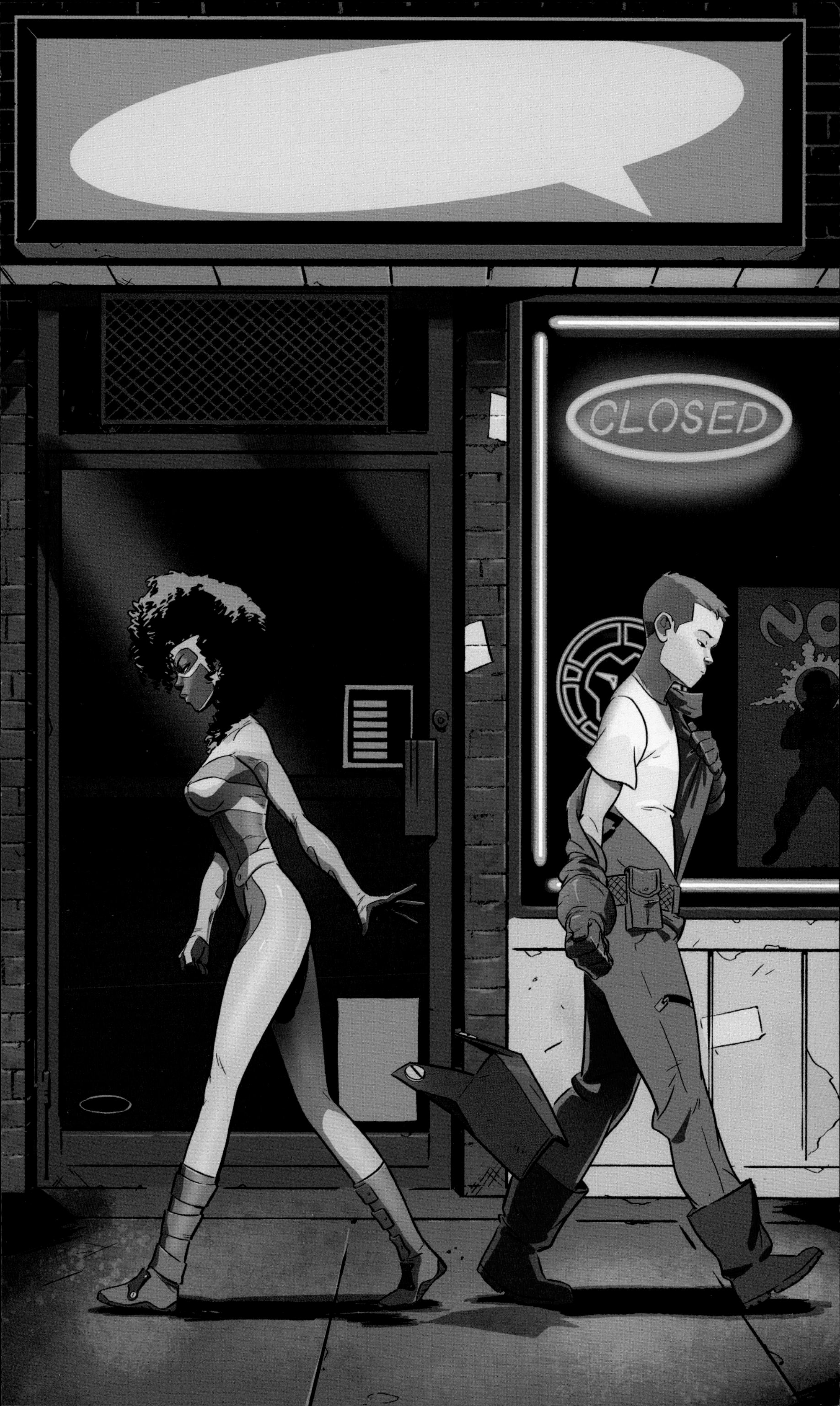
CLOSED

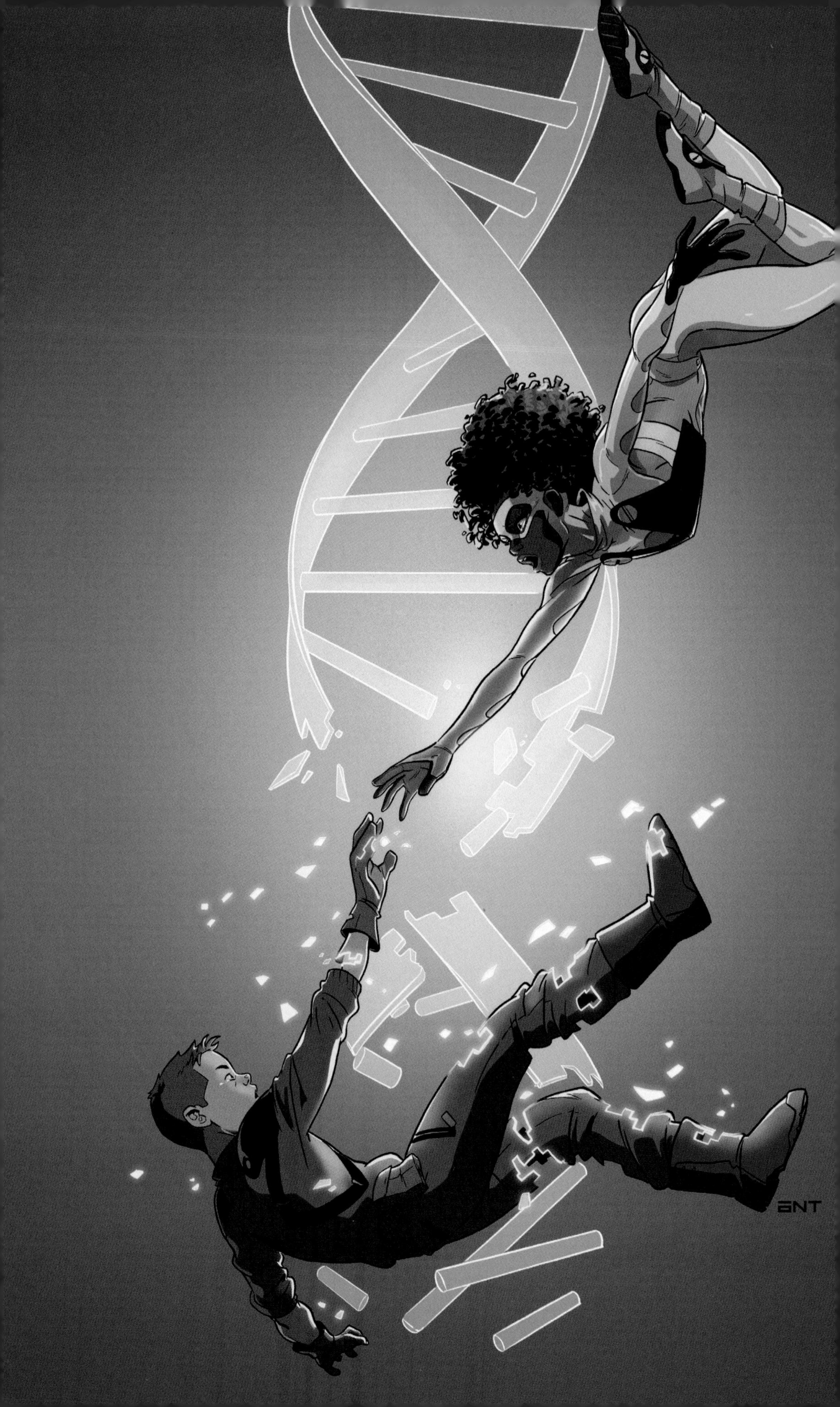
BNT

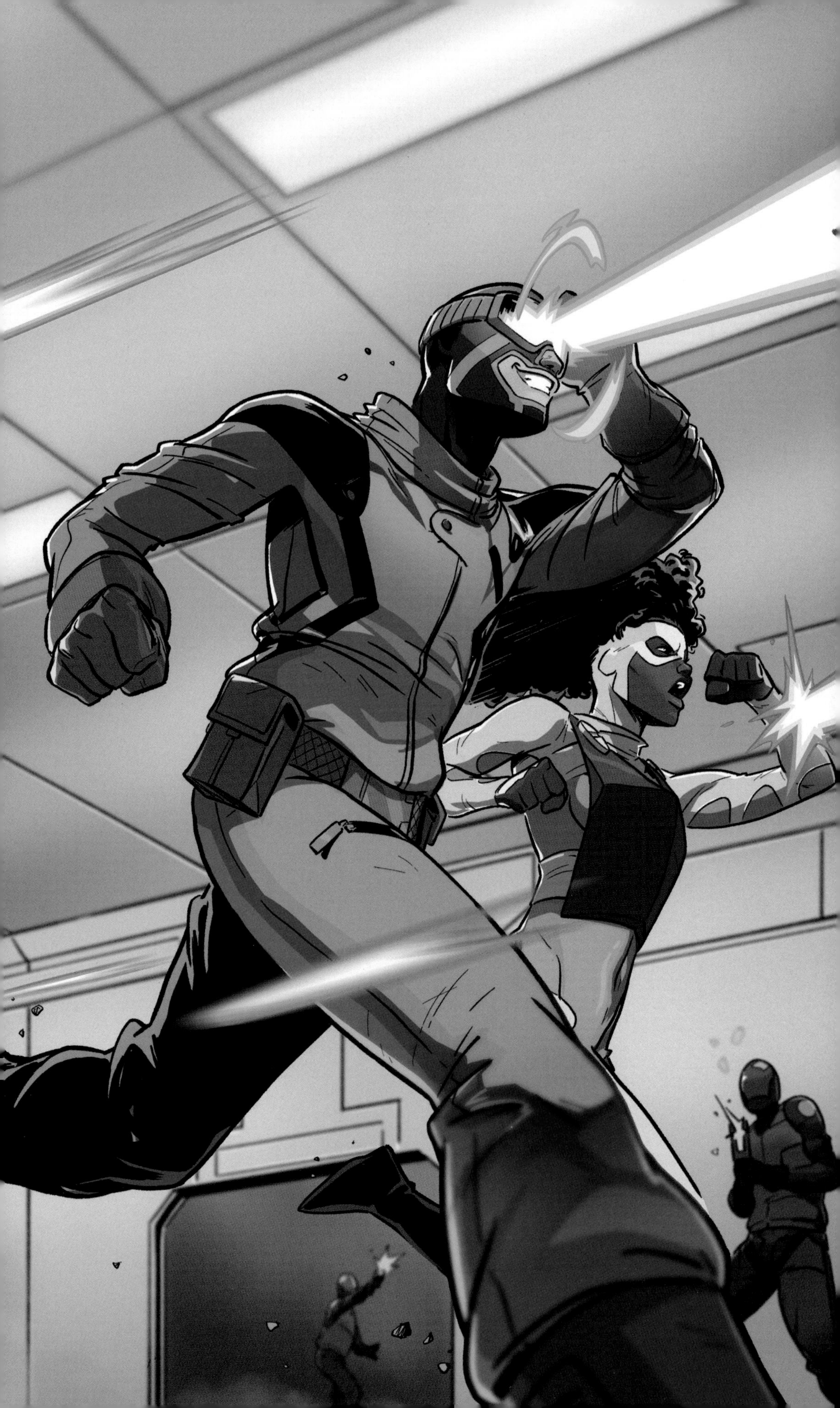

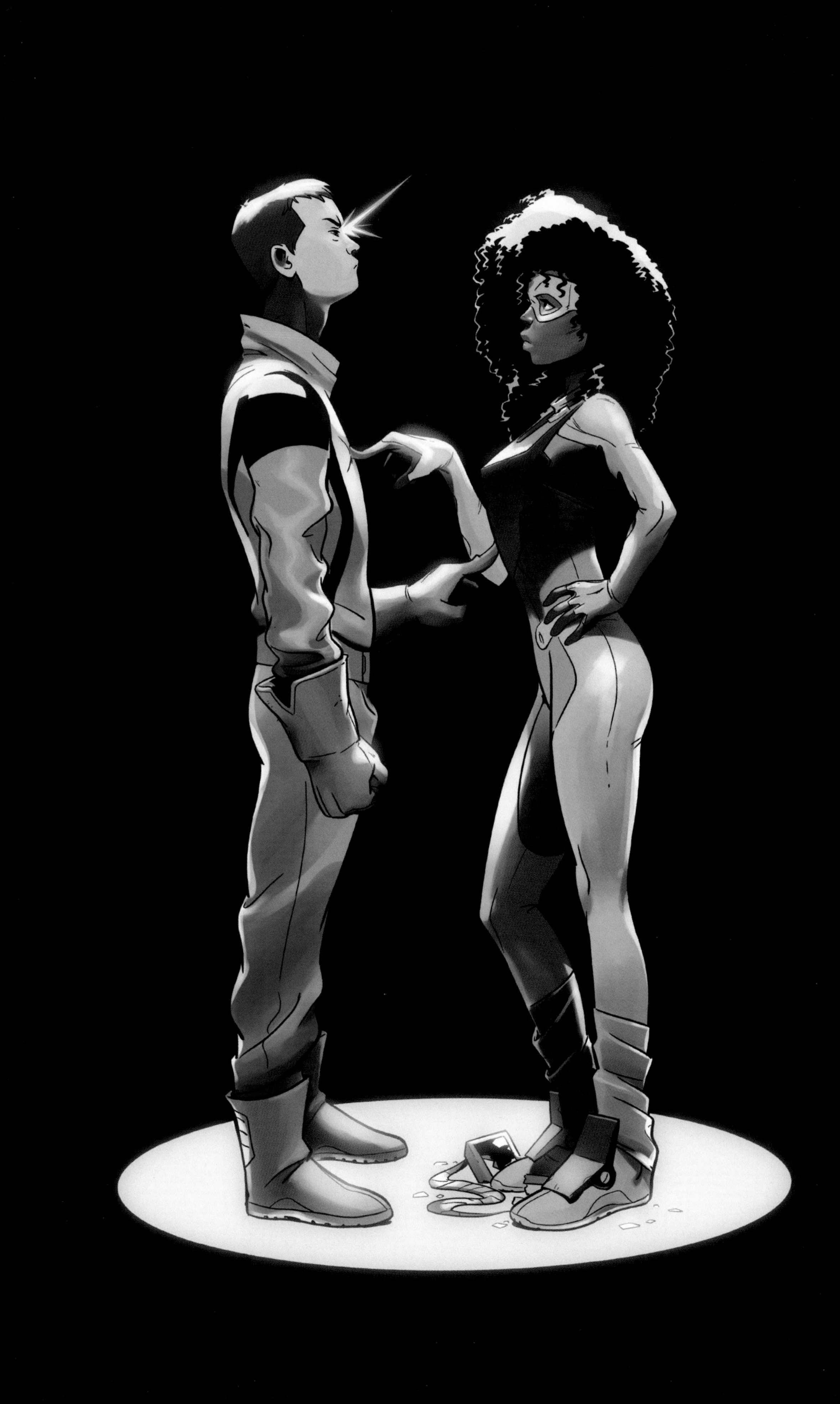

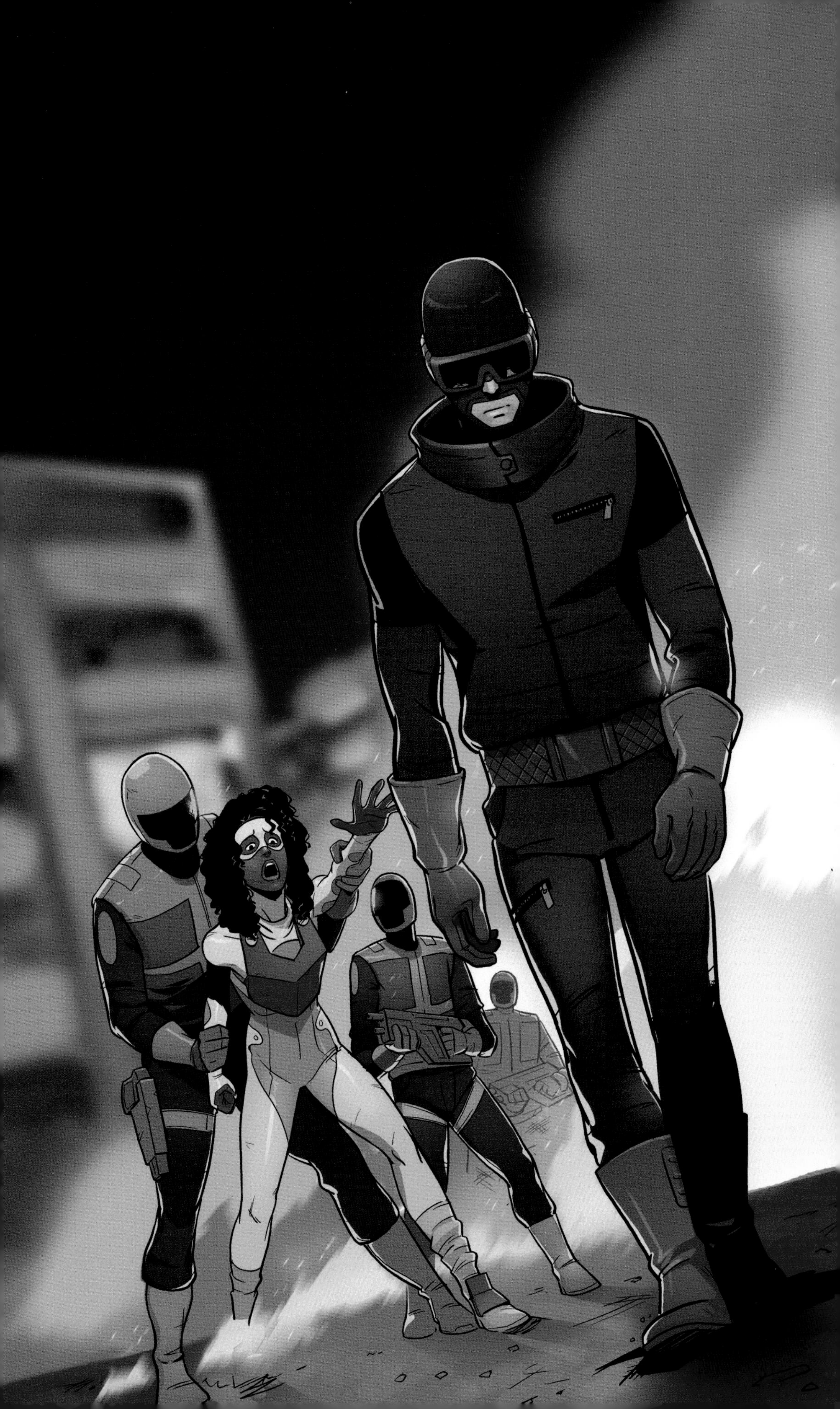

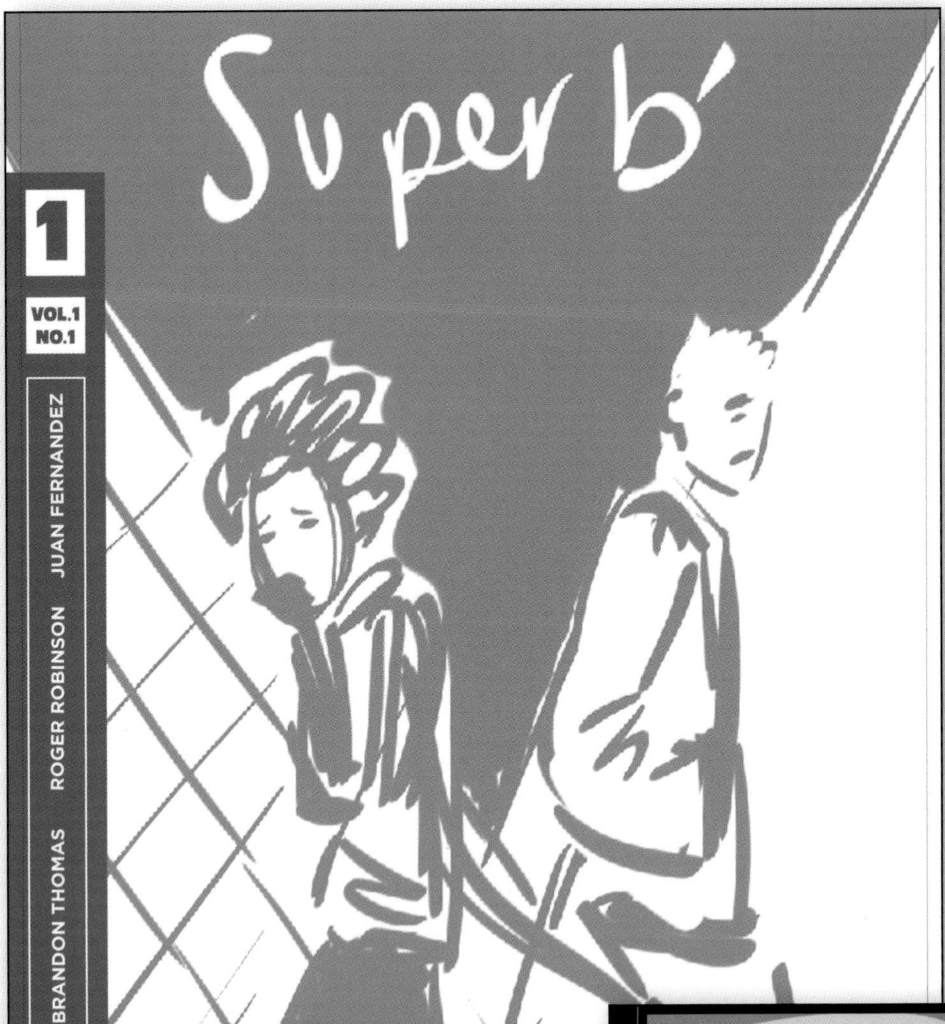
Superb
1
VOL.1
NO.1
BRANDON THOMAS
ROGER ROBINSON
JUAN FERNANDEZ
CATALYST PRIME

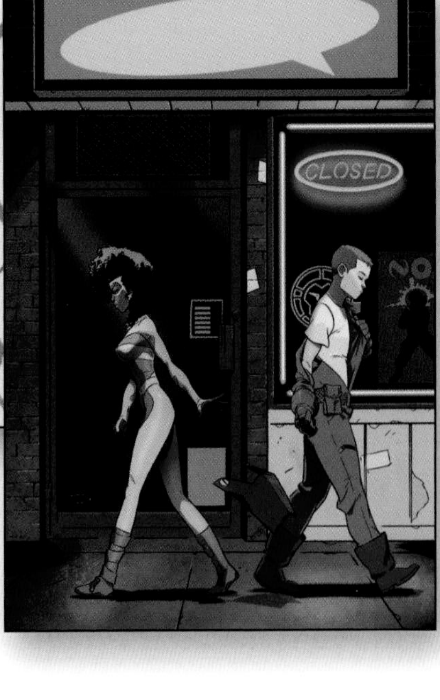
CLOSED

SUPERB COVER SKETCH FOR ISSUE #10

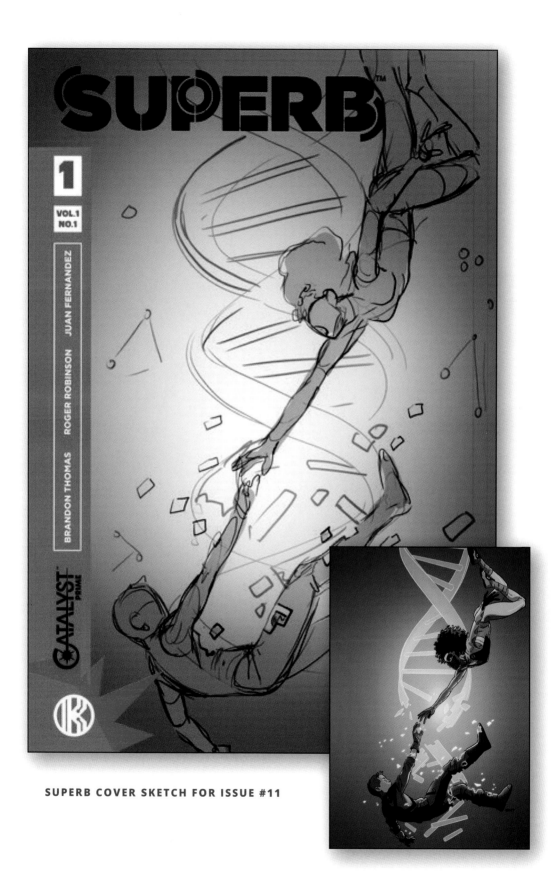

SUPERB COVER SKETCH FOR ISSUE #11

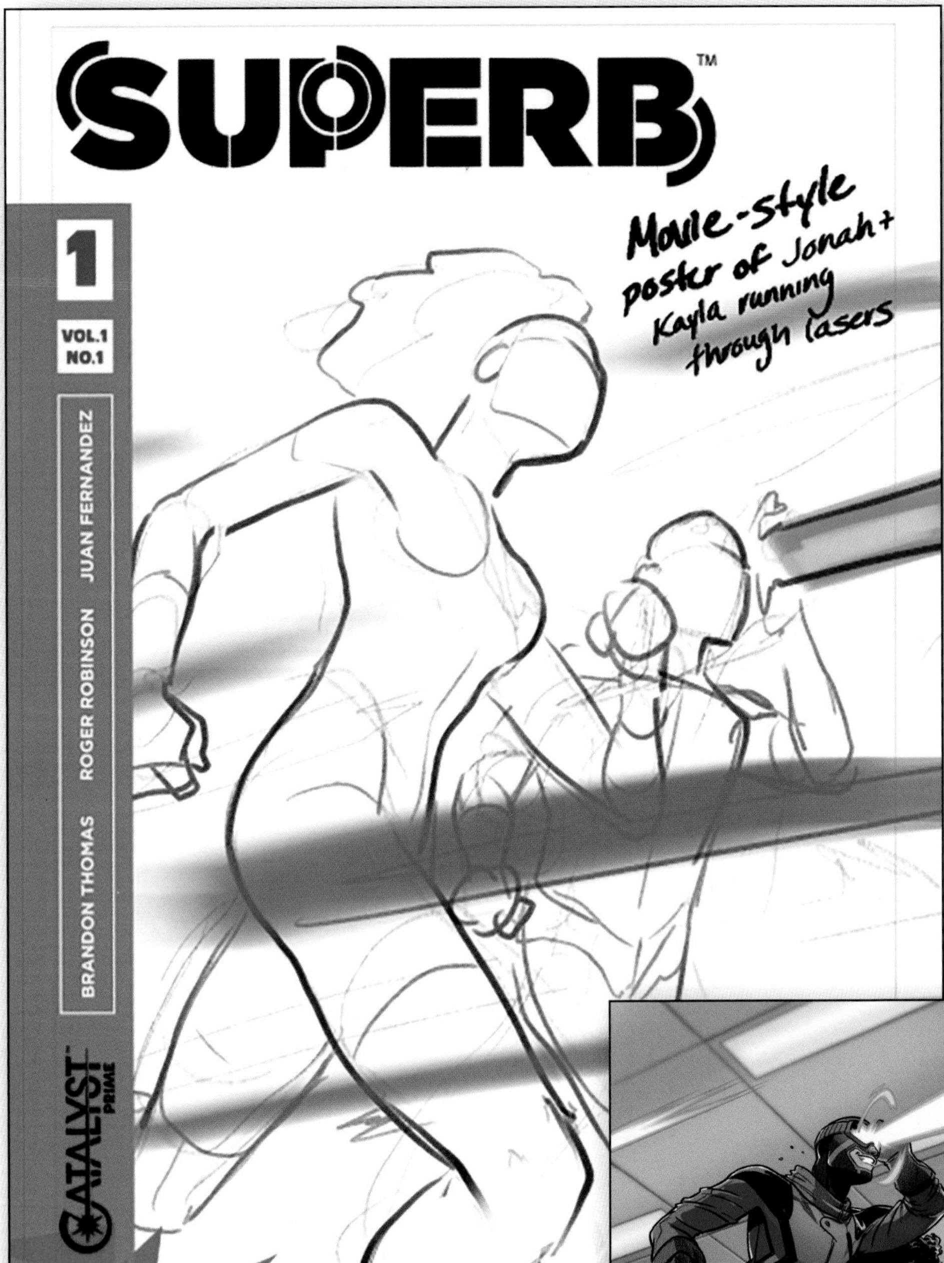
SUPERB™
1
VOL.1
NO.1
BRANDON THOMAS
ROGER ROBINSON
JUAN FERNANDEZ
CATALYST PRIME
Movie-style poster of Jonah + Kayla running through lasers

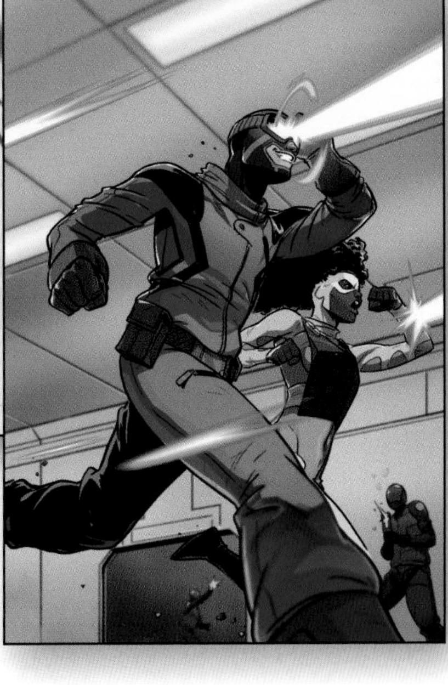

SUPERB COVER SKETCH FOR ISSUE #12

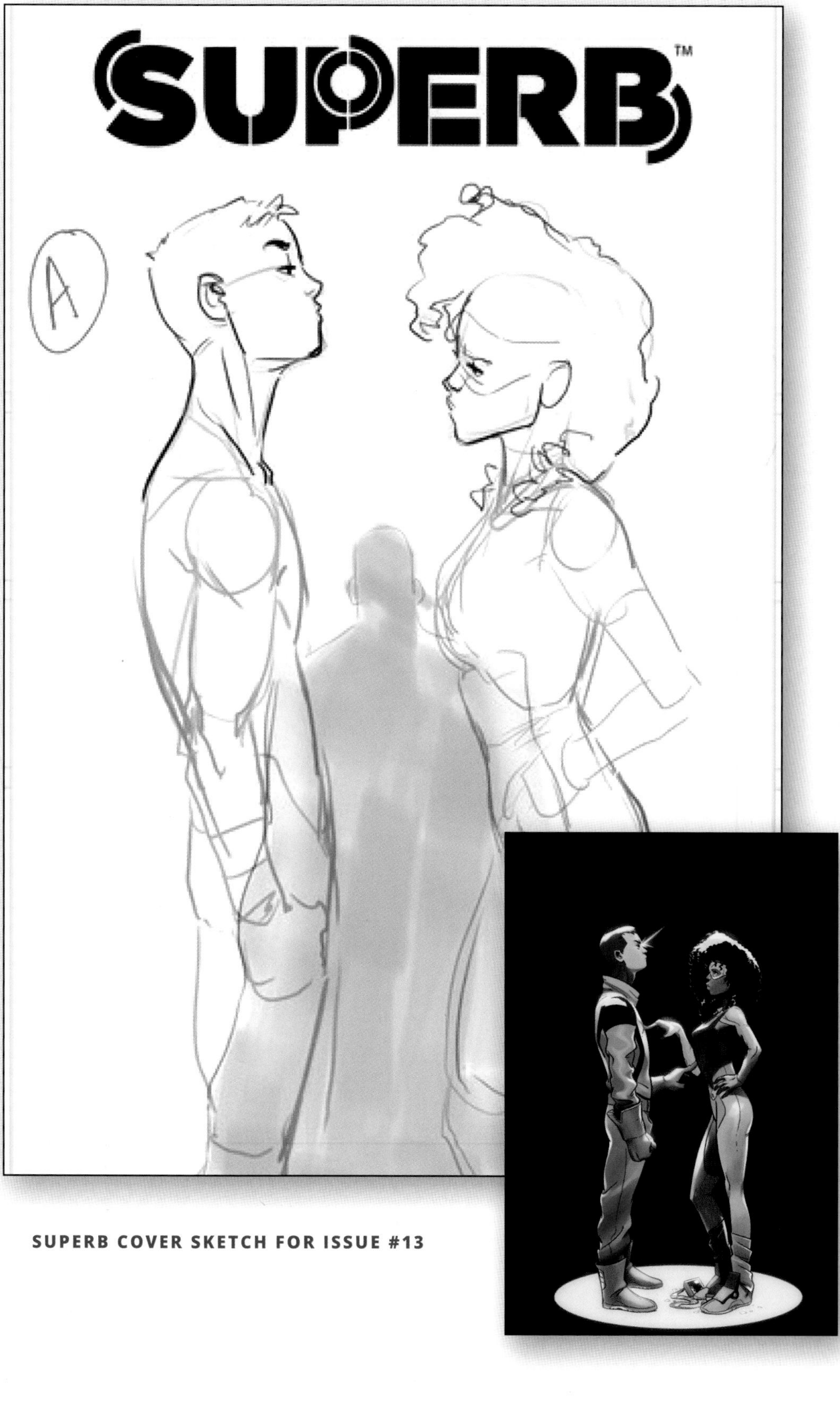
SUPERB™
A

SUPERB COVER SKETCH FOR ISSUE #13

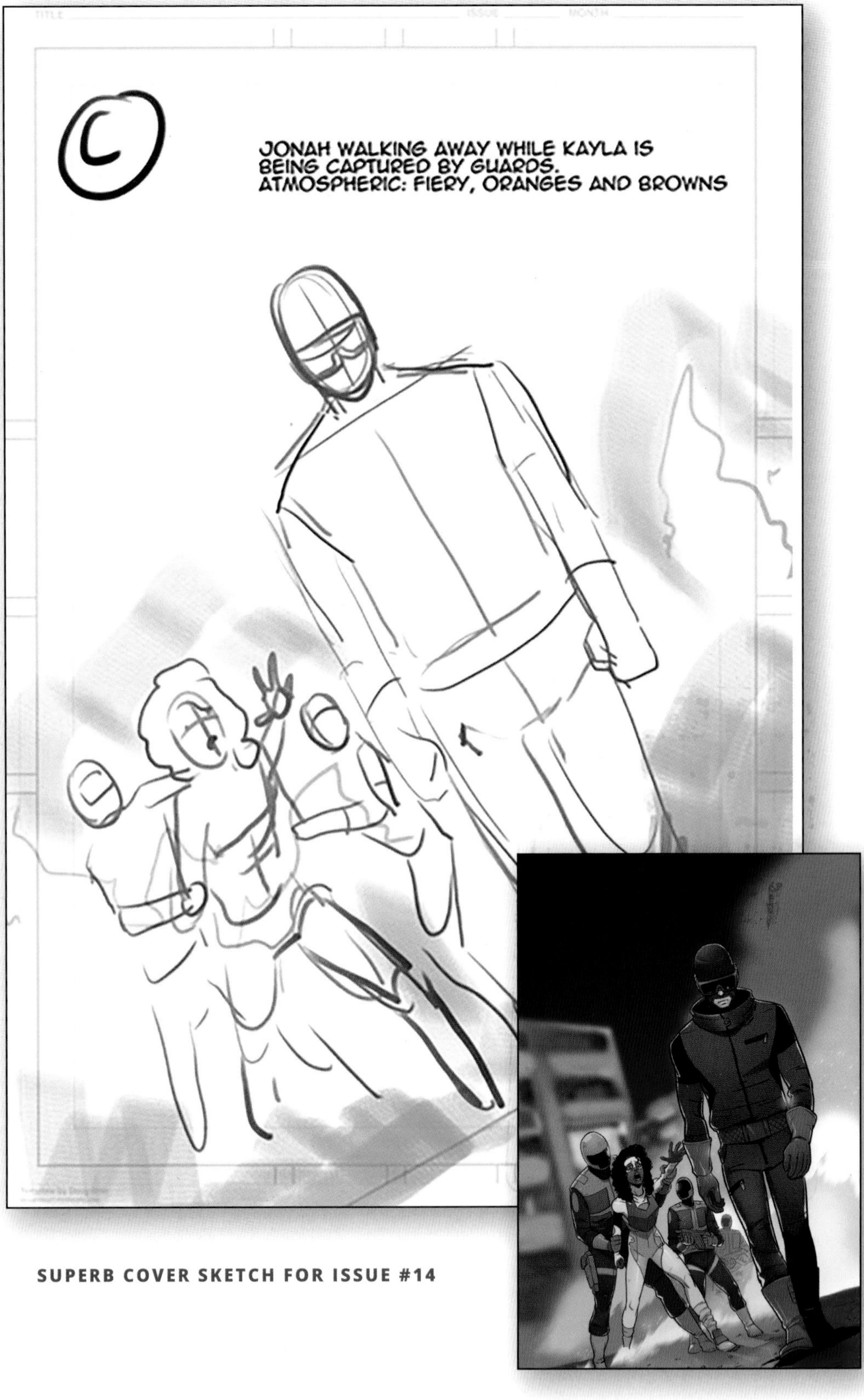
C
JONAH WALKING AWAY WHILE KAYLA IS BEING CAPTURED BY GUARDS.
ATMOSPHERIC: FIERY, ORANGES AND BROWNS

SUPERB COVER SKETCH FOR ISSUE #14